Best wishes

Jo Canning

The Greengroce

The Greengrocer

The Consumer's Guide
to Fruits and Vegetables

by JOE CARCIONE
and BOB LUCAS

Chronicle Books
SAN FRANCISCO

ACKNOWLEDGEMENTS

MANY FRIENDS AND associates have assisted in the production of this book. Special recognition is given to Judith Maraniss Weber for her editorial assistance and Lois Gamble Robinson, R.D., and Audrey H. Paulbitski, R.D., who reviewed the sections relating to nutrition. The illustrations were executed by the talented pen of Wendy Wheeler. The authors assume sole responsibility for the content.

CONTENTS

Introduction   *vii*

Vegetables   *1*

Fruits   *129*

CONTENTS

INTRODUCTION

THIS IS BASICALLY a book for consumers. And that includes all of us because food is the one thing we all have in common, regardless of where or how we live.

Every day, millions of consumers make millions of choices in produce. They reject spinach in favor of beans. They choose a McIntosh apple rather than a Delicious. They debate the merits of red vine-ripened tomatoes at 49 cents per pound against smaller ones at a lower price. If they're adventurous they decide to put something exotic like a kiwi fruit in their shopping cart. Hopefully, these decisions are based on knowledge of quality, nutrition and economy—not on habit or chance. This book is designed to make your choices easier and more rational.

People haven't always had this luxury of picking and choosing. They accepted the food available and were glad to get it because for most of human history most of mankind has been hungry. Even today, this is true in many parts of the world. In this book you'll read about Roman emperors eating asparagus and Catherine de Medici enjoying artichokes. These facts would never have become history if they weren't unusual. Would anyone have bothered to record that they were eating cabbage? Or turnips? Today you don't have to be a member of nobility or even especially rich to be able to enjoy these vegetables.

Even your great-grandparents would be amazed if they could visit the produce department of a modern supermarket. Pineapples and oranges available every day of the year? Impossible. Not to mention papayas, mangoes, broccoli, avocados. They wouldn't even recognize some of the fairly common produce items.

But your great-grandparents had something that we're only rediscovering now. A feeling of connection with nature. For too many years food was looked on as just another product. The growth of agriculture as Big Business and impersonal supermarket merchandising had a lot to do with it, but mainly it was the consumers' willingness to accept "convenience foods" and processed foods that put fresh produce into a decline for a while. Just in the time that this book has been being written, the pendulum has begun to swing back: more people are more interested in getting back to basics, and there's nothing more basic than fresh produce.

Fruits and vegetables are grown, not manufactured. They have genetic differences by species. They have family differences by varieties. And they have individual differences, too, just as people of the same race or the same family will vary in size, coloring or state of health.

The produce business has changed tremendously in the past 20 years or so. Produce isn't as seasonal as it once was because of improved transportation, better storage and refrigeration facilities, and the opening of vast new growing areas. For instance, it used to take ships five days to get Hawaiian pineapples dockside in San Francisco. Now they may arrive by air freight in a matter of hours. This means the fruit can be picked when it's riper and, therefore, sweeter. Or, look at apples. We enjoy crisp flavorful apples year 'round because of controlled-atmosphere storage which, without additives, keeps fruit in a state of suspended animation until it's marketed from storage.

Unfortunately, there have been some sacrifices along the way. In the interests of producing fruit and vegetables that can be marketed for longer seasons and be transported greater distances, some extremely flavorful produce has decreased in quantity or disappeared from the market completely. Some varieties of apples and grapes, for instance, have been phased out in favor of the standardized varieties that have better keeping qualities. And perishable produce, such as currants, costly to harvest and difficult to ship, becomes rarer each year.

All in all though, we are offered an amazing variety of high quality fresh produce, of high nutritional content and superior flavor. This produce is a better buy than processed foods in every way. Compare the cost and nutritional advantages of a 10-pound sack of "spuds" against the advertised convenience of a box of instant mashed potatoes or frozen French fries. You'll pay up to eight times as much for the processed potatoes and lose up to 50 percent of the original vitamin C. Any processing, canning or freezing reduces the natural vitamin content of food. (Incidentally, this includes your own cooking.) Processors try to get around this at times by "enriching" their products. But putting some refined vitamins and minerals back to replace those that have been lost doesn't amount to the real thing. For one reason, fresh fruits and vegetables contain a multitude of trace minerals and natural elements that are vital to human nutrition. In our metabolism one often depends upon and interacts with another, even though the amount is minute. Processors can't possibly reconstitute the complex balance and so, again, fresh is best if you want to be on the safe side nutritionally.

Which brings up the question of "organic" produce. The quotes are there because there are no standards to define this term at present. It's being stretched like a rubberband by some growers and some retailers, and often used to justify the marketing of inferior produce at exorbitant prices. I hope this situation won't result in the public rejecting the idea of buying fruits and vegetables produced as naturally and chemically-free as possible. But often what's marketed commercially doesn't measure up to what dedicated "organic gardeners" produce for their own use. I'll admit that appearance isn't everything. Thin-skinned oranges may show russetting or small brown spots and still be perfectly good. But there's no reason why produce retailed as organic should look so bad. At least, the standards for condition and especially freshness described in this book should apply equally well to produce that is sold as organic. Wilted old lettuce or rubbery carrots will have lost most of their taste and nutritive value even if they were grown in the Garden of Eden.

Skepticism is also recommended when it comes to nutritional claims. That even applies to some of the information in this book. Nutritive content will vary—sometimes drastically—depending on soil, weather conditions, age and varieties of a particular item. And sometimes public relations men, especially associations representing one produce item, will get carried away with the benefits of their com-

modity. So, you'll sometimes find claims for fruits and vegetables that are misleading, although not necessarily false.
Take watercress, for instance. Any nutritionist will tell you
it's an excellent source of vitamin A. True. But is one sprig
decorating a platter going to do very much for you? No.
Nutrition charts often analyze foods by the pound or by 3½-
ounce (100-grams) portions. That's good for a school or hos-
pital dietician, but not much use to the homemaker. So, in
this book we've attempted to give general information for
the amount normally consumed—½ grapefruit or a medium-sized tomato, for example. And, with produce such as
watercress, we've tried to suggest ways to take advantage of
its nutritional excellence in food preparation.

Visiting a wholesale produce market would be an eye-
opener for most of you. (In more ways than one—for instance, the peak hours run from about midnight to six in the
morning.) You'd see crates, lugs, cartons of beautiful fresh
produce—picked at its prime, carefully protected to keep its
quality and freshness. It's a shame what happens to some of
this produce once it's shipped out of the wholesale market.
There's no excuse for the condition of some fruits and vegetables sold at retail. Don't stand for it. If you don't think the
store you've been shopping at has the standards of quality
you have every right to expect, look for another one that
does. And, once you find a retailer who doesn't "dink" his
berries, or advertise "jumbo" cantaloupes without specify-
ing actual size, (after reading this book you'll know what
these terms mean), stick by him—he deserves your encour-
agement, financially and otherwise.

There are a few general rules to follow with fruits and
vegetables: Use your eyes to judge freshness and quality.
Buy in season whenever possible for flavor and economy.
But avoid produce advertised as "first of the crop." The
price will be high and it may have been harvested a week
or so prior to full maturity. Buy locally-produced fruits and
vegetables whenever possible because nothing can equal
the flavor of vine- or tree-ripened produce. Rinse all produce well before using—this doesn't mean soaking. Don't
overcook, you'll lose flavor and nutrition.

Beyond this, consult the chapters on individual fruits and vegetables for specifics. By the way, in this book produce is categorized by its use, not its botany. Why, for instance, put tomatoes under fruit and rhubarb under vegetables when you're going to use the tomatoes for salad and the rhubarb for dessert? This is a book for consumers not botanists.

Individual chapters have been divided into sections on varieties, seasons, marketing practices, buying tips, nutrition and suggested methods of preparation. Hopefully, the information will encourage experimenting with produce new to you, as well as choosing the best quality fruits and vegetables at the best prices, and serving your family nutritious, good-tasting meals.

JOE CARCIONE
BOB LUCAS
San Francisco
July 1972

Vegetables

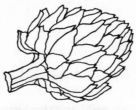

ARTICHOKES

THE LAST TIME I drove through Castroville, California, a banner reading "Artichoke Capital of America" was still stretched across Main Street. It's been there as long as I can remember. I don't argue at all with the claim, it's true, but I always feel like suggesting that the lettering be changed to "Artichoke Heart of America."

Now I'll make every artichoke-lover who lives where this vegetable is considered a "fancy" item turn green with envy. In season you can stop at roadside stands near Castroville, about 80 miles south of San Francisco, and buy enough for several families for $1. These stands also sell the dried purple artichoke blossoms that look like giant thistles. For good reason, artichokes are a member of the thistle family.

They originated in the Mediterranean area and were cultivated first in southern Italy and Sicily. The ancient Romans considered them a delicacy and devised ways to preserve artichokes in vinegar or brine. They were served at the banquets of wealthy Romans throughout the year. Centuries later, when Catherine de Medici left Florence to become Queen of France, she took her own cooks—and artichokes—along. This was the start of the French "haute cuisine." They've been popular in France ever since and French colonists were the first to introduce artichokes to the U.S., in Louisiana.

Varieties The only commercially-grown variety of any importance is the Green Globe.

This is as good a place as any to say that the Jerusalem Artichoke isn't a variety of artichoke at all. And it isn't from Jerusalem, either. It was originally called girasole, the Italian word for sunflower, because it belongs to that species. That was misheard as Jerusalem, and the artichoke was added because it was thought to resemble one in taste. This tuberous vegetable is not often found in produce departments today.

Seasons Artichokes are on the market almost all year 'round, but the supply peaks between March and May.

Marketing Practices Artichokes are always referred to as "chokes" by farmers, wholesalers and retailers. They vary greatly in size, ranging from an ounce to a pound in weight, and are graded small, medium and large. In addition, you sometimes find really tiny ones, called baby artichokes.

Depending on size and availability, artichokes may be sold by the each, in multiple units ("3 for . . ." or "6 for . . ."), or by the pound.

How to Buy The most important thing to look for is a compact green head with tightly closed leaves. A good test for freshness is to rub one artichoke against another in the produce bin. Fresh ones are crisp and will sing or squeak.

Once the artichoke has started to spread and open up like a rose it's past its prime. At this point, they will already have lost moisture and started to wilt. The longer they remain on the counter the more noticeable the condition gets as the artichoke begins to shrivel and the fresh, bright, green color takes on a sickly grayish or tannish cast. Obviously, these are artichokes to avoid.

But learn to tell the difference between discoloration from age and from temperature changes during growing. Cold weather damages the outside leaves of the artichoke, freezing the outer leaves, which will peel and turn black within a day. However, don't let a discolored frosted artichoke stop you from buying it, because the inner leaves and the edible part are not affected.

Artichokes are fairly delicate, but you can refrigerate them about 4 days or so in a closed container or plastic bag.

Nutrition Artichokes vary in caloric and nutritive value not only by size, but by the stage at which they're picked. A cooked medium-sized artichoke can range from 8 to 44 calories. They provide small quantities of various vitamins and minerals.

How to Use You can be as simple or as fancy as you want with artichokes. You can "manicure" them by trimming the tips of all the leaves and going to a lot of bother, but I don't think it's necessary. The simplest way is to cut the stem off so it's even with the bottom of the artichoke. In this way you can stand 4 or 5 up in a pot with 2 or 3 inches of water. Then the artichoke is not completely water-cooked. It is steamed and boiled at one time. This method is excellent for stuffed artichoke, as the stuffing will not be water-soaked, or run out because of too much water. Lemon may be added to the water to prevent discoloration during cooking. Cook the artichokes until the stem end is tender, about 20 to 40 minutes. When the "choke" is done, drain it well and serve on its own plate, with your favorite sauce on the side. Hollandaise or lemon-butter often are used when the artichokes are served hot, vinaigrette sauce or mayonnaise when they've been chilled.

Some people worry about how to eat artichokes and avoid them because they think they'll do something "wrong." Nonsense. Just do what comes naturally. Pull off a leaf and dunk it in the sauce. Put it in your mouth and pull the leaf through your teeth, scraping off the tender flesh. Discard what's left. When you get to the center, scoop out and discard the thistle-like choke. Cut the tender nut-flavored bottom that's left into bite-sized pieces. Dunk in sauce and eat.

Artichokes can also be stuffed, with garlic, parsley and bread crumbs, then boiled. Or with meat and then baked. For fancy luncheons and such, extra-large artichokes are pre-boiled and then the individual leaves are served as hors d'oeuvres. The tender end of the leaves can be topped with crab, shrimp or your favorite filling.

Baby artichokes are an excellent addition to meat or vegetable stews. The technique is to trim the tops of the leaves then slice the artichoke from north to south so the base holds the leaves intact. These slices can also be boiled and then marinated in olive oil, garlic and vinegar to serve as an antipasto or salad—or they can be sauteed with eggs to make a delicious artichoke omelet.

AVOCADOS

I BROKE INTO the produce business at about the same time avocados became popular, in the early '30s. Then, many people called them alligator pears and we promoted them as an exotic passion fruit with medicinal properties.

Yet the avocado is a native American with a long history. The name itself is supposed to come from the Central American Indian word *ahuacatl,* and can be traced back to the third century B.C. in Mexico and Guatemala. During Pre-Columbian times, avocados spread into South America. We know the Aztecs and Incas cultivated them from records kept by Spanish explorers dating back as far as 1519.

The avocado finally moved north when a horticulturist named Henry Perrine planted some in southern Florida in 1833. Spanish missionaries probably introduced them in California. At the turn of the century the first commercial plantings were made in Florida and southern California. The California ranches were practically wiped out by the great freeze of 1913 and, of the more than 100 varieties that had been planted experimentally, only one survived successfully. It was given the name Fuerte, which means strength in Spanish. (Forget any Spanish you know, produce men pronounce it few'-er-tee.)

Varieties About 10 varieties are now grown commercially. But one of the most popular is still the hardy Fuerte. It makes up about 50 percent of the entire California harvest every year. The Fuerte is pear-shaped, with thin pliable skin that's green, lightly stippled with yellow. Other common winter varieties are the Jalna, Zutano and Bacon.

The main summer variety is the Hass, easy to identify by its thick, rough, leathery skin. The skin of the mature fruit is green when picked but has turned black by the time it's ready for eating.

There's a special kind of avocado you can sometimes

find on the market, fresh or canned. It's green like a pickle and shaped like a pickle. As a matter of fact, some people call it a pickle avocado. It's also known as a seedless or cocktail avocado. Try one for a delicious treat. It's actually a bite-sized Fuerte without a seed. These unusual avocados grow on the same trees with regular fruit, but never develop seeds because their flowers aren't pollinated. Unless you know how, you may find it rather messy getting the "meat" of this seedless variety out of its skin. The best way is to cut it in half lengthwise, scoop out the seed skin in the center, and then press the skin with your fingers to squeeze out the fleshy part you eat.

By the way, the Calavo isn't a variety of avocado. It's a trade name applied to quality fruit produced by members of a large California cooperative. They deserve a lot of credit for helping to educate consumers and promote the avocado industry.

Seasons Wild avocados produce small fruit weighing only a few ounces for several months in the spring. The domesticated varieties you find on the market yield fruit that weighs up to a couple of pounds for about nine months of the year.

Winter is the major season and the supply reaches its peak in January. The summer varieties are available from June to late summer. The hardest time to find good avocados on the market is September.

If cherries, peaches, plums, and most other fruits aren't picked at just the right moment, the crop is lost. Avocados aren't as temperamental. The tree acts as a natural storehouse, so fruit can be held on the tree for months and just become more mature, nutritious and flavorful. This lets the grower choose his marketing time and "store" his fruit on the trees from November clear into April or May.

Marketing Practices Avocados are a very competitive produce item. The basic price is set by the packers and shippers and is based on supply and demand. The wholesaler and retailer then mark them up to cover handling.

Size and variety are the main factors professionals consider in pricing avocados. The size is figured by the number that fit into a standard container. To produce men size 40, that is two layers of 20 in a standard container, is large. Weight also determines the price, since heavy fruit indicates high oil content and good flavor. In these two qualities, incidentally, I've found California avocados better than those from Florida, but I may be slightly prejudiced.

Since avocados that are marketed commercially are fairly uniform in size, they're usually sold by the each. But occasionally—especially when some of the larger summer varieties are on the market—you'll find them priced by the pound. Be sure to weigh them. A heavy avocado may cost more than you want to pay.

The small seedless avocados, also known as cocktail or pickle avocados, are sold by the pound and usually are rather expensive.

It would be nice if you could look at newspaper ads and find which store is offering the best buy in avocados. It really gets my goat when I see "large" avocados advertised and they are not large.

When the retailer orders from the wholesaler there's no misunderstanding about the size he'll receive: a large avocado will weigh about 10 ounces, a small one seven ounces or less. But, when he offers it to you, a small or medium sized avocado can suddenly become large to him. There are no regulations requiring the retailer to describe the size and weight of the items he has for sale clearly. I think there's a great need for some.

Since retail stores don't have to list the variety of the avocados they sell, either, picking a good one can be a tricky business. For instance, the Bacon variety, which has less flavor and oil, may be wholesaling for much less than the Fuerte, but the retail price may be the same. Your only protection is to recognize the difference between the two varieties: the Bacon is more oval, with a fuller neck end.

How to Buy Your major decision is whether you want a ripe, ready-to-eat avocado or one that will soften up later at home. This second choice is your best bet. Actually, retail produce men should display and identify both kinds to make it easy for customers to find the kind they want.

In earlier, non-supermarket days, customers weren't allowed to handle the fruit. The wholesaler or retailer conditioned the fruit until it began to break or turn. That is, the avocado would have a little give when pressed and would ripen in a matter of hours or a day. They were then put in a large commercial refrigerator, where the temperature and humidity could be carefully controlled, until they were put on display. When a customer asked for a ripe avocado the retail produce man would carefully select a good ready-to-eat fruit. Today, however, delicate avocados are often displayed in supermarket bins, the same as potatoes, where some customers who don't know any better are tempted to squeeze and bruise the fruit.

Under these conditions you're better off to plan ahead a few days. Buy a hard but mature avocado and condition the fruit until it's ripe and ready-to-eat, the way professional produce men used to.

Choose a solid avocado with a full neck, showing it has fully matured on the tree. It will look pretty in a fruit bowl for the three to five days it takes to ripen at home. Or, better yet, put it on top of your refrigerator where the temperature is warm and even. You can speed up the process by placing your avocado in a paper bag, or wrapping it in foil, to confine the gases from the fruit that aid ripening.

Occasionally, you may be able to buy hard, windfallen fruit at a reduced price. These are casualties of a windstorm in the growing area that blew much of the fruit off the trees. Windfalls are identified very easily because they have no stems. They can be a good bargain. Just pour a little wax into the stem end and the avocado will ripen normally. If you don't seal the stem, air will enter and make the fruit turn black and take on a strong flavor as it ripens.

But what if you need a ripe avocado for dinner tonight? Here's what to look for. Pick one up carefully. Hold it in the palm of your hand and press it gently. The avocado should feel slightly soft under the skin or have a little give (like a ripe peach). With green varieties such as the Fuerte, choose one with soft, dull-looking skin that has a velvety feel. Avoid any that are glistening in appearance and hard. Look for an avocado with the full, symmetrical neck or stem end that indicates mature fruit. Watch out for finger marks and dark, soft spots. They usually indicate bad areas under the skin.

By all means avoid soft-skinned green varieties that are turning black or have black spots. They'll usually be soft and mushy. They may also have a strong medicinal taste that will turn your family, especially children, away from eating avocados forever.

Most retailers expect a certain amount of spoilage in such delicate fruit as avocados. A good produce man will sort over his avocados as often as every three or four hours to eliminate damaged fruit, either marking it down for quick sale to bargain hunters or throwing it away.

A ready-to-eat avocado or one ripened at home will keep in prime condition, uncut, in the refrigerator for four to seven days. Refrigerator grates will cause indentations on ripened avocados, so place the fruit on a dish. And, finally, never place an unripened avocado in the refrigerator.

Nutrition The smooth, creamy texture of the avocado is a dead giveaway of its high oil content. Unlike most fruits, which tend to be high in starch or carbohydrates, avocados can contain as much as 16 percent oil. But it's mostly unsaturated yet you can enjoy them in moderate amounts even if you're on a low-fat diet. They are a good source of vitamin C and contain fair amounts of vitamins A and E, as well as thiamin and riboflavin. They also provide good amounts of iron and potassium. An average-sized avocado half contains 167 calories.

Uses as Food Avocados, with their delicate nutty flavor and buttery texture, can be used as a fruit or as a vegetable. Most of us limit their use to salads, but in parts of Mexico and Central America, where they're a staple daily food, avocados are even used in soups and stews.

The best-known and most popular Mexican avocado dish, of course, is guacamole. (wah-kah-moh'-leh). It's made by combining mashed avocado with tomato, chopped onions, chili, some garlic and, often, lime juice. The balance of the flavoring is up to you. The Mexican people use fresh coriander and salt and pepper to taste. They serve guacamole with tortilla dishes, refried beans, or whenever its smooth texture contrasts with other dishes. North of the Border, guacamole has become a popular party dip, accompanied by chips and fresh vegetable sticks.

You're probably most familiar with avocados in salads. Avocado slices and grapefruit sections are one popular combination. Avocados also go well in a tossed green salad, along with tomatoes and other fresh vegetables. An avocado half, with anchovies and a tart vinaigrette dressing, makes a delicious salad or appetizer.

Cut in half—and pitted, of course—the avocado makes a beautiful natural cup for a variety of foods. Try them with seafoods such as crab, shrimp and tuna, or with chicken or cottage cheese.

For me, the simpler the better. I like the avocado in its simplest form—on the half shell, flavored with salt and pepper and lemon juice or vinegar.

A well-known food writer, M. F. K. Fisher, tells a story about receiving a box of avocados from her father's California ranch when she was at school back East. Instead of enjoying the fruit, her classmates considered her an awful snob who was trying to impress them. Today, thank goodness, avocados have lived down their reputation as a luxury item and are used in large quantities on both the East and West coasts. If you haven't acquired a taste for them, you're missing out on a unique and nutritious fruit that has the added advantage of being in peak supply in the middle of winter.

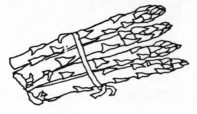

ASPARAGUS

TO OTHER PEOPLE a robin or a crocus may be the first sign of Spring, but to an oldtime produce man it's asparagus, which he always just calls "grass."

The name, however you pronounce it, comes from an Old Greek word meaning stalk or shoot. The plant is a member of the lily-of-the-valley family that originated in the eastern Mediterranean, where it still grows wild. Before asparagus was used for food it was considered a cure for heart trouble, dropsy and toothaches. It was even supposed to prevent bee stings. Early Roman records give detailed instructions on how to cultivate asparagus, how to cook it, even how to dry it for use out of season. Asparagus seems to have traveled wherever the Romans did, including England. It was brought to this country by early colonists, who often called it "sparrow grass." It spread westward with them as the country was settled.

Today California produces 60% of all the asparagus grown commercially in the United States. New Jersey, Washington and Massachusetts are also major producing states.

Varieties In the early 'thirties almost all the 'grass we sold was white or very light green. Now the green varieties are most in demand. Except for color there's not much difference between varieties of asparagus. Most grown now were developed to resist asparagus rust, which practically destroyed the asparagus crops all over the United States in the early 1900's. The lighter-colored asparagus you see will most likely be Conover's Colossal or Mammoth White. The dark green ones are probably of the Martha Washington or Mary Washington varieties.

The white asparagus that comes out of a can can be any variety, cut out of the ground when the tips first broke through the soil. The part of the stalk that's never been exposed to the sun will be white.

Seasons   Ninety-six percent of the year's fresh asparagus comes into the produce market between March and June. April and May are the peak months.

California supplies almost all the 'grass on the market early in the season. The growing cycle moves north from the Imperial Valley into the Salinas and Stockton areas. New Jersey produces half the country's crop in May and June.

Marketing Practices   Asparagus is one of the most perishable commodities we handle. It comes into the wholesale market in crates that have gone through a shower of ice water to reduce the temperature of the stalks. The process is called hydrocooling and is designed to keep the chemical composition—sugars and vitamin C mainly—and to prevent decay from developing.

Many other crops have been mechanized but asparagus is still hand-picked. Actually, I should say hand-cut. For example, at Morris Crudelli's asparagus ranch in San Joaquin County, California and the Harden Farms in Salinas, a special knife is inserted in the ground near the shoot and tilted to cut it off above the root. About half the length of the stalk should be underground growth, with some white on the butt end. This more woody portion keeps the asparagus from losing moisture and freshness.

Asparagus is one vegetable that's really entered the jet age. While most is still trucked to market, air freight shipments increase each year. One California grower uses 90,000-pound payload cargo jets to supply European markets. Within 17 hours after leaving the packing plant, his asparagus is being sold in London, Paris, Frankfurt or Zurich.

Asparagus is priced either by the pound or the bunch. Bunches usually weigh in at 1½ to 2½ pounds.

Compared to more staple produce items, asparagus is expensive. But when you consider the hand labor, processing and special handling each stalk gets, it's worth every cent you pay for it.

How to Buy   Look for firm straight stalks with tips that are well-formed and tightly closed. They should be green for about two-thirds of their length. Large size is considered desirable by most people, but as great a cooking authority as James Beard enthuses about ". . . slim and succulent stalks, and occasionally a very thin kind similar to wild asparagus that is extraordinarily good if properly handled."

Avoid limp wilted stalks and ones that are flat or angular. They'll probably be tough and stringy. Slightly wilted stalks can be freshened by placing them in cool water for a while.

Asparagus should be used as soon as possible after you get it home. If you have to keep it a day or two, wrap the butt ends with damp paper towels before placing the stalks in the vegetable crisper of your refrigerator. When you're ready to cook them, rinse the stalks in cold running water and drain to eliminate any sand or grit. Then snap off the tough woody part of each stalk at the point where it will break easily.

Nutrition   Asparagus is a delicious way to get needed vitamins C and A. It's a good source of potassium and very low in sodium. Another advantage: there are only about 35 calories to a large serving.

Uses as Food   I can't think of anything much worse than mushy overcooked asparagus. It should be what we call "al dente," which means firm enough to bite into. There's a long tradition behind this. The Emperor Augustus supposedly ordered executions carried out "quicker than you can cook asparagus." To him, that meant instantly.

There are three different ways to quick-cook asparagus. You can place the asparagus flat in boiling water for about 10 minutes. Or you can steam-boil it by standing the stalks upright in about an inch of water and boiling them uncovered for five minutes, followed by 10 minutes steaming in a covered pot. The third way is to cut the stalks diagonally into pieces about 1½ inches long and pan-cook them in butter for about three to five minutes.

The simplest way to serve asparagus is with melted

butter and perhaps some lemon juice. Hollandaise is another, more elaborate, sauce that's very popular. Or, you can sprinkle the cooked asparagus with Romano or Parmesan cheese and put it under the broiler until heated. When asparagus is served cold, in salad, a vinaigrette sauce is usually used to dress it.

In San Francisco many of the small Oriental restaurants feature Asparagus Beef in season. Short pieces of fresh asparagus and paper-thin slices of beef are pan-cooked over small stoves right at your table. In two or three minutes you have a meal as delicious as any that would take hours of preparation.

Finally, there's one dish I really recommend for lunch. It's asparagus on toast with a thin slice of ham, preferably Italian prosciutto, and covered with cream sauce.

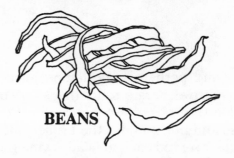

BEANS

JUST THE OTHER day I read a highly-respected nutritionist's public apology in the newspaper. She was referring to how "standard" American diets used to be considered better than ethnic ones, and specifically to the use of beans, when she said: "When I think of what we used to do years ago, I'm embarrassed."

Her statement probably made an awful lot of people say "I told you so" in Japanese, Chinese, Spanish, Italian and other languages, because beans are a good source of protein, equal to meat in some cases. The Japanese "tofu" or soybean cakes are an outstanding example of this.

Every continent has its own varieties of beans and, luckily, most of them are available in the U.S. today. Lima beans and green snap beans originated in the Americas, soybeans and Chinese long beans are native to the Orient, and fava beans have grown in Africa and Asia Minor since prehistoric times.

Varieties   I could write a whole book just on beans if I included all the varieties that are dried. But here I'll only talk about those commonly sold as fresh produce.

GREEN SNAP BEANS: many people still call them string-beans even though the commercially-grown ones have been nearly stringless for years. The Kentucky Wonder, a flat variety about 12 inches long, used to be the preferred variety. Now it's been replaced by the Improved Kentucky Wonder. Other popular varieties—round, rather than flat—are the Blue Lake, Contender, Harvester and Wade. They all average 5 to 6 inches in length. Yellow wax varieties were once popular but are being phased out rapidly by major producers today.

ITALIAN BEANS: you may know this type as Romano beans. They've been a favorite in Mediterranean countries for a long time but are just beginning to catch on in the U.S. The size varies from ½ to ¾ inches in width and 5 to 7 inches in length.

CRANBERRY BEANS: you're probably more familiar with this bean in dried form, also known as the red bean or red pea. The pods, like the shelled beans, have little flecks and stripes of red. They're a favorite in Mexico and the West Indies, where they're used in all sorts of thick soups and rich stews, as well as being mixed in with rice and meat dishes.

CHINESE LONG BEANS: this bean is sometimes called the Yard-Long Bean and that's no exaggeration—they do grow that long. I think you could almost call them spaghetti beans because they're also thin and pliable. These beans have a distinctively different flavor that reminds some people of asparagus.

LIMA BEANS: in the old days these beans were a big fresh produce item, now competition from frozen Limas has just about driven them off the fresh vegetable counters. When you do see any of these pale green beans with flat broad pods, try them, they're delicious.

FAVA BEANS: these shiny green beans are often called broad beans or horse beans because of their large size. They can be up to 18 inches long.

Seasons Green snap beans are available year 'round. California and Florida are the big domestic producers. Some are imported from Mexico, too.

Italian beans are available, in the San Francisco market at least, from July through September.

Fresh cranberry beans are harvested in California in September and October, and somewhat earlier in Florida.

Chinese long beans are fairly common throughout the year—in San Francisco, at any rate.

Fava beans are generally on the market in April, May and June.

Marketing Practices Perhaps you've already noticed a recent problem with fresh beans. Some large commercial producers have introduced mechanical harvesting to reduce labor costs and the machines tend to snap off the bean below the stem, exposing the meat. If the beans are going to be processed immediately, I guess it doesn't matter, but when marketed fresh the exposed part starts to decay and sour. Beans (and other produce, for that matter) don't keep well when cut into. So, currently, mechanical harvesting is obviously not desirable for fresh use.

All types of fresh beans may be sold loose by the pound or pre-packaged in plastic bags.

How to Buy- Let me tell you how a good professional chooses his beans. Young fresh ones have a pliable velvety feel, definitely not hard or tough. I have great respect for the ability of Chinese produce buyers. They just press their hands into the crates gently—if the beans feel hard they keep on moving. They can tell fresh young beans without even looking at them.

But you should buy with your eyes. Look for freshness, tenderness and good color. Avoid any that look coarse, wilted, or have defects from mechanical harvesting.

All green beans are perishable, but they can be stored in a plastic bag for several days in the refrigerator.

Nutrition   The nutritional and caloric content of fresh beans varies according to the variety. And, since standard reference works limit themselves to the most commonly used fresh varieties, I have to plead ignorance except for green snap beans and Lima beans. A cup of cooked snap beans contains about 50 calories, Limas about four times that amount. Limas are a fairly good source of protein; green snap beans a source of vitamins A and C and some calcium.

Uses as Food   All varieties should be rinsed before cooking. Snap beans, Italian beans, Chinese long beans and small immature fava beans are cooked and eaten pod and all. Just snap off the stem ends, cut into pieces and cook in a small amount of water.

Lima beans, cranberry beans and large fava beans should be shelled, like peas, and then cooked in a small amount of water until tender.

I really look forward to the time when fresh cranberry beans are on the market because they're great in minestrone and this Cranberry Bean Soup, a great favorite of mine: Shell 3 pounds fresh cranberry beans and place them in 3 quarts water, along with a medium-size onion, sliced, 2 or 3 sliced garlic cloves and a tomato cut into small pieces. Add 2 tablespoons olive oil, salt and pepper to taste, and cook slowly until the beans are softened (about two hours).

Here's another Carcione special that I call Springtime Vegetable Stew, because that's when all its ingredients are at their best: First shell 1 cup young tender fava beans and 1 cup peas, then trim very small fresh artichokes (keep going until they're about the size of the marinated ones you see bottled in your supermarket) and slice them in quarters from top to bottom. Place all these vegetables in a saucepan with about ¾ inches of water. Add 1 medium-sized spring onion, one diced garlic clove, and 2 or 3 tablespoons of olive oil. Bring to a boil, then reduce the heat and barely simmer for 20 to 30 minutes.

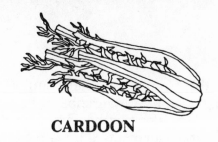

CARDOON

THE LEAFY MIDRIBS of this vegetable, tender and fleshy when cooked, are a favorite of Italians, and people of Italian descent, who call it cardoni. Its history is closely related to the globe artichoke but its appearance is quite different. In the field, mature cardoon plants look like rangy thistles with stalks up to five feet high. It's said that in Argentina the domesticated garden plants raised for the Italian community have escaped and are now flourishing as an irritating weed on the Pampas.

In the market cardoon looks like an oversized bunch of clip-topped celery with regular rows of little spurs on the edges of the stalks.

Seasons   Cardoon is primarily a fall and winter vegetable.

How to Buy   Choose bunches that are young-looking with fresh dark green leaves on the top end. Avoid big spread-out bunches or ones that show signs of age. Store in the refrigerator as you would celery.

Uses as Food   The flavor of cardoon is a pleasant combination of celery and globe artichoke. The innermost tender shoots can be eaten raw like celery.

To cook, remove and discard the large tough outer stalks. Rinse well, separate the stalks and pare off the spurs on the sides and the string part off the outer surfaces. Then cut into sections and boil in a small amount of water, or steam until tender, about 12 minutes. (A little lemon juice or vinegar added to the water will prevent the white flesh from discoloring.) Drain, season with salt and pepper and, if you wish, add butter or other dressing of your choice.

A favorite Italian way of preparing cardoon is to parboil it, then dip it in egg batter or bread crumbs and fry.

BEETS

BEETS ARE GROWN commercially in 31 of the United States, but don't bother looking for any if there's a field of sugar beets or chard within several miles. It isn't that they're not compatible, just the opposite. They're all first cousins and intermarriage is frowned upon because the offspring will be neither beets nor sugar beets nor good green chard.

All three developed from a wild, slender-rooted species that was common in southern Europe, especially in sandy soil along the sea. The beets we grow—with large, round, red roots—are fairly modern as vegetables go. They didn't develop until the sixteenth century and only a few varieties were available as recently as a hundred years ago.

Varieties The beets we see in the produce market are all globe-shaped or slightly flattened. Growers concentrate on the Crosby Egyptian and Early Wonder varieties because they grow to marketable size quickly. Sometimes the Detroit Dark Red is available, too, but most of the crop goes to processing plants to be canned or bottled.

Seasons Beets grow best in a cool climate, and they are available every month of the year. June through October are the peak months.

Marketing Practices There are many different ways of selling beets. You aren't likely to find all of the styles in any one produce department. Most stores will have beets tied in small bunches with the tops uncut or trimmed about six inches from the root. They are usually priced by the bunch.

You may also find them loose and sold by the pound. These beets may have short-trimmed tops, about four inches long, or be topped to within a half-inch of the beet root.

In some parts of the country beets are topped and prepacked in film bags, priced by the bag.

How to Buy That old saying about good things coming in

small packages is true with beets. Little ones will be young and tender. The large mature ones you see may store better, but they're apt to be tough and have a woody texture.

The beet root should be smooth and firm. Avoid any that look soft, flabby, rough or shriveled. The tops, if any, should look fresh.

Nutrition   Beets are low in calories—there are about 35 to 40 in ½ cup.

Beet roots absorb minerals directly from the soil and these essentials, which we often forget to consider in our diet, are their main nutritive value. Cooked they provide large amounts of potassium, as well as magnesium, calcium, sodium and phosphorus.

The tops that most of us throw away are good sources of vitamin A, calcium and iron. Cook them like spinach.

Uses as Food   Menus in European restaurants always list what we call beets as beet roots. And, of course, they're correct. In southern European countries you'll find them mainly in salads. In the north, where they're more of a staple, beets are used in other ways. Scandinavians often serve them pickled. But the most famous European beet recipe is borscht, native to Russia and Poland. This beet soup is served either hot with boiled potatoes or cold, with sour cream. On a hot day, especially, a bowl of beautiful pink cold borscht is a refreshing start to dinner.

In this country Harvard beets, glazed with a sweet-and-sour sauce, are a popular dish. The name probably comes from the color—the Harvard football team is sometimes called "the Crimson."

At home we boil our beets (they take a fairly long time to get tender), then peel and slice them and serve with a little oil and lemon. If any are left over we put them in the refrigerator to add to salad the next day.

By the way, never cut into beets *before* cooking. They will "bleed" and the beautiful red pigment will end up in the cooking liquid, leaving the beets you serve without a lot of their attractive deep wine-red color. Vinegar or lemon juice will help "set" the color while cooking.

BROCCOLI

WHY DID IT take Americans so long to discover broccoli? It's a mystery to me, because it's one of the oldest members of the cabbage family and the Greeks and Romans were eating it more than 2000 years ago.

But aside from some Italian immigrant families who brought "broccali" seed from the Old Country to raise in their backyard gardens, this delicious vegetable was almost unknown to the American public until the 1920's. Then D'Arrigo Bros., enterprising growers in Northern California's Santa Clara Valley, started shipping sample crates back East and promoting the "new" vegetable on that newfangled contraption, the radio. The demand skyrocketed and by the early 1930's broccoli was both an established crop and an accepted part of the American diet. Now more than 100 million pounds of fresh broccoli is marketed each year.

Varieties A major variety is the Italian Green, commonly called the Calabrese after the Italian province of Calabria. It has a large central head covered with bluish-green flower buds, called curds. Another popular variety is the De Cicco, similar to the Calabrese but lighter green in color.

Chinese broccoli, also known as Gai Lon, is more leaf than flower. It's light green, with a long shank, big leaves and a small flower bud.

Seasons Broccoli is on the market year 'round in good supply. California is still the major producer, although broccoli is grown in quantity in Arizona, New Jersey, New York, Oregon and other states, as well.

Marketing Practices All grades of broccoli are supposed to be fresh and young, with compact bud clusters. Size is the main factor that determines how a bunch is graded. U.S. Fancy, for instance, must have stalks 2½ inches in diameter and between 6 and 8 inches in length.

Broccoli is almost always sold in bunches, sometimes

wrapped in transparent film, weighing between 1½ and 2 pounds and priced by the each or by the pound.

How to Buy A broccoli inspector probably wouldn't agree with me but size isn't really important. Age is. The stalks should be tender and firm, not woody. The heads should be compact and dark green or purplish-green, depending on the variety. The tiny flower buds should be tightly closed. Yellow buds or ones that have started to flower indicate overmaturity. Broccoli should smell fresh. Avoid any with a strong, pungent odor. Of course, reject any bunches that look wilted or shriveled.

Plan to use the broccoli you buy as soon as possible.

Nutrition When prepared correctly, broccoli is more than worth its weight in vitamins and minerals. Just look at what you get in one large cooked stalk: one-and-a-half times the vitamin C needed daily, half the vitamin A and significant amounts of riboflavin, iron, calcium, potassium and other nutrients. All that and just 32 calories.

Uses as Food Do you know people who take beautiful green broccoli and cook it down to watery gray-green mush? For heaven's sake, try to educate them. Broccoli should never be cooked past the point where it's just tender or "al dente."

Here's how to do it: rinse well in cool water and freshen up the butt end, cutting off any woody portions. Then divide the thick stem into quarters by cutting two slits from the bottom almost up to where the head forms. This guarantees that the stalk will cook through by the time the more delicate buds do.

It's best to steam broccoli in about an inch of water, removing the cover from time to time, to let the steam escape. (This keeps the broccoli green.) Test with a fork in about 15 minutes; it should be ready.

Some people dress broccoli with lemon and butter, or Hollandaise sauce, or grated cheese. I prefer to marinate the cooked broccoli in a casserole with a little olive oil and minced garlic before serving.

BRUSSELS SPROUTS

AS YOU DRIVE south from San Francisco along the cool foggy coast of San Mateo, Santa Cruz and Monterey counties, you pass about 85% of the Brussels sprouts grown in the U.S. Through the car window all you can see are fields of tall sturdy stalks. But up close they're just about the strangest-looking plants you've ever seen. Growing around each stalk in neat rows are tiny round knobs that look like miniature cabbage heads. That's exactly what they are. Brussels sprouts are a member of the cabbage family that produces numerous small heads instead of one large one.

Brussels sprouts are one of the newest vegetables we have and one of the few that originated in Northern Europe. (It shares these distinctions with rutabagas.) Supposedly they originated first near Brussels, Belgium. In 1623 one botanist described some plants he'd heard of but never seen that "bear 50 heads the size of an egg." Two hundred years later an American botanist improved on the story by writing about "thousand-headed cabbage."

Varieties The average consumer wouldn't be able to see any difference between the four or five commonly-grown commercial varieties. Two of the more popular ones are the Jade Cross and the Long Island Improved.

Seasons Brussels sprouts are harvested and marketed in the U.S. from mid-August through the first week in May. Imports from Mexico supplement the supply in March and April and account for almost all the sprouts on the market between May and July. Prices stay fairly steady all year with a slight dip from January through March.

Marketing Practices Most produce gets graded higher as the size gets larger. Brussels sprouts are an exception. Smallness is desirable for good quality and taste, so U.S. No. 1, the highest grade, specifies that "the diameter of each brussels sprout shall be not less than one inch and the length not more than 2¾ inches."

Brussels sprouts are still sold loose by the pound, but you'll find some packed in 10-oz. wax cups that are priced by the package.

How to Buy Let the U.S. grading system be your guide. Look for small, firm, compact heads with bright green color. Wilted yellow leaves are a sign of age. Other sprouts to avoid are large puffy ones or heads with black spots or holes that indicate insect damage.

I usually advise to shop with your eyes. With sprouts use your nose, too. Old ones have a strong odor.

Brussels sprouts are highly perishable and your retailer should display them on refrigerated counters. The refrigerator is the place to keep them at home, too. Don't wash until you're ready to use them—and that should be within a day or two.

Nutrition Brussels sprouts are an excellent source of vitamin C. Six or seven cooked sprouts contain more than the recommended daily allowance for adults, along with a good amount of vitamin A and some thiamin and iron. This amount contains 36 calories.

Uses as Food Before cooking Brussels sprouts wash them thoroughly in cold water. Then slice off a little of the butt end—not too much or the leaves will fall off. Cut an X into the stem so the sprouts will cook through quickly. Place in a small amount of lightly salted water at a high boil. Cook in a covered pan for about 6 to 8 minutes, then drain and add butter, salt and pepper. You can season with lemon juice or nutmeg, too, or serve the sprouts au gratin or with sliced almonds or chestnuts.

For something a bit unusual you might try shish kebab with cooked brussels sprouts alternated on the skewer with chunks of beef and tomato wedges, then grilled.

One more thing, some people object to the cabbagy smell Brussels sprouts have while cooking. No explanation is ever given, but it's said that adding a walnut to the pot cuts down the cooking odor.

CABBAGE

TWO BILLION POUNDS of fresh cabbage are marketed each year in the United States. Just imagine the amount of coleslaw or corned beef and cabbage that represents! Almost 10 pounds a year for every man, woman and child. The only vegetables eaten in greater quantity are potatoes, lettuce and tomatoes.

Cabbage has three unbeatable things going for it: it's versatile, inexpensive and grows almost anywhere. You can find cabbage growing along the subarctic shores of Labrador and Newfoundland, in the semi-tropical areas of Florida, and every climate in between.

This ability to grow wherever it's planted is probably why it has survived since pre-historic times. Botanists think it's the most ancient vegetable still grown today. No one knows where or when it originated, but cabbage has been cultivated for more than 4000 years. The Celts probably introduced it to the lands they invaded—from the Mediterranean lands in the south to the British Isles in the north, and to the east as far as Asia Minor.

Early colonists introduced cabbage to North America. Most of the varieties grown in the United States today originated in Germany or Holland.

Varieties Only a few of the several hundred varieties of cabbage are grown commercially. They fall into five main European types, plus one Oriental.

The Domestic is the most important commercial type. It's an early to mid-season crop that's a favorite for making sauerkraut. The heads can be round or flat in shape, with leaves that are crumpled and curled. The Flat Dutch is a popular variety of Domestic cabbage, producing heads that weigh between 5½ and 6½ pounds.

The Danish is a solid-headed type that's marketed late

in the fall, and from storage through winter and spring. The heads can be round or oval, with smooth leaves.

The Pointed type is sometimes called green cabbage. It comes into the market in early spring. The Early Jersey Wakefield is a variety that produces small heads, weighing about 2 to 3 pounds, with fine flavor.

Red cabbage actually ranges from magenta to purple in color. It's great for pickling and making colorful, nutritious salads. Several varieties are of commercial importance. One is the Red Acre, a globe-shaped variety that averages about 4 pounds per head.

The Savoy type is sometimes known as curly cabbage. It's easily identified by its crinkled leaves. The heads are loosely formed, usually flattened in shape, and yellow-green in color. One popular variety is the Savoy King Hybrid. It weighs about 4 pounds and is good for salads.

Chinese cabbage, also called Napa Cabbage, is becoming increasingly popular and can now be found outside centers of Oriental population. It's about time because it's a delicious and versatile type of cabbage that can be used either in salads or as a cooked vegetable. Sometimes this type is called celery cabbage because it looks like a combination of Romaine lettuce and celery. It forms an erect, nearly cylindrical head like Romaine, but the individual leaves are blanched white at the bottom and pale green at the top, like celery. Sometimes this type will be marketed under its oriental names: *pe-tsai* in Chinese, *hakusai* in Japanese.

Seasons Cabbage is on the market all year 'round. It's grown in practically every State but the major producers are Florida from December to April; California from November through April; Texas from November through February; New York from mid-July through mid-November; and Wisconsin from mid-July through mid-October.

Marketing Practices Cabbage is graded for size as well as quality. Most cabbages on the market are U.S. number 1, with the additional classification of small, medium or large.

They are usually displayed in bulk and sold by the pound. But when the size is very uniform some retailers will price cabbages by the head.

How to Buy   Look for firm heads that feel heavy for their size. The color, whether green or red, should be bright. Avoid cabbages with wilted outer leaves or puffy appearance. Excessive trimming of the butt end causes dehydration, so reject any that look as if they've been overly "butted."

When buying Chinese cabbage avoid any very large, hard heads. They may be overmature and taste strong or bitter.

You can keep most varieties of cabbage at least a week. Just rinse in cool water, cover with plastic wrap and store in the crisper of your refrigerator.

Nutrition   Depending on the variety, 3½ ounces of raw cabbage will supply between one-half and all the vitamin C an adult requires daily. Over-cooking will reduce the vitamin C content markedly—don't do it. Cabbage also contains small amounts of other vitamins and minerals.

The food-energy in a 3½-ounce serving varies from 14 calories for raw Chinese cabbage to 31 for raw red cabbage.

Uses as Food   The Irish have corned beef and cabbage, the Germans have sauerkraut, the Russians and Poles have cabbage soup. It seems that everywhere cabbage is grown there's a different way of preparing it.

Whoever called America the "melting pot" must have been thinking of cabbage, because we've taken over all these ethnic cabbage specialties and made them our own. Just consult any good cookbook and you'll find New England Boiled Dinners using cabbage, Pennsylvania Dutch sweet-and-sour cabbage, and many others.

Be adventurous and combine different colors and varieties of cabbage when you make coleslaw. Vary the flavor by experimenting with curry powder or horseradish in the dressing.

And, when you cook cabbage, try steaming not boiling. (10 to 15 minutes for wedges, 5 minutes if it's shredded.) I call it cabbage al dente, but I leave the cooking to my wife —after all, her maiden name was Ahern, which should qualify her as a cabbage-cook.

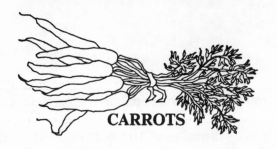

CARROTS

IF YOU'VE EVER walked down a country road and noticed the weeds with white, umbrella-shaped flowers called Queen Anne's Lace, you've really been looking at carrots in their wild state.

No one seems to know exactly where or when cultivated carrots developed. Different types are found all over the world. In Egypt they still grow carrots with small purple roots. The Japanese raise some giants that are over three feet long.

An art museum may seem like that last place to find out about vegetables, but old Dutch paintings can clue us in on how carrots developed in Europe. In the sixteenth century artists painted them in purple and yellow. Our familiar orange-colored carrots finally show up a hundred years later.

When carrots moved from Holland to England during Elizabethan times, they became popular immediately—and not just as food. Ladies thought the feathery, fernlike carrot leaves were so pretty they used them for decoration in their hair.

The carrot may be a common vegetable but it's an American aristocrat. It arrived *before* the "Mayflower." Carrots are given credit for helping to save the colonists at Jamestown, Virginia, from starvation during the winter of 1609.

Actually, carrots were an important food crop in all the early settlements. They were easy to grow and, vital in the days before refrigeration, they would keep all winter in cool, dark, underground "root cellars."

Generations of children have grown up hating carrots and that's a shame. If you think you dislike carrots I'll bet I know the reasons. You were served what produce men call "horse carrots"—meaning large, mature ones—and they were probably overcooked. Also, children (and adults for that matter) hate being told to do what's good for them. Carrots were supposed to make your hair curly (they won't) or improve your eyesight (an overstatement, although they will help keep your eyes healthy and prevent night blindness). Maybe carrots just need what public relations men call a "new image."

Varieties If you're a home gardener the variety you plant is important. But it's not very practical to try identifying carrots in the produce department where you shop. One thing's sure, they will all be of the Mediterranean type, that is elongated and orange-colored.

Chances are the ones you buy will be either the Imperator or the Nantes variety. They average seven inches in length and about an inch and a half in diameter, tapering slightly toward the root.

You may also see a short blunt variety called the Chantenay. They're usually about five inches in length and two inches in diameter.

Seasons There are large supplies of fresh carrots on the market every month of the year. The major producing states —California, Texas and Arizona—harvest and ship carrots year 'round. Other states supply local markets, especially in the spring.

Marketing Practices Some carrots still come into the markets with their tops on. Retailers often call them "fancy" and sell them by the bunch at a premium price. It's good psychology because they look fresh and attractive to customers. You've probably bought some yourself, thinking they were "better." I hate to disillusion you but they may have grown in the same field as the topless ones in the next bin. So, since you'll just discard the leaves anyway, I'd advise you to pass them by and save some money.

Carrots without their greenery, we call them cliptop, are sold loose by the pound. They're usually your best value.

More and more cliptop carrots come packaged in cello bags weighing a pound or a little more. It's difficult to tell how fresh the carrots are inside the wrapping, especially since some are designed with a dark-colored band that hides the stem end of the carrots, where the signs of age appear. I'm willing to give the packer the benefit of the doubt and consider this printed band is just for decoration, but I'd still avoid buying a pack like this if possible.

How to Buy   Assuming you can see the carrots you're buying, what should you look for? Small, well-shaped, fresh-looking ones in general. I hate to be negative about carrots but it's really more a question of what to avoid: Shriveled ones with wilted foliage. Limp, rubbery ones. Cracked ones.

The stem end is the most important place to look. If it's black or deeply discolored, the carrot is old. If it's large, and the carrot has a thick neck, the lighter-colored core will be large, too. This core is actually a fibrous pipeline that carries nutrients from the ground to the leaves. For eating purposes it should be small because the good taste comes from the deep orange outside that stores the sugar.

Carrots will keep well in your refrigerator, but for best nutrition and flavor use them as soon after buying as possible. Before storing remove the tops, if necessary, rinse in cool water and put them in a plastic bag.

Nutrition   Doctors used carrots before cooks did. Ancient Greek physicians prescribed them as a medicinal herb tonic. Today we value carrots mainly for the vitamin A they provide, unaccompanied by the saturated fat found in other food sources such as egg yolks and butter. One 5½-inch carrot will supply you with 6000 units of vitamin A, even more than the recommended daily allowance.

Some authorities, notably Dr. Jean Mayer of Harvard, consider that carrots must be cooked to be nutritionally valuable but the more commonly-held view is that raw or cooked they're a prime source of vitamin A. In fact, a normal portion of carrots ranks second only to liver in vitamin A content.

That vitamin A, essential for healthy eyes and good bone and tooth formation, is actually visible in the carrot. Carotene, which gives carrots their characteristic orange color, converts to vitamin A in your body.

If you're counting calories, reach for a carrot when you

crave a snack. Twenty-five thin carrot sticks will add just a little more than 20 calories to your daily intake.

Uses as Food   I can't understand why anyone should make a big deal out of preparing carrots. Go ahead and call them rabbit food if you want, but they're best raw. If you don't want to chomp them rabbit-style, then slice them into green salads or shred them for coleslaw. Some people like carrot and raisin salad.

At health food bars you'll find carrot juice and I think it's really great. Some people say it's too sweet, however, and prefer to mix it with other liquified vegetables in a vegetable juice cocktail.

Of course, there are many delicious ways to cook carrots. Baby carrots cooked briefly in butter are a treat. Larger ones go well in stews or can be baked along with a roast. I even know people who use them for cakes—very good ones, too.

CAULIFLOWER

IT'S PRACTICALLY A sure bet that if Shakespeare or Benjamin Franklin isn't responsible for a memorable quote, Mark Twain is. And he is the one who said cauliflower is "cabbage with a college education." He was right about cauliflower being a member of the cabbage family, even the name means "cabbage flower."

Cauliflower is native to the Mediterranean and Asia Minor and has been cultivated in that area since at least 600 B.C. The English called it "Cyprus coleworts" in olden days because it came there from the island of Cyprus. It was imported from France and sold in the London markets in the early 1600's.

Cauliflower grows best where the climate is cool and the air is moist. That's why you'll find the major commercial cauliflower crops growing along the cool foggy coast of California and the Atlantic-cooled farming areas of New York State.

Varieties In Italy cauliflower is very popular. Italians are a colorful people and so is their cauliflower: bright purple and bright green.

But in the U.S. the public accepts only creamy ivory-white cauliflower. There are probably more names and trade names than there are actual varieties. The small compact Snowball type is most popular—Early Snowball, Super Snowball and Snowdrift are three of the most widely-grown varieties. The Danish Giant is a larger, more leafy variety, grown mainly in the Midwest.

Seasons Cauliflower is available year 'round and the price stays fairly steady.

Marketing Practices Cauliflower may be cello-wrapped or unwrapped. In the produce market unwrapped cauliflower has always been called naked pack. These days the heads come in with the green leaves that surround the flowerets, or curds, trimmed to the bare minimum. They're called naked bikini pack. (Don't ask me how anything, including a cauliflower, can be naked with a bikini on, or accuse me of putting down cauliflowers by regarding them as sex objects, I didn't make up the names.)

I feel that wrapping is okay for shipping because it keeps the delicate white curds from bruising. About 90% of the pack is wrapped.

But here in San Francisco, close to the major growing area, I do feel the wrap has hurt local sales. The wrap hides the natural beauty and appeal of the fresh cauliflower and probably affects impulse sales.

There's only one grade: U.S. No. 1. It stipulates a clean compact head, white to cream-colored, and not less than 4 inches in diameter.

Most pricing is by the each and this saves time at the checkout counter. But, if the heads aren't uniform in size, and if your retailer doesn't play fair by having a couple of prices based on size, the buyer shopping for a small family is going to get less for his or her money.

How to Buy   Look for compact white heads with any leaves that remain green and fresh-looking. Avoid heads that are loose and spread out, a sure sign of overmaturity. And don't buy any with a speckled appearance or smudges, unless they're discounted in price.

Sometimes you'll see heads with a few small leaves poking through the head. Don't worry. This won't affect the eating quality at all. In fact, some retailers mark these heads down and they make a good buy.

Refrigerate cauliflower in a plastic bag before using, within a few days if possible. The leaves should be removed and the curds well-washed in cool water before using.

Nutrition   Cauliflower isn't as valuable nutritionally as its close relative, broccoli. But it does contain an excellent amount of vitamin C, as well as some iron. A cupful of raw flowerets contains 27 calories, ⅞ cup cooked, 22 calories.

Uses as Food   A head of cauliflower cooked whole and dressed with cheese sauce, almonds or bread crumbs is very attractive and flavorful. Cauliflower can also be used in casseroles and Japanese tempura. By all means never overcook cauliflower or you'll turn this fine vegetable into a mushy mess.

But I like cauliflower raw. The flowerets make a crunchy, spicy addition to salads. And they're great with dips for hors d'oeuvres. Here's the recipe a White House chef created for the reception following the marriage of a President's daughter. It was served with cauliflower, cherry tomatoes, carrot sticks and other raw vegetables. Cream ½ pound Roquefort cheese with ¼ pound cream cheese until soft and smooth. Add heavy cream (about 1 cup) slowly until the mixture is of "dip" consistency. Add a dash of Tabasco sauce and mix well. Then fold in 1 cup finely-chopped watercress. Heap the dip in the center of a platter and surround with the cauliflower and other vegetables.

CELERIAC

CELERIAC IS AN interesting variety of celery which is grown for its root rather than the tops. Actually, it's sometimes called celery root or celery knob. Celeriac is a popular vegetable in Europe but it's almost unknown in the U.S. I'm willing to bet that outside of large cities where supermarkets carry it in small quantities, you'd have trouble finding any.

If you see an irregularly-shaped roundish light-brown root about the size of a baseball, it's probably celeriac. Dents on the sides and a few little roots on the bottom should confirm your identification. Sniff the cropped greens on top and you'll smell the rich odor of celery.

Seasons Celeriac is available year 'round with more volume during the fall and winter months.

How to Buy Look for medium-sized roots with fresh green tops. They should be firm and clean. Press the top of the root, a soft spot on top indicates decay. Reject any with sprouts on top of the root, too, that's a sign of age. Aside from this, my only bad luck has been with large ones that may have a hollow or soft, pithy center.

Uses as Food Celeriac is one of the few vegetables that must be peeled before using. Maybe that's one reason it's never caught on. If some enterprising processor diced it and put it in a freezer carton my guess is that it would sell well.

Until then, here's how to go about preparing celeriac: remove the ¼-inch-thick skin with a potato peeler and dig out the deeper root spots with the tip of the peeler.

Cooked, it can be used to flavor stews and soups. It can be served creamed or au gratin as a hot vegetable. But it's probably best just to make it into a simple salad. Peel, boil whole for about 10 minutes, or until tender, cool, and then dice and mix with mayonnaise flavored with herbs at hand, chopped chives or parsley, for example. Chill and serve as a side dish.

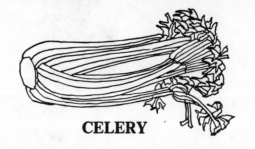

CELERY

IN THE HEYDEY of the railroads, local specialities were bought for the dining car and sold fresh to passengers along the way. A stop at Kalamazoo, Michigan, meant celery. The first seed had been brought there from Scotland in the 1850's and it became a commercial crop grown by Dutch settlers in the area.

Cultivated or wild, this member of the parsley family got its start around the Mediterranean. In its wild form it's called smallage, still grown for flavoring. The Greeks had a word for celery: selinon. It's mentioned in Homer's *Odyssey*, dating from about 850 B.C.

Up to fairly recently, as food goes, celery was used medicinally only; it was considered too bitter to eat even as late as the sixteenth century. In the next century an English naturalist wrote, "Smallage transferred to culture becomes milder ... whence in Italy and France the leaves and stalks are esteemed as delicacies, eaten with oil and pepper."

Today celery ranks fifth in dollar value among vegetables sold at retail in the United States. California and Florida account for 80% of all celery marketed, but Michigan still produces some, along with several other states.

Varieties Up to the 1930's people felt celery had to be blanched (white). Fortunately mild sweet green celery is now available and accepted, a much better choice nutritionally.

Celery is usually classified by color. There are green varieties of two main types: Utah, developed in the region of the Great Salt Lake, is stringless and has a nutty flavor. Summer Pascal is darker green. In the trade green celery, regardless of type, is called Pascal.

The other group is golden. The major one is called Golden Self Blanching. It is a standard variety in France and has yellowish leaves and stalks that blanch to a light yellow-ish color.

Seasons Celery is available every month of the year in fairly steady supply. The largest quantity is on the market in May, the least in September. But prices do fluctuate. In one year, I've seen celery selling on the wholesale market as low as $3 a crate and as high as $11.

Marketing Practices It's hard to imagine how small celery seed is—a million seeds to the pound, in fact. Celery is al-most always started in greenhouses or cold frames and then transplanted into the fields. When the stalks are blanched, sunlight is cut off (so chlorophyll doesn't develop) by anchor-ing paper in place with wires or by placing boards on either side of the plants.

Most harvesting is still done by hand, the bunches are then washed and pre-cooled, usually by spraying with cool water, a process called hydrocooling.

Celery is packed 18 to 48 bunches to the crate. The smaller the count the larger the bunches.

More and more small-sized celery is pre-packaged in cellophane or polyethylene bags, either by the packers, wholesalers or retailers, and sold as celery hearts.

There are a number of standard grades for celery based on "quality" and "condition." As the produce ages, condi-tion especially is subject to change, so you really have to judge for yourself. To keep celery looking fresh retailers often butt the bottom of the bunch (the technique is fully explained in the chapter on lettuce). It's a good idea, there-fore, to look a bunch over top and bottom before you buy.

How to Buy When a professional buyer looks for good cel-ery the first thing he does is pick up a bunch and pull the stalks apart to see if the inside is woody or has developed an overgrown seed stalk in the center. (Please don't try this on your own in a retail store.) Shop with your eyes instead. Is the bunch well-shaped and does it look fresh? If so, buy it. Avoid pithy or woody-looking stalks. If it's limp and pliable with wilted or yellow leaves, shop elsewhere. Your retailer should always display his celery in a refrigerated rack.

Celery is fairly perishable. It should be kept cold and moist until you use it at home.

Nutrition If you tried to invent a snack for dieters, you couldn't improve on celery. There are just eight calories in three inside stalks or one large outside one.

Green varieties have a little more vitamin A than blanched ones, both have the same amount of vitamin C, about one-sixth of what you need daily. Celery is a good source of two essential minerals, sodium and especially potassium.

Uses as Food I'm sure most people serve celery mainly as an appetizer. For cocktail party fare it's often stuffed (blue cheese dip is one good combination). But don't forget the other uses for celery. It's a standard ingredient in poultry stuffing, stews and vegetable soups, such as Minestrone.

I like to encourage people to use produce in new ways. So how about trying this recipe for fried celery? The quantity serves four. Clean celery stalks and cut into ½-inch pieces until you have 2 cups. Heat 2 tablespoons olive oil or butter in a skillet, add the celery and stir over high heat for two minutes. Don't go away, keep stirring. Add 4 tablespoons water, 1½ teaspoons salt and ½ teaspoon dill seed. Cover and steam for five minutes, shaking the pan now and then to keep the celery from sticking. Serve immediately.

CHICORY, ENDIVE & ESCAROLE

BELGIAN ENDIVE IS actually blanched chicory. Escarole is broad-leaved endive. There's hopeless confusion between the botanical and common names of these three salad greens. If you can keep them straight you're doing better than many professional produce men I know.

All are members of the same family. Endive and escarole are closely related, chicory is a more distant relative. They all probably originated as herbs growing wild in southern Europe or the Near East. The ancient Egyptians and Greeks used endive-escarole as a vegetable. Chicory can't be traced back that far—there's no record of it being cultivated until the early 1600's.

By the start of the nineteenth century these salad plants were being grown in the United States. Today endive, escarole and chicory account for one-quarter of all the greens marketed. The main producing state is Florida, followed by New Jersey, California and Ohio. Oddly enough, almost all Belgian endive is actually imported from Belgium.

Varieties All the endive sold commercially is of the curly-leaf type. It grows in loose heads with curly narrow leaves. The outer ones are dark-green and the color gets progressively lighter toward the center. There are two main varieties: Ruffec, with white midribs or stalks radiating out from the crown, and Green Curled Pancalier, very similar except the midribs are rose-tinted.

Escarole is actually broad-leaved endive. The leaves may be straight or waved. The most widely grown variety is the Full Heart Batavia. The heads measure 12 to 15 inches across, with leaves that are deep-green, slightly crumpled and closely bunched. The center or heart is often blanched, that is, lack of exposure to sunlight makes it whitish in color.

There are three types of chicory. The head type used for salad greens has finely-cut feathery leaves with dark green edges and almost white centers. Varieties such as Magdeburg, Brunswick and Zealand chicory are grown for their thick roots, which are dried and used as coffee substitute or additive. This bitter-tasting "coffee" is very popular around New Orleans.

I've left the best for last—Witloof or Brussels Witloof. Most retail produce departments bill it as French or Belgian endive. This variety is forced in darkness to develop a compact cluster of blanched leaves. These five- to six-inch long hearts of chicory, shaped like short thick cigars or torpedos, are pure white shading to a light yellowish color at the tip.

Seasons   Endive, escarole and chicory are available all year in fairly even supply. In general they grow best as an early-spring or late-fall crop, so more may be on the market, and less expensive, during these months.

Marketing Practices   The standard grade is U.S. No. 1. Since these greens are perishable, not much below this standard is ever shipped to market.

Usually bunches are not uniform in size or weight, so they are priced by the pound. Don't be put off by the seemingly expensive price of Belgian endive. An average head, adequate for a family salad, will weigh little more than ¼ pound.

How to Buy   These varieties are more perishable than lettuce and any retail produce man who knows his trade will display them in a refrigerated rack and sprinkle them often. Like all salad greens, the endive, escarole and chicory you buy should be fresh, young, tender and crisp.

Reject any bunches that look flabby and wilted or show insect injury. Avoid green-leaved varieties that have turned yellowish. Blanched types, such as Belgian endive, should never have frayed brown edges or small reddish-brown spots on the midribs.

Witloof or Belgian endive usually gets the special display treatment it deserves. Often you'll find these small heads arranged in careful rows in the small wooden crate in which they were imported or shipped. These crates often are air freighted from Europe, which adds to the cost.

Endive and escarole will keep three to eight days in the vegetable crisper of your refrigerator. They should be washed thoroughly under cold running water, then drained and blotted dry with paper towels before being stored in a plastic bag.

Chicory is more perishable. Plan to use it within a couple of days. Place the unwashed greens in a plastic bag in the refrigerator and remove and wash leaves individually just before you add them to your salad.

Nutrition In common with other greens, these three are excellent sources of vitamin A. They also contain a fair amount of iron and other minerals. The calorie count is about 20 in an average serving.

Uses as Food Small amounts of endive, escarole and chicory can really add flavor and interesting texture to a mixed green salad. The outer leaves have a spicy pungent flavor and the center parts are milder.

Belgian endive, with the leaves separated on a salad plate, is delicious with a simple dressing of oil and vinegar.

In Europe these greens are often cooked and served as a hot vegetable. Here's an unusual Italian recipe for escarole and lentil soup you may want to try for something different: Cook one pound of lentils in 8 cups of water for an hour, until almost all of the liquid is absorbed. Then saute a chopped onion, minced garlic clove and a tablespoon of chopped parsley in three tablespoons of olive oil. Add one-inch pieces of escarole leaves to the onion mixture and simmer for 15 minutes. Combine, juice and all, with the lentils. Season to taste with salt and serve hot with grated Parmesan cheese on top.

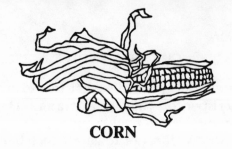

CORN

I DON'T KNOW why people say "as American as apple pie," when it really should be "as American as corn-on-the-cob." Corn has been the most important crop in the Americas as far back as records exist, and even before.

Corn probably originated as a type of gigantic grass growing on the slopes of the Andes. Cultivated forms spread from tribe to tribe throughout South, Central and North America, sustaining all the pre-Columbian civilizations. Very little corn seeds itself to grow as "volunteer corn," so its cultivation meant the end of nomadic life and the start of a stable society with an assured food supply. The arrival of corn was such an important event that every Indian culture has its own legends of gods, goddesses or sacred animals bringing it as a gift for man.

It's not surprising, then, that all the early European explorers found fields of corn being cultivated, from South America clear up into Canada. Crew members on Columbus' first voyage were amazed to see fields of corn stretching 18 miles long in Cuba, as well as Indians smoking cigars made of tobacco with cornhusk wrappers.

The Pilgrims were introduced to corn soon after they landed. The story goes that a friendly Indian named Squanto showed them how to plant corn with a fish head under each mound to fertilize it. If he'd known what would happen to the Indians later he might not have been so helpful.

By the way, the Pilgrims are responsible for the name corn, which just meant grain to them. They differentiated between European grains and this strange new kind by calling it Indian corn. In Europe our corn is still called maize, which is closer to the Indian word for it. I suppose we really should be saying maize-on-the-cob but I'll stick to corn, if you don't mind.

Varieties Over 200 varieties of sweet corn are now grown in the United States. Most are recently-developed hybrids, crosses between two varieties that hopefully combine the best characteristics of both parents.

Stores usually advertise or post signs when the corn they're selling is Golden Bantam or Country Gentlemen, a white variety, because they know their customers will recognize the names. Actually, these are far from being the most widely grown varieties.

Most commercially-grown corn comes from Florida and you've probably never heard the names of the most popular varieties produced there. They are Iobelle, very productive in midseason; Florigold, at its peak in the spring; and Illinichief Super-Sweet, noted for its sugar content, as the name suggests.

Seasons Corn is on the market every month of the year, but May to September are the peak months. From December through April just about all sweet corn comes from Florida.

Marketing Practices Most corn comes into the produce market in large wirebound crates. Retailers have different ways of displaying and selling the ears. Sometimes they are sold as is, with the husks and silk still attached. Other retail produce men strip all but a few of the inside leaves and trim the stalks close to the ears. When corn is pre-packaged in bags or trays, the ears are completely cleaned and stripped of husks, silk and stalks.

Corn sold in bulk, whether stripped or not, usually is priced in multiple units of three or six. In summer, when the supply is greater, it may be sold by the dozen. The pre-packs are priced by the bag or tray.

How to Buy As soon as corn is picked the sugar in the kernels starts converting into starch. So the fresher you can get it, the better. People who grow corn claim you should run, not walk, from the field to the kitchen where the pot of water is already boiling and ready. Unfortunately, most of us can't get corn this fresh.

The next best thing is to keep it cold until used. Corn is always refrigerated until it arrives at the retail outlet and retail stores should display it in refrigerated racks. The ears should never be piled high because even this tends to generate heat and "cook" the ears.

Most produce men will tell you that leaving the green husks around the ears keeps moisture in and preserves quality. But experimenters at some agricultural schools claim to have proved just the opposite. I don't want to get into the controversy, so I just suggest avoiding any ears (with or without husks) that have dented kernels, the sign they've lost moisture and will taste tough. I consider this the most important thing to look for when you're buying corn.

If you're choosing corn that hasn't done a strip-tease, look for ones with fresh green husks. Then check the stem end to see it isn't dry or discolored. The silk ends should be free from decay or worm damage. Next, pull a portion of the husk back about two inches or so and check whether the kernels look well-filled, milky and tender. They should be large enough so there's no space between the rows. Avoid ears with immature white kernels or overmature large ones that look tough.

Use the corn as soon as possible after you get it home, keeping it refrigerated until you cook it.

Nutrition   Corn is a good-tasting natural way to get carbohydrates. It provides small amounts of various vitamins and minerals. The yellow varieties are a fairly good source of vitamin A. The white varieties, once very popular, contain only a trace of this vitamin.

The kernels on a small five-inch ear of corn only have between 70 and 85 calories—but don't forget to count the butter you'll spread on it.

Uses as Food   In the produce market I've demonstrated how sweet and fresh my corn is by eating it raw. I doubt that many of you will do this.

But let me tell you what I found out years ago from the people who should know about corn, the growers. When I was arranging shipments for the wholesale market I usually found myself at a ranch during lunchtime. They would pick the corn just as the water came to a boil and throw the ears in for *one* minute. It came out sweet as sugar every time.

Still not long enough for you? Okay, eight minutes in boiling water, no more.

I'm tempted to stop right here but there are other ways to prepare corn. When you barbecue you can roast some ears right along with the steaks or hamburgers. Just remove the husks, spread softened butter or margerine on the kernels, and wrap the ears in aluminum foil. Put them over the hot coals for 10 to 15 minutes on each side.

Off the cob, corn can be used in chowders, fritters, puddings and relishes. One of the best corn dishes is one of the oldest: succotash. This combination of corn and Lima beans was an Indian staple. A smart move on their part because it's delicious and practically a balanced meal in itself.

48

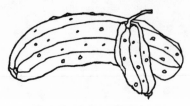

CUCUMBERS

IF YOU'RE "COOL as a cucumber" exactly how cool are you? Precisely 20 degrees cooler than the outside air on a warm day, according to scientific tests.

Cucumbers and hot weather seem to go together. These relatives of the musk-melon originated in the valleys of India between the Bay of Bengal and the Himalayas. Long before history was recorded, cucumbers spread westward. They are one of the few vegetables mentioned in the Bible —"We remember the fish which we did eat in Egypt freely; the cucumbers, and the melons . . ." (*Numbers*). The Greeks and Romans enjoyed them, too. A Roman naturalist described how cucumbers were forced and grown out of season for the Emperor Tiberius, who demanded they be available every day of the year.

Columbus brought cucumber seeds, along with other vegetable seeds, to Haiti in 1494. Very soon French, English and Spanish explorers were reporting that Indians were growing them from Florida clear up into Canada.

Today cucumbers are grown commercially in 18 states, with the greatest amounts coming from Florida, North and South Carolina and Virginia.

Varieties Cucumbers can be divided into slicing and pickling varieties. The most common eating variety is the Marketer. They have smooth, dark green skin and are usually between 6 inches and 9 inches long, tapering at both ends.

Another eating variety that seems to be coming into the market in increasing numbers is the English, Holland or European variety. It is long and skinny, with light green skin. They may grow as much as 2 feet long, but are at their best when they are about 12 inches to 15 inches in length. They are very thick-meated and seedless. The reason for this is that they are parthenocarpic, a long word meaning the cucumber blossom isn't fertilized. Insects would foil this whole plan, so English cucumbers are kept cloistered in greenhouses. This raises the price quite a bit.

The Armenian cucumber, also called Syrian or Turkish, looks very much like the European cucumber because it is long and narrow. But it's field-grown, paler green and the blossom end is often curled. It's a very good cucumber that may be passed over because of its odd shape and size. Most come into the San Francisco market from nearby between July and November. This cucumber should be firm, but even when soft or flexible the taste is crisp and hard. It has small soft seeds and thick meat. I recommend it highly.

Lemon cucumbers get their name from their shape and color, not their taste. They're the size of an extra-large lemon with greenish-yellow skin. The taste and flavor are more subtle than green-skinned types. They are available on the San Francisco market from July to November. Whitish skin indicates immaturity, yellow-orange color over-maturity—avoid both. They should be peeled before using because the skin is tough.

Pickling cucumbers range in size from the small West Indian Gherkin to large ones such as the National Pickling, which can be used for large dill pickles.

Seasons Cucumbers are available all year thanks to imports from Mexico, which supplement the home-grown supply from mid-November to early April. The peak season is May through August.

Marketing Practices The cucumbers you buy will probably be graded U.S. No. 1 or U.S. Fancy. U.S. No 1 should be well-colored and well-formed, and U.S. Fancy even more so.

When fully mature, cucumbers have hard seeds and no market value. So they're picked before they get to this point. Then the skin is waxed with a commercial preservative. It's supposed to prevent evaporation and keep the cucumbers crisp longer.

The longer English variety are usually cello-wrapped, often with a little label informing you that they are seedless, burpless and non-bitter.

Cucumbers are sometimes sold by the pound, but

mostly by the each. The Fancy grade is usually so uniform in size that they are sold by the each. U.S. No. 1 can be sold either way. English cucumbers are admittedly luxury items. The price for them is usually about double that of their American cousins.

How to Buy   It's more a question of what not to buy. Over-mature cucumbers will have a puffy appearance and the color will be dull, sometimes yellowed. Other cucumbers to avoid are old ones that look wrinkled or shriveled (the flesh will be tough and bitter), and ones with dark sunken areas that indicate decay.

Cucumbers can be stored in the refrigerator for about a week. Put cut pieces in cellowrap.

Nutrition   A big cucumber—7½ inches long and 2 inches around—will contain about 25 calories. That makes them great for anyone on a weight-reduction diet. They contain small amounts of various vitamins and minerals.

Uses as Food   Today most people like cucumbers simply and quickly prepared, sliced and tossed into a salad. An old-fashioned favorite was to marinate sliced cucumbers and sweet fresh onions in a vinegar and water solution until dinnertime. When drained they made a nippy side dish.

And then there are pickles. Here's an easy, foolproof and delicious recipe: Wash and dry 30 small cucumbers. Place in a crock with 10 sprays of fresh dillweed. (If there's a Farmer's Market in your vicinity, one of the stalls is sure to have it.) Boil 4 quarts water with a cup of coarse (Kosher or crystal, *not* rock) salt. Cool. Add 4 large garlic cloves, 4 tablespoons vinegar, 4 bay leaves, ½ teaspoon mustard seed and 4 chili peppers (the little yellow wax ones in bottles are fine). Pour over the cucumbers. Be sure the liquid covers them. Cover with a cloth, a plate and a stone to weight it down—it's traditional. Turn every couple of days. The pickles should be ready, crisp and tangy, in ten days to two weeks. And, if you're saying, "what no alum?," it's left out on purpose because if you use too much your pickles will come out softer than without any at all.

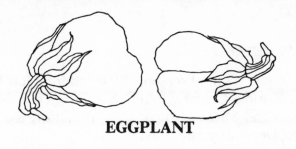

EGGPLANT

IN TURKEY THERE'S a popular eggplant dish called "The Imam Fainted." This story explains the name: An Imam, or Moslem priest, married a beautiful young girl who brought 12 jars of olive oil (the size Ali Baba hid inside in the "Arabian Nights" story) as part of her dowry. One of her charms turned out to be a talent for cooking eggplant. The Imam ordered her to serve it every night. For eleven nights he enjoyed the dish, but on the twelfth—no eggplant. When he asked why she told him, "All the olive oil is gone." And the Imam fainted. The recipe is for baked eggplant stuffed with chopped tomatoes, onions and garlic . . . and lots of olive oil.

Eggplant is most widely-grown and eaten in the same parts of the world that produce olive oil: Turkey, Greece, Spain and Italy come to mind. But it was domesticated originally in China and India and carried west by Arab traders. Small brightly-colored varieties were introduced in Italy in the sixteenth century. Besides the purple color we know, there were white, gray, green, brown and striped varieties. Maybe whoever named the vegetable was thinking of Easter eggs.

Spanish explorers brought them to the New World. They are one of the few vegetables that thrive in the tropics that we grow in this country.

Varieties In Europe eggplant is called Aubergine, and that's the name you'll find it under in some cookbooks. White as well as purple eggplant is still grown there, but most of the commercially-grown eggplant in the United States is a dark lustrous purple color. The main varieties are Black Beauty, the most common in California, Florida Market, New York Purple, New Hampshire and Black Magic. A small elongated Japanese variety also is seen more and more in San Francisco markets.

Seasons Eggplant is available all year around in fairly

steady supply. It's most reasonably priced from July through August. Florida, California and New Jersey are the major producers and Mexico is now a big producer, too, mainly between December and May.

Marketing Practises   The eggplant you buy probably will be graded U.S. Fancy or U.S. No. 1. Either grade should be firm, well-colored and free from injury or disease. The difference between the two grades, more of interest to the bulk buyer than the consumer, is often a beauty contest, with the shaplier eggplant walking off with the honors.

Most people buy eggplant by the each. Usually it's priced that way, too, although I've seen it sold by the pound occasionally. One exception is the smaller eggplant, like the Orientals. You'll sometimes find two of them in a film bag, sold as a unit.

How to Buy   Look for firmness and good color which means bright, shiny and dark. The cap should look fresh and green. Heft the eggplant to determine if it's heavy for its size, the way it should be. Avoid any that feel flabby or look shriveled. Eggplant bruises easily, so watch for signs of decay that show up as dark brown spots on the surface.

Aside from these do's and don't's, choosing the best eggplant is usually a tossup. The ones you see on display probably grew in the same field, and regardless of shape or size will all taste alike. So it's best to buy according to how much you need and how you intend to use it.

Unless you refrigerate eggplant it will start losing moisture and become soft and shriveled. It's delicate so don't pile other produce on top of it. Perhaps the best advice is just to use eggplant as soon as possible.

Nutrition   One-half cup of cooked eggplant (not including what it's cooked in or with) contains just 19 calories and contains small amounts of various vitamins and minerals.

Uses as Food   If you've been avoiding eggplant because you don't know how to cook it, just look in any good cookbook and you'll find dozens of recipes, ranging from simple to complex. One widely-read book on French cooking lists 27 recipes; a popular American cookbook contains 17.

It can be baked whole, either plain or stuffed. And it can also be sliced or cubed before cooking. Here authorities differ. We recommend salting and pressing eggplant to remove moisture before cooking, especially before frying, others say that's an old wives's tale. You'll just have to decide for yourself.

Eggplant makes delicious French fried chips and fritters. You can sauté it or alternate with meat on a skewer. Very often eggplant is combined with tomatoes, onions and peppers. But the best-known dish is undoubtedly Eggplant a la Parmesan. Here's my recipe: Cut 2 medium-size eggplants crosswise into ¼-inch slices. (You can peel and remove some of the moisture as described above before frying to keep the olive oil from splattering all over the kitchen.) Sauté in olive oil until lightly browned on both sides. Then cover the bottom of a casserole with Neapolitan sauce (see Tomatoes). Add a layer of eggplant and cover with grated Parmesan or Romano cheese. Continue filling the casserole with layers of sauce, eggplant and cheese until all the slices are used. Bake 45 minutes in a 350-degree oven.

FLORENCE FENNEL (FINOCCHIO)

JUST SAYING THE word, "finocchio" is usually good for a snicker in San Francisco, because it's the name of a tourist nightclub featuring female impersonators, guaranteed to shock retired schoolteachers from Iowa who visit there on regularly-scheduled bus tours.

But to most Italians and people of Italian descent, finocchio is a popular vegetable that's part of the fennel family. It's related to celery, which it resembles somewhat in looks. It has feathery leaves, round stalks and a large bulbous root with the sweet aroma of anise or licorice.

Other members of the fennel family are often confused with this species. There's sweet fennel, a dwarf variety used for its tender stalks; common fennel, which grows as tall as 6 feet, and is grown for its seeds, used to flavor breads, pastries and candies; and the herb anise.

Only one variety of Florence Fennel or finocchio is marketed. The season starts in September and continues on into May. It's stocked in small quantities and usually priced by the pound.

How to Buy Look for bulbs that are fresh, solid and crisp. Avoid any with cut stalk surfaces that are yellowed or show signs of age. Bunches that show flowers in the central seed stems are overmature. You can store finocchio in a plastic bag in the refrigerator for a few days before using.

Uses as Food Some recipes call for the stalks, but the bulb at the bottom is what's used most often. It has a sweet, mild, slightly licorice flavor. The trimmed bulb can be sliced and eaten with dip or added to salad. Finocchio can be boiled, braised or steamed and covered with cream sauce.

FRESH HERBS & SPICES

WHETHER THE LEAVES, roots or seeds of these plants are used they have one thing in common: flavor that stimulates our senses of taste and smell. Their strength, usually due to the essential oils they contain, made ancient people believe they had magical qualities and they were used in medicines and potions (yes, love potions, too), as well as for flavoring food. Before the days of refrigeration, herbs and spices were used in great quantities to cover the smell and taste of food we'd probably throw out today as "bad." At present herbs and spices are used much more subtly to enhance the flavor of other produce, and most people agree that a little goes a long way.

Herbs were common in North America from the days of the earliest European settlers. Some were brought from Europe, others were cultivated native plants. They were especially popular in herb teas, used as tonic and refreshment. If you've ever visited the beautifully reconstructed village of Colonial Williamsburg in Virginia, you've seen the extensive herb gardens, laid out in the formal English tradition.

But herb-growing doesn't have to be elaborate. A small corner of a garden, a windowbox, or even the window sill in a city apartment can be used to grow herbs. Of course, dried herbs are available in bottles and boxes, but I encourage you to grow your own or buy fresh ones whenever you find them available in your produce department or a nearby farmer's market. These are the most common ones you'll find fresh:

Parsley Parsley is familiar to all of us as a garnish we politely push aside and leave on a plate or platter. The early Romans and today's Italian chefs, too, take this herb more seriously as an essential ingredient in basic recipes. It originated in the Mediterranean region and is related to celery and carrots. The Romans fed it to their chariot horses to make them run faster and ate it themselves to prevent drunkenness. It's not recorded whether it actually accomplished either purpose.

There are more than 30 kinds of parsley, but the variety you'll find most often in your supermarket is called Neapolitan or Italian parsley. In larger cities it's available at all times, sold by the bunch. Some markets, in San Francisco at least, give some free at the checkout counter to regular customers who ask for it, much as florists will include some ferns with cut flowers.

Parsley should look fresh and green. Avoid any that is wilted-looking or has yellowed sprigs. When you get it home place the parsley in a pan of cool water for 10 minutes or so to restore moisture and crispness, then shake off excess water and refrigerate in a plastic bag. Parsley is perishable and should be used within a few days.

In quantity parsley is very rich in vitamins C, A and iron. A few decorative sprigs aren't going to do much for you nutritionally, however.

Chopped parsley, mixed with butter or olive oil and other seasonings, makes a fine sauce for boiled new potatoes, carrots and many other vegetables. It's also an excellent addition to stuffings, stews, soups, sauces and omelets.

Chives Chives are an unusual member of the onion family because the foliage rather than the bulb is all that's eaten. Chives in many varieties grow wild and are cultivated, too, practically everywhere you can think of: Mongolia, Japan, the Philippines, as well as Europe and North America.

The grass-thin hollow leaves may be chopped and used as a nourishing garnish on soups, salads, omelets and cooked dishes. Chives are often combined with cottage cheese, cream cheese or sour cream as dips, spreads and dressings. The Japanese use the pretty violet-colored flower, dried or fresh, as a colorful garnish and pungent addition to many dishes.

In your market you may find small bunches of chives, or small plastic tubs of freeze-dried chives. But the best way is to buy the pretty little pots of chives that many produce departments feature from time to time. Then your supply will be constant since new leaves will grow to replace the ones you snip off to use.

Sweet Basil   This aromatic herb is a favorite of Italian people who call it "basilico." Its flavor is like spicy cloves and is a natural complement to traditionally-Italian favorites such as tomatoes and veal. If you use a lot of it, as I do, I recommend growing your own. It doesn't take much room, the plant won't grow much taller than 18 inches. And the leaves you pick will be really fresh and aromatic.

If you've never seen fresh basil in the market you shop at, try this experiment when fresh basil is in season, from spring into late August. Sidle up to your produce man, whisper "Joe sent me," and ask him for fresh basil. You may get a blank stare. On the other hand, he may reach down behind the counter and come up with a bunch, hidden away where it wouldn't be damaged by handling. The reason for all this intrigue is that fresh basil is very perishable. Once you get it home, wrap the root ends in wet paper towels, seal the whole bunch in a plastic bag, and refrigerate at once. I suggest using fresh basil the same day you buy it.

It's easy to test the aroma this herb will add to your dishes. Just pick one leaf and crush it between your fingers and smell the delicate aroma. There are many uses for basil —from seafood cocktails to flavorings for soups like bean, pea and tomato, to lamb and beef stews, to hamburgers, meat loaves, pork roasts, veal and beef dishes.

But my favorite is Pesto, or Italian green herb sauce, served with noodles, spaghetti or other pastas. In season you can make a large batch and freeze it for winter use. This amount serves four: Chop 2 cups of washed and drained basil leaves, along with 2 or 3 cloves of garlic and a couple of sprigs of parsley. When these ingredients are chopped very fine, add ½ cup olive oil, about 1 cup freshly grated Romano or Parmesan cheese, and a little salt and pepper. Use immediately, or store in the refrigerator for a week or two.

Dill   When I say "dill" you probably think "pickles." But there are other ways to use the leaves and seeds of this pungent herb. It's native to Europe but has spread throughout the world.

Fresh dill is occasionally seen on the market, sold in bunches, which may be several feet long. It should have a fresh green appearance.

Dill can be used in avocado or seafood cocktails, with fish, cottage or cream cheese, and with many vegetables. And, of course, for those pickles. For an easy foolproof dill pickle recipe, see the chapter on Cucumbers.

Anise This herb is a close relative of Florence Fennel, which is served as a vegetable. It has the same sweetish licorice taste. Bunches are seen occasionally in San Francisco markets. The leaves can be used very sparingly in meat stews, stuffings for fish, and with vegetables such as beets and carrots. The seeds can be sprinkled on coffee-cake or mixed with fruit.

Mint Mint used to be a lot more popular than it is now. But mint jelly is still a standby with lamb and what would a mint julep be without it? Occasionally you'll see one of the many varieties of mint in the market. Its pungent and refreshing flavor makes it a colorful addition to summer punches and drinks. But it can also be used in fruit cups, especially with melon, cooked with fish, or even added to cabbage, carrots, green beans or potatoes for an interesting change of taste.

Ginger Root The ginger plant produces beautiful brilliant flowers. What you see in your supermarket or Oriental grocery isn't quite as pretty. It's a light brown root easily identified by its flat irregular shape, with toe-like growths of various sizes protruding out from the sides. Ginger originated in Southeast Asia and has been used in Oriental cooking since very ancient times. One of the wonders Marco Polo found in Cathay in the thirteenth century was ginger—he mentioned seeing vast plantations devoted to growing it. The Spaniards brought it to the Western Hemisphere in the sixteenth century.

The ginger root contains an aromatic oil that gives it its

pungent smell and a substance called "gingerin" that's responsible for its bite and almost peppery taste.

Ginger root is a tropical plant. Chances are the ones you see in your store arrived from Jamaica, Hawaii or the Fiji Islands. It usually sells by the pound and may seem quite expensive—but remember, a little goes a long, long way. Unless you're planning to make ginger marmalade or crystalized ginger candy (both traditional Scottish favorites for some unknown reason), settle for a smallish tuber on your first try. It is usually marketed in clean condition and stores quite well when refrigerated. Since you're most likely to use very small amounts at any one time, some experts recommend peeling the whole root with a potato peeler, wrapping in foil and freezing. It will keep for months and the frozen root is actually easier to grate than the fresh. Just grate off the amount you need, rewrap what's left and replace in the freezer immediately.

Those who should know say that fresh ginger root is a must and cannot be replaced by the powdered product.

Ginger and Oriental cooking go together—whether it's Indian curries, Japanese soups, or Chinese ginger beef. Consult a good Oriental cookbook for these exotic recipes and many more.

Horseradish Root If you can find horseradish sold fresh, you'll never be willing to settle for the bland bottled stuff that's passed off as grated horseradish. The horseradish root looks rather like an overgrown irregular parsnip. It's large, white and fleshy. Horseradish, which is a must for some Jewish people during the Passover season, is mainly used as a condiment for meats and seafoods. Like ginger root, it can be frozen and grated as needed.

GARLIC

PEOPLE HAVE STRONG feelings about garlic. In Sicily, where my family came from, it's indispensible in everything but dessert, while the mere mention of garlic is offensive to many Englishmen. The French fall somewhere in-between, gastronomically as well as geographically. Most American cooks would agree with the French that a delicate undertone of garlic enhances the flavor of meat and salads. However, they might not go as far as one famous French chef, who claimed that his success came from chewing a small clove of garlic and then breathing gently on the salad!

Garlic, like its close relative the onion, is native to western Asia and the Mediterranean. Its strong taste led to the belief that it gave strength to those eating it. Egyptian slavemasters fed it to the laborers who built the Great Pyramid of Giza about 3000 B.C., and an inscription on the pyramid told the exact cost of the garlic, radishes and onions consumed during its construction. The Roman nobility, who avoided garlic themselves, included it in soldiers' rations to make them strong and heroic.

There's probably more folklore connected with garlic than with any other vegetable. In many parts of the world it's believed that anyone carrying or wearing garlic is protected from the "evil eye." Witches, and even vampires, are supposed to vanish at the sight of it. It's been used as a folk-medicine cure for "improving the voice, intellect, complexion, and promoting the union of fractured bones and helping to cure all the ills that flesh is heir to," as one Englishman wrote of its use in India. It's easy to laugh these claims off until you remember that "witch doctors" were using molds to cure infections long before penicillin was grown synthetically, and the same goes for many other "modern" medicines.

Varieties Garlic is a bulb, like the onion, but inside the papery skin are smaller individually-wrapped sections called cloves or buttons.

There are three major varieties marketed. The Creole or American, a white-skinned variety, is strongest of the three in flavor and aroma. The Italian or Mexican variety is recognizable by its pinkish or purplish outer skin. The Tahitian variety is the largest, the bulbs run 2 to 3 inches in diameter.

Seasons   Garlic is on the market all year. The supply peaks in March and April and again from August through October. California, Louisiana and Texas are the major U.S. producers and additional supplies are imported from Mexico, Italy and France.

Marketing Practices   All garlic used to be sold loose on the counter. Some still is but, more and more, you'll find a couple of smallish bulbs or even individual cloves packaged in a box, cellobag or cellopack tray. This is unfortunate because good-size stock is hard to package in small standard-size containers, and processing adds to the cost. Don't blame the retailer, it came about because too many self-service customers helped themselves or concealed garlic bulbs in bags of less-expensive onions.

How to Buy   Forget variety and look for a good-size bulb with big cloves. They're easier to work with and save time. Well-matured garlic is cured or dried in storage for some time before marketing. It should be firm, dry and have a paper-like crackly skin.

At home store the garlic bulb in a cool dry place away from foods which may pick up its aroma. A capped jar in a cupboard convenient to the counter or table where you prepare food is ideal.

Nutrition   Garlic contains the same nutrients as onions. But since you'll consume so little, its major benefit is lending flavor and excitement to the food it accompanies.

Uses as Food   I've heard that in any recipe that calls for cooking garlic along with other ingredients, if you add the clove without removing its skin, the flavor will come through without the aftertaste or smell. You might try this if you or members of your family have a built-in aversion to garlic.

Some people prefer to use a mortar and pestle or a garlic press (you can find one in the gadget section of any housewares department), but all that's really needed to prepare garlic is a sharp knife. Remove a clove from the bulb and bang it with the knife-handle to loosen the skin. Peel and then mince by cross-hatching it and slicing.

Any southern Italian, Sicilian or Spanish recipe is sure to call for garlic. The cloves add flavor to the tomato sauce that's used on pasta, meat and vegetables and, with parsley, are used when stuffing or breading meat or fish.

Roasts gain flavor when tiny slivers of garlic are placed in slits made in them with the point of a knife before cooking. Large salad bowls should be rubbed with garlic or have a garlic-impregnated crust of French bread included before the salad ingredients are added. Minced garlic also adds flavor to marinades and salad dressings.

Hot slices of garlic bread are a delightful accompaniment to any Italian dinner. It's easy to make, here's how: Add minced or pressed garlic to butter you've softened and creamed and blend together. (About 4 cloves garlic to ¼ pound butter.) Then cut a loaf of crusty French or Italian bread partially through, so the slices are still attached but can be easily broken off for serving. Spread the garlic butter generously in each "slot" and wrap the loaf in aluminum foil. Place in a 350 degree oven until toasted—about 10 to 15 minutes should do it. Bring the loaf to the table wrapped, and open only to break individual slices off. This keeps the aroma in and the bread warm.

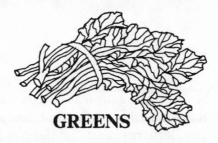

GREENS

CHARD, COLLARD, DANDELION, KALE AND MUSTARD

THIS CHAPTER IS about a mess of pottage. If you think you don't like greens, I can imagine your answer right now. But that's mess as the Army still uses the word and pottage as in pot-herb.

Sophisticated city-dwellers, especially in the North, often have a pitying or condescending attitude toward poor underprivileged rural folk who have to live on greens. They shouldn't. All of these leafy green vegetables are chock full of vitamins and minerals.

Collards and kale are both primitive members of the cabbage family that don't form heads. Actually the only difference between them is the shape of their leaves. Both have been grown since prehistoric times and their exact origin, probably in Asia Minor or around the Mediterranean, is unknown. The Greeks grew them both; so did the Romans who introduced them to France and Britain. For almost a thousand years they were the chief winter vegetable in England. By 1669, maybe even earlier, these greens were growing in "the Colonies." Now the South grows and consumes most of these greens.

Chard, or Swiss chard, is the most ancient member of the beet family. It never develops the large fleshy red root we associate with beets, and it is grown for its succulent stems and leaves. Today's chard is very similar to that grown in prehistoric times in the Near East, Asia Minor and the Mediterranean regions. Aristotle wrote about red chard in the fourth century B.C., light and dark green varieties developed later and a Swiss botanist described its yellow form in the sixteenth century.

Mustard is also called Indian Mustard in reference to its origin in India. Yes, it is the plant that mustard seed, used in pickling and ground into the familiar condiment, comes from. But the large pungent leaves are edible, too. Pliny the Elder, the Roman writer of the first century, said mustard cured epilepsy, lethargy, and "all deep-seated pains in any part of the body." He also prescribed it as an effective cure for hysterical females—it's lucky for him there wasn't a Women's Lib chapter in Ancient Rome.

The dandelion is a weed of the chicory family that grows wild throughout Asia, Europe and North America and annoys gardeners everywhere. But it's a collector's item as a raw or cooked vegetable and for making wine. The name comes from the French *dent de lion,* lion's tooth, referring to its saw-edged leaves. In Colonial America, dandelion greens were used as a spring tonic and were thought to be a cure for heart trouble and rheumatism.

Varieties Collards have leaves that are tall, broad and smooth. The Georgia is a popular old variety; others are the Blue Stem, Cabbage, Green Glaze, Louisiana and Vates Non-Heading.

Kale has curly leaves that are large and hardy. The main types are Scotch, Blue and Siberian.

Chard has red, yellow and green varieties. Those grown in the U.S. today are of the red or white-stemmed green variety. A major one is the Fordhook Giant, with large leaves that have thickened midribs.

Mustard, growing wild, makes California's hills a blaze of yellow color in springtime. Local Italians call this wild mustard Calutzi. Among the commercially-grown varieties are the Elephant Ears, with large plain leaves, and the Fordhood Fancy and southern Curled, both curly-leaved varieties.

Dandelion greens can be gathered wild. Golfers occasionally encounter women, usually quite elderly, collecting them from the edges of fairways, about the only open space left in much of the country these days. The commercial varieties are less bitter than their wild relatives and usually have blanched stems. The main ones are the Thick Leaved, American Improved and the Common French.

Marketing Practices   All of these greens are bunched and priced by the bunch.

Nutrition   All are exceptionally good sources of vitamin A and contain fair amounts of vitamin C and riboflavin, as well. They also contain important minerals, such as iron and calcium.

An average portion will contain between 20 and 30 calories.

Uses as Food   In the seventeenth century an Englishman wrote: "Mustard is so necessary an ingredient to all cold and raw Salleting, that it is very rarely, if at all, to be left out." I've been leaving it out of my salads because it's a little strong for my taste, about three times stronger than watercress, which it's related to and resembles in taste, but you might try it and decide for yourself.

The more usual way of eating mustard and the other greens is steamed or boiled. In the South they are stewed with salt pork and eaten with cornbread to sop up the "pot likker." Migration from the rural South and the growing popularity of "Soul Food" has made greens more than a regional dish.

Here's a recipe you might try: Fill a large kettle with 4 cups of water and bring to a boil. Add a ham shank with about a pound of meat on it. Simmer a ½ hour then add 2 pounds of chopped mixed greens (1 pound collards, ½ pound each, kale and mustard) and salt and pepper to taste. Cook covered for ¾ hour, or until all the liquid is absorbed. Then remove the ham shank, dice the meat and mix into the greens. Serve hot with cornbread.

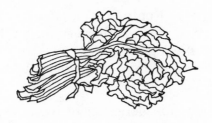

KOHLRABI

I WISH I had a nickel for every person who walks by a display of kohlrabi wondering what it is and how on earth you use it. If you speak German you should have at least part of the answer: *Kohl* means cabbage and *Rabi* means turnip. This strange-looking vegetable is a member of the cabbage family that has a turnip-size bulb—actually a swelling or enlargement of the stem—growing just above the ground, with turnip-like leaves sprouting from it. Its taste resembles a turnip, too, but the flavor is more delicate.

This cabbage-turnip is a newcomer as vegetables go, less than 400 to 500 years old. It's also one of the few that originated in Northern Europe. Kohlrabi was first described in 1554, and by the end of the 1500's was known in Germany, England, Italy and Spain. Records of its cultivation in the United States go back to 1806.

Varieties In Europe fancy varieties of kohlrabi with frilly, deeply-cut leaves are grown for ornament. In this country only two varieties are common. The most widely-known is Early White Vienna, actually light-green in color, and Early Purple Vienna, with purple skin and creamy-white flesh.

Seasons Kohlrabi is available almost the year around. You're more likely to find it in your local store between May and November, and especially in June and July, when the supply peaks.

Marketing Practices Kohlrabi is marketed in such insignificant amounts, compared to other vegetables, that there are really no set marketing standards.

It is displayed in bulk and priced by the pound or bunch.

How to Buy Look for globes about the size of large eggs. The larger-sized ones will probably be woody and tough. You should also avoid kohlrabi with growth cracks or

blemishes. The condition of the tops is an additional indication of quality. They should look young, green and fresh.

Kohlrabi will keep a week or more in the refrigerator,
but it's better to use it as soon as possible after buying.

Nutrition   Kohlrabi provides excellent amounts of vitamin
C. The tops, like other greens, are a good source of vitamin
A. Two-thirds of a cup, cooked, contains 29 calories.

Uses as Food   Kohlrabi can be marinated in French dressing
and eaten raw. Usually, though, it is cooked, either by steaming or boiling. Before cooking, cut off the greens. (If they
look young and tender, save them to cook like spinach.)
Rinse the kohlrabi and remove the skin of more mature-
looking ones. Then quarter, dice, or cut into slices or julienne strips.

An interesting way to serve kohlrabi, either raw or
steamed and then chilled, is in a "hot bath." That's a literal
translation of the *Bagna Cauda* sauce that the Piedmontese,
in the section of Italy near the French-Swiss border, use for
vegetables, as well as fish and meats. It's best to make this
sauce, or dip, in a chafing dish, since it should never brown
or boil. Cook ½ cup butter, ¼ cup olive oil and 6 thinly-
sliced garlic cloves for about 15 minutes. Add 4 ounces (2
cans) of anchovy filets, minced, and stir until they dissolve
into the sauce. Keep the Bagna Cauda hot for dunking. I
wouldn't stick to just kohlrabi, I'd provide a variety of raw
or pre-cooked vegetables—from artichokes and broccoli to
yams and zucchini. It's a real conversation dish for a cocktail
party or buffet dinner.

LEEK

AN ENGLISH POEM called "The Philosopher's Banquet"
offered this advice:
   If Leekes you like, but do their smelle dis-leeke,
   Eat Onyons, and you shall not smelle the Leeke;
   If you of Onyons would the scente expelle,
   Eat Garlicke, that shall drown the Onyon's smelle.
   As you might gather from this, the leek is one of the
mildest members of the onion family. It's also one of the
largest, resembling a giant green onion with wide flat leaves.
   Since Biblical times leeks have been known in Egypt
and other lands bordering the Mediterranean. The Romans
were fond of them, especially the extremely vain Emperor
Nero who believed they improved his singing voice.
   Phoenician traders, visiting the British Isles for the tin
that's been mined there for thousands of years, introduced
the leek to Wales. It's been the Welsh national emblem since
640 A.D., when the Welsh scored a victory over the Saxons,
at least partly because of the leeks pinned to their hats,
which kept them from attacking each other by mistake. In
Wales it's still traditional to wear a leek on St. David's Day
to honor their patron saint.
   In France leeks are called the asparagus of the poor and
widely used. I don't know why they've never gained the
popularity they deserve in this country.

Varieties   Commercially-grown varieties are all quite similar. The best-known are probably the Broad London, also
called Large American Flag, and the Giant Musselburgh.

Seasons   Leeks are on the market throughout the year. The
peak months are September to November and again in May.
New York City and the East Coast get large supplies from
New Jersey. The San Francisco Bay Area supplies the West
Coast.

Marketing Practices   Leeks are almost always sold three or four to the bunch. Unfortunately, the price per bunch is fairly high because of the lack of demand and resultingly low sales volume.

How to Buy Look for well-shaped, medium-sized leeks. The tops should be fresh and green, while the root end should show several inches of blanched or white skin. Avoid those with obvious signs of age or mishandling, such as ragged or wilted greens, or overmature bulbs, which may have splits and be tough and stringy.

Leeks store pretty well, but unless you're a weekend shopper I'd use them at once. If you do store them for any time, place them in a plastic bag and refrigerate.

Nutrition A whole bunch of leeks contains just 52 calories. They are richer in nutrients than other members of the onion family. They contain a fair amount of vitamin C, calcium and phosphorus, and are a good source of potassium.

Uses as Food Before using make sure your leeks are well-washed and free of grit, which often collects in the neck. One French cooking authority—and French chefs do know their leeks—recommends cutting two slits down into the neck, one north to south, the other east to west, and then rinsing thoroughly.

Leeks can be boiled or braised and served either with butter, white or cheese sauce. Try them in meat stews or the Scottish cock-a-leekie, a one-dish meal of chicken, barley and leeks. Leeks can be eaten raw, too. Thin slices of leek can be an interesting "new" salad ingredient.

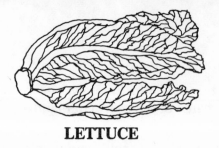

LETTUCE

LETTUCE IS ABOUT the only produce that's managed to avoid the food processors. You won't find it canned, frozen or dehydrated. Just fresh, the same way King Nebuchadnezzar is supposed to have served it in ancient Babylon. The royal cooks must have gathered the wild lettuce that's native to Asia Minor, the ancestor of our modern varieties.

Wild or cultivated, leaf lettuce was known all over the ancient world in the countries bordering the Mediterranean, and even in China. By the Middle Ages more compact forms, such as Romaine, were being grown, and head lettuce was common in Europe as early as the sixteenth century.

In every colony on this continent, lettuce was one of the first garden vegetables planted. Although lettuce is still grown in almost every state today, commercial cultivation is more restricted. For instance, California and Arizona produce 80% of the marketed crisp-head lettuce, the kind you probably call Iceberg.

The recent history of lettuce shows how fast food technology changes. Not too long ago lettuce, which is very fragile and perishable, was packed in ice in sheds close to the fields where it was picked. After the heads were cut and cleaned down, that is the loose outer leaves removed, they were placed in large wooden crates: a layer of lettuce heads, then ice, then paper, then lettuce, and so on, layer after layer, until the crate was full. The icing gave the popular name Iceberg to crisp-head lettuce and it's stuck.

Icing was expensive because of the labor and shipping weight involved. So a vacuum-cooled process was developed: cardboard containers filled with lettuce are cooled quickly to about 32°, removing heat and some moisture. The lettuce is then shipped to market in refrigerated trucks or boxcars. Today some lettuce, stripped of most outer leaves and cellophane-wrapped, is even air-freighted to Europe.

Varieties   There are four types of lettuce you're apt to find in your produce department. I recommend trying some different varieties if you're in a rut with Iceberg, in my opinion the least interesting in taste and texture. Here they are, in order of importance:

CRISP-HEAD   the most popular type, which you buy as Iceberg. It has a solid head of tightly-wrapped pale green leaves. The varieties grown are either the Imperial type, with large but thin cabbage-like crumpled leaves, or improved strains of the Great Lakes type, with thick darker green leaves that have a fairly tough texture.

COS OR ROMAINE   easy to recognize by its large loaf-shaped head. The long narrow leaves may look coarse and stiff, but they taste tender and sweet. The common varieties are named Dark Green and White Paris.

BUTTERHEAD   as the name suggests the soft tender leaves of this type of lettuce have a buttery texture and flavor. The heads are usually small and round with loosely-packed yellowish-green leaves. This delicate lettuce is very perishable and doesn't ship well, so it's found mostly near its growing area. Butter lettuce is most popular in the East and Midwest. The best-known varieties are Boston, with a medium-large head formed by loosely arranged broad leaves of a light-green color, and Bibb, with a smaller more compact head of short dark-green leaves edged with dark-red. Limestone is Bibb lettuce grown in limestone soil, mainly in Kentucky and Indiana. It is considered a delicacy and is often featured, a la carte, in expensive restaurants.

LOOSELEAF OR LEAF   this fairly hardy type doesn't form into heads at all. The leaves, which can be smooth or curled, branch out from the stalk without overlapping. The varieties you'll see most often are Red, with crinkled leaves that shade from green to a reddish-bronze color at the tips, and Australian or Salad Bowl, with beautiful light yellowish-green leaves that are scalloped and curly.

I've seen many sub-varieties of lettuce come and go in the time I've been in the produce business. Each change is usually for the better. Department of Agriculture scientists and other agricultural researchers are constantly coming up with lettuce that is more disease-resistant, ships better and has improved taste and texture.

Seasons You'll find lettuce available in almost equal amounts every month of the year. From December into March most of the crop comes from California and Arizona. As hotter weather approaches, production moves north into Colorado, New York, New Jersey and the midwestern states.

Marketing Practices Less than 10 years ago major growers and buyers met in Phoenix, Arizona, to set better, more uniform standards for marketing lettuce. Up to that time containers were bulge-packed, and sometimes filled to overflowing with hard mature lettuce, which is definitely not the best-tasting kind. So, this conference agreed on a flat pack in standard-sized pasteboard cartons. The hard white and overgrown types were down-graded in favor of the greener, more springy heads you'll find on sale today.

Since lettuce is so perishable, the name of the game is to get it to the consumer as fast as possible and in the best condition. This goes for the grower, the shipper, the wholesaler, and the retail produce man, as well.

Lettuce is displayed either in bulk or individually wrapped in perforated poly-film. Depending on the size of the heads and the supply of the particular variety, lettuce may be priced by the head or heads, or by the pound.

When a very perishable variety such as Limestone is marketed far from its "home," it becomes a luxury item. I've seen some Limestone priced as high as $3 a pound in San Francisco retail markets.

How to Buy You probably buy lettuce by appearance and texture. Generally speaking, you're right, but here are some additional tricks of the trade that should be helpful.

Heads of the crisp-head (Iceberg) type should be round and well-formed with fresh-looking green outer leaves. Avoid hard and heavy whitish heads. These are usually overmature and have a large bitter core. Professionals check the butt (or cut) end. It should smell sweet, not bitter, and have a creamy color. As lettuce gets older the butt end gets browner, finally turning almost black. Since no one would buy it in that condition, retailers often resort to "butting." That means they slice away the darkened surface of the butt end and remove the wilted outer leaves. So, even if you feel foolish doing it, the "nose test" can mean the difference between bitter and sweet-tasting lettuce.

Romaine heads should be full and closely-bunched with crisp dark-green outer leaves. Select butter lettuce heads that are fairly puffy, with leaves that are soft and waxy, forming loosely overlapping semicircles. Each of these leaves should support itself without signs of wilting. Even though the texture of leaf lettuce is soft, the leaves should be firm. Heads with wilted or slimy leaves should be avoided.

Don't expect to revive tired-looking lettuce at home. If controlled temperature and humidity in commercial units haven't kept this produce in good condition, your home refrigerator will never bring about a miracle cure.

Good produce can be kept in good condition though. A good rule of thumb is, the softer the lettuce the sooner it should be used. Leaf lettuce, for example, should only be stored for two to three days. The best method for all varieties is to wash the leaves quickly under cold running water, then drain and blot with paper towels before putting in a plastic bag and storing in the refrigerator. Never store lettuce next to apples, pears, plums, avocados, tomatoes or melons. They all give off ethylene gas as they ripen, which makes lettuce develop rusty-looking spots.

Nutrition   I'm sure you already realize that lettuce is low in calories, but do you know *how* low? A quarter of an average-sized head has only about 15 calories.

If you've been discarding the darker green outer leaves, you've been throwing away most of the vitamins and minerals contained in lettuce. It's safe to assume that the greener the leaf the richer the source of vitamins A, C and E, as well as iron, calcium and other minerals.

Uses as Food You're probably eating more salad greens than you used to. Everyone is, it seems. The per capita consumption of lettuce has more than doubled in the past 30 years.

Not all of this is in salad. How often have you heard the lunch-counter chant, "BLT to go"? The L is lettuce, of course. Almost every kind of meat or salad sandwich gains interest and nutrition with the addition of a crisp lettuce leaf. This includes Latin American "sandwiches," too, like tacos. They should never be served without shredded lettuce.

Larger leaves make natural cups for seafood or fruit salads. Again, don't just stick to Iceberg. Romaine or butter lettuce leaves are more attractive and flavorful.

In Europe, lettuce is often served as a hot vegetable as well as a salad green. French cooks either braise it or cook it with fresh peas.

But let's face it. The most natural and delicious use for lettuce is in a green salad. By that I mean a crisp sharp-tasting bowl or plate, not the soggy mess of wilted greens and thick dressing that often passes itself off as salad. What makes the difference? Bite-sized pieces of cold, moisture-free lettuce to which the dressing is added just before serving. Here's how to do it.

If you're using crisp-head, bang the head down on a counter or table, then the core should twist out easily, releasing the leaves. With other varieties, just break off the number of leaves you need. Rinse the greens for your salad in cold water and drain. Then wrap them loosely in a rolled-up towel and place on the bottom shelf of your refrigerator while you make your dressing.

I guess you can use bottled dressing. That is if you're willing to pay an exhorbitant price for the cottonseed oil and synthetic ingredients most commercial dressings seem to contain. I prefer the clean bite of the dressing that's called vinaigrette or basic French, poured over lettuce and tomato. The secret is using three parts of olive oil to one of wine vinegar. There's an old Italian saying that goes: "You need four men to make salad dressing—a generous man to pour the oil, a miser to add the vinegar, a wise man to sprinkle the salt and pepper, and a madman to mix it like crazy."

Salad can make a whole meal and a refreshing one, too, especially on a hot day. It could be a Crab Louis or a Chef's Salad with strips of ham, chicken and cheese. Another favorite is that California classic, the Caesar Salad. Some people say it actually originated in Tijuana, just over the Mexican border, during Prohibition. This quantity should serve four people:

Start the day (or night) before by crushing a garlic clove in ½ cup olive oil. Then, a few hours before serving, brown 2 cups of stale ¼-inch bread cubes (croutons) in ¼ cup of the oil, and drain on absorbent paper. Just before serving, break the washed and completely dried leaves from a large head of Romaine into a salad bowl. The rest of the ingredients can be combined right at the table—it makes an impressive and dramatic ceremony. Add salt and pepper to taste, then the rest of the garlic-oil, and toss until every piece of Romaine is coated. Break a raw (or coddled) egg into the bowl and squeeze in the juice of one lemon. Toss again. Next add ½ cup grated Parmesan cheese and the croutons. Give it one final toss and serve. If you want, you can cut 6 anchovy filets into small bits and add them to the salad, too, making sure to cut down on the amount of salt you use. If Caesar was the noblest Roman of them all, this recipe with his name occupies the same rank in the salad world.

MUSHROOMS

I CAN REMEMBER watching my father drop a silver dollar into a skillet of wild field mushrooms to be sure they were safe to eat. If the coin turned black—it never did—it was supposed to show the mushrooms were poisonous. Now I find that his foolproof test is absolutely worthless—at least that's what the mycologists, or fungus experts say.

Mushrooms and myths seem to go together. For one thing, they seem to grow like magic, springing up overnight from nowhere. And some contain enough phosphorus to glow in the dark. Combine these two with the fact that they often grow in rings and you have the origin of myths about "fairy rings," as well as stools (or umbrellas) for leprechauns.

The Egyptian Pharaohs, who were considered gods as well as kings, declared mushrooms sacred and reserved them for their own use. The Romans called them food of the gods, too, but allowed anyone to eat them on holy days and holidays. Even today some mushrooms are considered sacred. They're of the Psilocybe species, used by some Mexican and South American Indian tribes to induce trance-states and hallucinations, only during the most serious religious ceremonies, never "for kicks."

Commercial cultivation probably started in France during the reign of Louis XIV. One French cave contained 20 miles of mushroom beds. The U.S. mushroom industry started about 100 years later and in 1890 Kennett Square, Pennsylvania—still the mushroom capital of the United States—started commercial cultivation.

Varieties All the mushrooms commercially grown in the United States today are of a single species, *Agaricus campestris,* a descendant of the common field mushroom. In the East they're of the "Golden" type, in the West "Hawaiian Brown." From the names you'd probably guess that one is golden in color, the other brownish, and you'd be right.

There's very little difference, if any, in flavor or quality between the two. As I'm writing this, Eastern white mushrooms have become susceptible to virus infections, in spite of almost unbelievable precautions in growing them. This has no effect on the quality or safety of the white mushrooms marketed, but does interfere with production, so they are seldom seen now in most markets.

You can't talk about mushrooms without including some of the other varieties, even if they are available only dried or in cans. One gourmet-writer, Roy Andries de Groot, in his fascinating book, *Feasts for All Seasons,* says: "One of the saddest things about cooking in the United States is that we, as a nation, are so afraid of being poisoned by wild mushrooms that we restrict our entire supply to a single mass-produced type, which is the blandest of all the species. How different is this from France, where the skilled gathering of wild woodland mushrooms is still a thriving business, so that the corner grocery in even a small town can usually offer five or six different types."

In dried form, packaged in cellopack, you can find the Shi-i-take, or forest mushrooms, cultivated in Japan. They are grown on logs in what must be one-industry towns because in olden days this prayer used to be said for a good crop: "Please emerge, mushroom, otherwise we shall have to leave the village."

Mushroom powder made of dried wild mushrooms also is available in cellopack in some stores. And, some imported dehydrated soups use them.

In cans, you may be able to find the cep (also known as the steinpilz in German, porcino in Italian and stensopp in Danish) and the chanterelle (called pfefferling in German).

And then, of course, there's the "black pearl" or truffle. This fungus grows under the roots of young oak or beech trees, mainly in the Perigord section of France and the Piedmont section of Italy. They're tracked down and rooted out of the earth by female pigs or specially-trained dogs. The place you see truffles most often is as little black slivers in tins of imported Paté de foie gras.

Seasons Mushrooms are available throughout the year since all cultivation is indoors under controlled conditions not affected by weather. However, supplies are best from November through April, lowest from July through September. Perhaps when people take vacations from cooked meals the demand lessens and fewer are cultivated. That's just a guess though. Pennsylvania grows 62% of the national crop, California and Michigan account for another 26%.

Marketing Practices Driving south from San Francisco along the coast you'll pass a mushroom farm set back from the road. A large sign says: No Visitors.

That's standard practise wherever mushrooms are grown. The reason is that mushrooms are a fungus and to keep the strain pure all other fungi and bacteria must be eliminated from the growing area.

It takes two months for a mushroom crop to mature. That includes a week spent pasturizing the beds of synthetic compost material the mushrooms will be grown in. Meanwhile, pedigreed mushroom spawn is collected in laboratories that must be about the cleanest places on earth. All the air is filtered, ultraviolet light is used and the atmosphere is pressurized. The technicians working there wear sterilized gowns and masks, as well as rubber gloves.

When a mushroom crop is mature, and this doesn't mean large in size necessarily, it is harvested by pickers (really cutters) who wear miners' caps with lights on them as they crawl through the rows of beds. Some of the best pickers are women, but as recently as 30 years ago women weren't even allowed inside mushroom growing houses—it was thought even their presence would endanger the crop.

The mushroom harvest is then sorted by size, from small (under 1 inch) to extra-large (over 3 inches). Most mushrooms marketed are U.S. No. 1, which stipulates good shape, freedom from disease and closed caps.

Retailers sell them by the pound loose and in cellopack pint cartons, either whole or sliced. Mushrooms may seem expensive, but remember how light they are and how few you're apt to use. Because of controlled growing conditions the price is pretty stable throughout the year.

One more thing, apparently (and I've checked) there aren't any Federal or state laws against marketing wild mushrooms. Some cities—San Francisco is one—have local ordinances against them, but the main deterrent is retailers' fear of either losing customers very dramatically or at least promoting lots of lawsuits and damaging publicity.

How to Buy   The most important thing to look for is closed caps. This means that the covering of the cap should curl down over the edge and cover the gills, or dark fluted formation under the cap. When the cap opens out like a parasol and exposes the gills, it's a sign the mushroom has been hanging around the retailer's too long, because they are seldom shipped in this condition. These old mushrooms will have lost moisture and won't be as firm or as easy to slice.

I've heard of cases where customers have asked retail produce men for stuffing mushrooms and have been sold large open ones. Don't you ever fall for that. Any large mushroom becomes a stuffing mushroom as soon as you remove the stem.

Unless you intend to stuff them, I'd choose smaller mushrooms with short stems. You'll be getting more for your money. They should look fresh and unbruised, in addition to being tightly furled.

Mushrooms are highly perishable. They should be refrigerated by the shipper, the wholesaler and you. Store, with slightly damp paper towels over the mushrooms, on a flat surface where air can circulate around them. An easier way is to just store in a plastic bag—stored either way they should keep a week. Don't ever soak or peel a commercially grown mushroom, especially before storing.

Nutrition   Gourmets aren't the only ones who appreciate mushrooms. Weight-watchers and vegetarians do, too. They give a lot for a little. The trouble is, unless you eat them in quantity they're not going to do very much for you.

Four medium-sized ones, sautéed, will contain 78 calories. They have a higher mineral content than most vegetables, especially iron and copper.

In quantity, mushrooms are high in protein and a good source of the B-complex vitamins, especially riboflavin and thiamin, and contain most of the essential amino acids.

Uses as Food   First, a word on preparation. Never soak mushrooms. It's really not necessary even to rinse them. Just wipe them off gently with a damp towel and they'll clean up beautifully. And there's no sense in peeling them, either—you'll waste a lot of time and lose a lot of flavor. If a portion of the skin looks "bad," just cut it away. That's one of the advantages of mushrooms, they're 99.9% edible. That other .1% is the thin slice you should cut away from the very bottom of the stem.

Any soup, sauce, stew or gravy improves with the addition of mushrooms. Just make sure you don't overcook them. Ten minutes tops. Oh, and use a stainless steel or enameled pan, mushrooms will discolor aluminum.

Have you ever tried them raw? Just squeeze on a little lemon juice and slice into salads or serve whole as hors d'oeuvres.

They're great dipped in flour and sautéed; or fried with parsley, onions and garlic; or stuffed with meats and spices and baked.

Here's a good recipe to try for marinated mushrooms, sometimes called Mushrooms a la Grecque.

Simmer 1 pound small button mushrooms in 1 cup water to which you've added ½ cup olive oil, a garlic clove, a whole bay leaf, a couple of sprigs of parsley, the juice of 1 lemon, a large pinch of thyme, ½ teaspoon salt and about 8 whole black peppercorns. When the mushrooms are just tender (about 10 minutes), remove them to a large glass jar while you let the liquid cool. Then pour it over the mushrooms, cover the jar and store in the refrigerator. It will keep a couple of weeks. The marinade will get stronger as it sits, so keep it under control by fishing out the garlic, bay leaf and peppercorns when it gets spicy enough for you. You can serve them as antipasto or with salads.

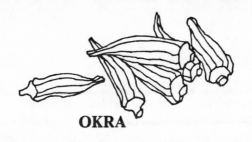

OKRA

OKRA'S INTRODUCTION TO the United States was not a happy one. It arrived on a ship filled with Bantu slaves. The name okra was known by in the Congo and Angola areas of Africa was shortened to "gumbo" and used to describe the well-known Creole dish that is halfway between soup and stew. Gumbo, especially popular around New Orleans, combines okra with chicken, shellfish or meat and filé, a Choctaw Indian seasoning made from dried and powdered sassafras leaves.

If you ever have the chance to venture off the beaten tourist track to Ethiopia and the Sudan region of the Upper Nile, you can still see okra growing wild, just as it did in prehistoric times. The plants, a relative of cotton, were carried to India and Egypt, where they are still used today as a cooking oil, coffee substitute and, of course, vegetable.

Varieties Commercial growers, New Orleans produce men, or really dedicated home gardeners may be able to discuss the characteristics and merits of varieties such as Perkins' Spineless, Louisiana Green Velvet or Lady Finger. But the average shopper is apt to be satisfied with distinguishing between green and white or ribbed and non-ribbed. In fact, that goes for a certain San Francisco produce man, too.

Seasons Okra cultivation in this country is limited to regions where long hot summers duplicate the climate of its African homeland. That means such states as Florida, Georgia and Texas. Okra is available year 'round, with the peak months occurring from July through October. Cuba used to export okra to the United States between November and May, but at present, Cuban okra is even harder to find than a Havana cigar.

Marketing Practices Okra is usually packed and wholesaled in three different sizes. Extra Fancy is small, Fancy is medium-size and Large is apt to be too tough for good eating.

Since okra is sold in bulk by the pound you can pick and choose the pods that are up to your own standard, remembering that the smaller ones are the most tender.

How to Buy   Okra pods must be harvested less than a week after the plant's flower opens or they will be tough and woody. That means you should choose pods from two to four inches long to be sure of getting young tender produce. In addition to large pods, avoid any that look dull and dry or shriveled and discolored.

You can store okra for a week or two. Just place the pods in a plastic bag inside the vegetable crisper of your refrigerator. But okra is rather perishable, and the best idea is to purchase it as needed for immediate use.

Nutrition   For most people okra is an interesting change, not a staple. Nutritionally that's okay, because it's not a basic essential, although it does supply some vitamins A and C, as well as potassium and calcium.

Uses as Food   You consume a lot of okra without knowing it. Thousands of tons go straight from the field to the food processors, where some winds up in vegetable soups and some, as a hidden ingredient, helps make catsup hard to get out of the bottle. So that mucilaginous (or, less elegantly, gooey) quality of okra does serve a purpose.

Most people think of gumbo in connection with okra cookery. But there are other ways to prepare it, as well. Simplest is to cook the washed and de-stemmed pods in a small amount of boiling salted water. The cooked okra can then be combined with stewed tomatoes or served with tomato sauce. Or you can cook the okra whole in my Neapolitan Sauce (see Tomato chapter for the recipe).

Another interesting way is to slice the pods, dip them in corn meal and fry. When you use this method you're duplicating the way the Egyptians prepared okra, according to an account written by a Spanish Moor who visited Egypt in 1216.

ONIONS

I'M NOT SURE that younger people even know the term, but in my day it was a real compliment to say, "that man knows his onions." It meant he really knew his business. I don't know where or when the expression originated, but I'll bet it goes way back. Choosing a good, fresh, sweet-eating onion requires real skill. I wish more retailers, as well as consumers, knew the tricks of the trade.

There's no record of the first men who knew their onions and domesticated them. It was somewhere in that section of Asia Minor known as "the Fertile Crescent" during prehistoric times. The Egyptians certainly knew them. Onions were not only used for food and medicine, but were considered a symbol of the universe and eternity because of their sphere-like shape.

In Europe onions were known and used extensively by the Greeks and Romans. In addition to the flavor they added to other foods they were eaten with, onions were thought to make soldiers brave. In Europe in the Middle Ages they were one of the few vegetables that were available to commoners as well as kings. They must have done a lot to make the stews and thick soups people ate day in day out a little more palatable.

Onions were also prized medicinally. There were claims they could cure almost anything, from dog bites to earaches to stings of "venemous worms," whatever they are. Onions were even prescribed for warts. You were supposed to cut an onion in half, rub it on the wart, tie the onion halves back together and bury them. When the onion decayed in the ground the wart was guaranteed to disappear.

The Spaniards brought onions to the West Indians on their early voyages. Thanks to Indians and settlers they spread rapidly. Today, literally billions of pounds of onions are grown in the United States each year.

Varieties Onions come in a bewildering number of sizes, shapes and colors, as well as specific varieties. I'll only be able to cover some of the more commonly-found ones.

The most strongly-flavored onions, used mostly for cooking, are the globe-shaped ones. They may be white, yellow or red in color. They're sometimes called the Creole type. Southport Globe is a popular variety.

Among the sweet early varieties are the Granex, a yellow hybrid that varies in shape from thick flat to almost globe; Italian Red, flat in shape and a California favorite for use raw in sandwiches and salads; the Red Torpedo, also called the Italian bottle onion, which is long and red.

Bermudas are large flat onions, either white or yellow, with a mild taste that seems designed for salads or hamburgers on a bun. Spanish onions are very large, round and mild in flavor, with color that ranges from yellow to rich red.

Pearl onions aren't a variety. They are small, round, white onions of various varieties that are harvested when less than 1 inch in diameter. "Boilers" are a little larger— from 1 inch to 1½ inches.

Even smaller are the green onions, often called scallions in the East. Again, they're not a separate variety, just small young onion plants harvested when the tops are green and the white bulbs are between ¼ inch and ½ inch in diameter.

Seasons With the exception of green onions, most types are more than slightly dried before they come to market. So, from storage, they are available as needed all year long. The globes and Italian Reds are available year around. You'll find Bermudas from March through June, Spanish onions from August through April, and the Red Torpedos, which don't store too well, only in the early summer months.

Green onions are available every month of the year.

Marketing Practices The produce business isn't quite as exciting as it used to be. For instance, in the old days if you were buying onions you had to be on the lookout for 'stove-piping.' (I think the term originated in Texas.) This is what would happen: Onions were shipped into the market in burlap sacks and a few unscrupulous growers would fit old chimney stovepipes inside the sacks during packing. They'd place inferior onions inside the pipe and good quality ones on the outside. When they pulled the stovepipe out of the middle of the sack the only onions that showed were everything onions should be. Many a buyer was surprised, and not pleasantly, when he found what was really inside that sack that looked so great when he bought it.

With today's strict inspection and grading there's no chance of your getting a stovepiped onion. As a consumer I wouldn't even be concerned about grades of onions. Leave that worry to the wholesaler who's "playing the market" in a much more basic way than any stockbroker, who only has to deal in paper, not perishable produce.

Most retail stores will offer three or four varieties, always including a yellow onion, a flat white and usually a flat red. One reason is that many shoppers routinely look for and buy a particular color.

Onions are most often sold loose by the pound, but you can also find cooking onions in cellopack bags ranging from three to ten pounds in weight.

Sometimes very large Bermudas and Spanish onions will be sold by the unit, since most people will buy one or two at the most.

Green onions are almost always sold by the bunch. Lately, a few are appearing in overwrapped trays.

How to Buy   If you're choosing onions loose from the bin, feel for firm dry ones that crackle or rustle when pressed gently. The outer paper-dry skin should look bright and smooth. Always check the neck or stem end for dampness, softness or woody centers. It seems almost unnecessary to warn against "sprouters"—they're old and I can't imagine what they'd be doing in a produce bin anyway.

Choosing the best mild variety for salads is the biggest challenge. The problem is that any variety gets stronger as the season progresses. A sharp experienced wholesaler can put his nose to a 50-pound sack and tell you whether the onions inside are mild. I'm sure your nose isn't this educated and I wouldn't even depend on most retail produce men, unless they've taste-tested their produce.

In general, don't overstock. If your family is small, especially, buy what you need loose by weight.

Bunches of fresh green onions may be sold whole or as clip-top. Look for bright fresh-looking tops and medium-length, clean white root ends. Bulbs over ½ inch in diameter won't be as sweet as the smaller ones. Green onions should be stored in a plastic bag in the refrigerator. All others should be put in a cool, dark, dry area. This usually means the bottom of a kitchen cupboard. If you've been storing potatoes and onions together, and I'm afraid most people do, your onions are probably sprouting or rotting sooner than they should because of the moisture the potatoes give off.

Nutrition Onions aren't exceptional in their nutritional content. But they add a lot of flavor with a minimum of calories—a medium-size onion (about 2¼ inches in diameter) will have 38 calories, 5 green onions about 45.

Uses as Food Each family, each nationality, each region of the country has its own favorite ways with onions. You can make French onion soup, a real gourmet treat, or you can boil them, or French fry them, or combine them with peas or other vegetables. Stews need them, so does liver. Just look in any cookbook and you'll find hundreds of recipes calling for onions. I've even found one for onions (Spanish) stuffed with onions (Pearl).

It's a shame to cook mild sweet onions, though. They belong in sandwiches or salads. Try a favorite of mine sometime early in the spring season: buy some red onions—preferably Torpedo or Italian Red—and slice them into a salad bowl with some tomatoes. Add olive oil and salt and pepper and serve.

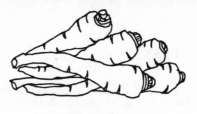

PARSNIPS

THIS ROOT VEGETABLE seems either to turn people on or turn them off, with no in-between. And, since I've been informed that one of the joys of being a wife and mother is NOT buying and serving foods you don't like yourself, many of today's children and adults, too, have grown up without ever seeing, let alone tasting, a parsnip. So first let me try to describe what a parsnip looks and tastes like. The parsnip looks like an off-white carrot with a fat top that tapers to a sharp point. Taste isn't so easy. It's not bland like a potato, although the texture is similiar. The best I can do is robust, with a unique nut-like flavor and a mild fragrance resembling celery.

Parsnips are cold-weather relatives of the carrot. They probably originated between the Mediterranean area and the Caucasus to the northeast. The Emperor Tiberius, who seems to have been the king of the gourmets as well as of the Romans, used to have parsnips imported from the area along the Rhine River, where they grew wild. The royal produce men must have known what they were doing because many a wild-parsnip gatherer has collected similar-looking (but very poisonous) water hemlock instead. By the mid-sixteenth century parsnips were being cultivated extensively in Germany. They were the staple food of poor people, the potatoes of their day.

Parsnips were introduced to North America by early settlers. Even the Indians took up parsnip-growing. Today they are grown mostly in market gardens around cities. Massachusetts, Illinois, Washington and Northern California are the largest producers, since parsnips need cold weather to convert the starch in the root into sugar. As a matter of fact, in olden days, farmers believed parsnips were poisonous until after the first frost.

Varieties and Seasons Several common varieties are the Improved Hollow Crown (also called the Guernsay, Ideal or Student), the All-American and the Harris Model.

Parsnips are at their best from October through January. Supplies are lowest in May, June and July.

Marketing Practices Parsnips are harder to harvest than some other large root vegetables because the root grows entirely underground. Grading practices connected with them are really of interest only to growers, Department of Agriculture inspectors and wholesalers.

Parsnips are sold clip-topped, either loose or in plastic bags, and priced by the pound.

How to Buy Look for smooth, firm, well-shaped parsnips. Small to medium size ones are best—large ones are likely to have woody cores. Avoid soft, shriveled parsnips, they're undoubtedly old and will be fibrous and pithy. Misshapen parsnips are uneconomical to buy because there will be so much waste in preparation.

Nutrition An average serving of cooked parsnips contains 66 calories. They contain little vitamin A, but do have some vitamin C and various essential minerals.

Uses as Food Before cooking, parsnips must be scrubbed, scraped and pared. They can be cooked whole or cut into slices, cubes, or julienne strips. They add sweetness to stews and soups or can be served alone. Parsnips should be steamed in a small amount of water until tender. To serve simply drain, add butter and salt and pepper to taste. Or, you could try this recipe (it serves six): Put 12 cooked parsnips, split lengthwise, into a baking dish. Now combine crushed fresh pineapple (1 cup), fresh orange juice (½ cup), brown sugar (2 tablespoons), plus grated orange rind, ginger, nutmeg and salt to taste. Pour over the parsnips, dot with butter and bake in a 350 degree oven for a half hour.

PEAS

> "Pease porridge hot,
> Pease porridge cold,
> Pease porridge in the pot
> Nine days old."

I'M SURE YOU learned this centuries-old nursery rhyme as a child without ever realizing that pease and peas were one and the same. And to me, for instance, porridge meant oatmeal and nothing else.

From the Middle Ages up through the seventeenth century pease porridge—sort of like our split pea soup—was *the* winter staple all over northern Europe. Peas were among the few vegetables that could be dried and used throughout the months when nothing else was available. As a matter of fact, this use for peas was discovered more than 5000 years ago. They've been found at the site of Swiss lake dwellings that date back to the Bronze Age and in what remains of ancient Troy.

It wasn't until new varieties with better flavor were developed that people started eating green garden peas fresh. But when they did, peas were a bigger fad than hula hoops or skateboards. In France in 1696, Mme. de Maintenon wrote: "The impatience to eat them, the pleasure of having eaten them, and the joy of eating them again are the three points of private gossip ... it is both a fashion and a madness."

The climate in England was ideal for growing peas, and their cultivation became widespread. So many varieties were developed there that they were called "English peas." The phrase is still used in the South to distinguish them from Southern peas, which we Yankees call cowpeas or black-eyed peas.

Varieties There are so many characteristics that can distinguish varieties of peas that an Austrian monk, Gregor

Mendl, developed the whole science of genetics by observing generations of peas. Just a few possibilities are tall or dwarf, small or large pod, smooth or wrinkle-seeded, early or late. Combine a few of the traits: dwarf-early-wrinkled or tall-large pod-smooth and you can see why there are more than 1000 varieties grown in the United States today.

Commercial or garden peas may be either wrinkle-skinned or smooth-skinned types. This means that when *dried* the peas either remain smooth or become wrinkled. Wrinkled varieties tend to be sweet and smooth varieties tend to be not so sweet. I know of no way to distinguish between these two types except to taste test. Commonly-grown wrinkled varieties are the Little Marvel, Freezonian, Progress No. 9, Wando and Alderman. Smooth-seeded varieties are the Alaska and Radio.

Two special types deserve your attention, too. First, Chinese peas or peapods—you may know them as sugar peas or snow peas. The French call them *mange-tout*, or eat-all, and that's the best description. The peas inside are tiny and the pod is tender so they are eaten whole.

The other type is the Southern, or black-eyed type, also known as cowpea. Unlike garden peas, which are native to Asia, cowpeas originated in Africa. They were brought to this country by slave traders and are still popular in the South. Northerners are apt to call them beans, but by official government decree, as of July 13, 1956, they're peas.

Seasons   The Mexican crop makes fresh peas available year 'round. In winter and early spring, Mexico, California, Texas and Florida supply the market. Later in the season northern states, from Washington in the West to New Jersey in the East, come into production. May through August is the peak season.

Marketing Practices   I can remember when fresh peas were one of our biggest sellers on the wholesale market. I'd venture to say that 3000 sacks—and that's got to be 240,000 pounds—would be sold on the San Francisco produce terminal on a good day. Nowadays 10,000 pounds would be considered a heavy shipment.

I'll bet the answer to this decline is sitting in the freezer section of your refrigerator right now. Frozen peas, of course. I can't argue that fact that they're not convenient, but I think I sure can make a case for fresh peas on the basis of taste if you're willing to compare the two. I've noticed lately that some of our ecology-minded younger generation is "discovering" fresh peas. Good for them.

U.S. No. 1 is the common grade on the market, although there is a Fancy grade, too. The standard calls for well-filled pods that are neither overmature nor too small.

Garden peas and Chinese peas are sold loose by the pound. In the South, black-eyed peas are, too. In the North, however, you're apt to find fresh ones already shelled and packed in cello-bags.

How to Buy Look for small, shiny green pods that are rather velvety to the touch. Don't buy any pods filled to the bursting point. These are old or mature and the peas inside will taste tough or mealy because the natural sugar has started converting to starch. Also reject any pods that are faded or discolored.

You can always tell how fresh peas are by breaking a pod open and tasting one of the peas inside. But here's a professional trick that works just as well. Press down gently on the pea pods on display in your retail produce department. Push them around a little. If the pods squeak against each other they're fresh. We used to be able to predict whether peas were fresh or not without ever opening a sack, just by using this "squeak test."

Keep peas unshelled in your refrigerator and use them as soon as possible after you buy them. The English writer Charles Lamb had the right idea when he wrote a friend that moving to his new home near Covent Garden, London's produce district, meant he'd be able to eat his peas fresher.

Nutrition Peas contain some riboflavin and vitamin A. They are a good source of thiamin and niacin, vitamin C and iron. And they provide very good amounts of protein.

There are 84 calories in ½ cup of shelled raw peas and 71 calories in ½ cup of cooked ones.

Uses as Food   You can hunt through every cookbook you own and chances are you won't find a single mention of the way peas are best—raw. Yet all you have to do is watch anyone, child or adult, shell peas and watch how many go into the mouth instead of the saucepan.

If you must cook them, use as little water as possible and keep the cooking time to a minimum. The French cook peas with lettuce and use as liquid only the water that clings to the leaves after rinsing.

Peas and carrots are a popular combination, but there are others I like better. Try peas with sauteed mushrooms, boiled pearl onions, or with small boiled new potatoes in cream sauce. By themselves, peas take on added flavor with the addition of mint or basil. Or try peas with a sliced new spring onion and a little garlic, olive oil, salt and pepper. Place in a pan with a little water and cook slowly for 15 to 20 minutes.

Cooked peas can be served chilled in vegetable salads. Another good combination is with small shrimp.

Chinese peapods should be stir-fried in oil, perhaps with a small amount of soy sauce. Take a tip from the best Chinese restaurants and combine them with crunchy water chestnuts.

PEPPERS

IT HAPPENS EVERY day. A man is sent out to bring one thing back for dinner and comes home with something quite different. Take Columbus, for example. He set out to get *Piper nigrum* (pepper) and came back with *Capsicum annuum* (chili pepper) instead. He meant well. No European had ever seen the plant dried black peppercorns came from. But they were hot and so were the strange vegetables he found in the West Indies. The mistake was a natural one—even today some people think both come from the same plant.

This native American hot pepper, often called chili (from Chile), was soon widely adopted and cultivated by the spice-hungry Europeans and then spread to most tropical areas of the world. In India, where they are known as chillies, they became so common that centuries later botanists claimed they were native to that area. The pimiento, a sweet mild pepper, became so popular in Spain that it was reintroduced to the Western Hemisphere from there. And another mild bright-red variety has made Hungary the world's paprika-producer up to this day.

Varieties There are hundreds of types and varieties of peppers and it's almost a rule of thumb that the smaller the pepper the more pungent the taste.

Big sweet peppers, usually called Bell because of their shape, can be green or red in color. They aren't different varieties, it's just that the red ones have been harvested when fully ripe and sweet (they were green first). The California Wonder is perhaps the most popular variety.

When it comes to the small hot chili peppers, you better know the variety you're buying and proceed with caution. The *Green,* or *Fresno,* is a small dart-shaped green chili about 1½ inches long and not too hot. The *California Long Green,* or *Anaheim,* is longer and fairly mild. It's often used

for stuffing to make the delicious Mexican dish, Chiles Rellenos. The *Serrano* is a small thin green or red chili pepper
that's very hot. The *Yellow Wax,* also known as *Guero* or
Carribi, is hot enough to bring tears to your eyes when you
eat it. It's sometimes used for pickling. There's also the
Jalapeno, thinner and longer than the Fresno, and really hot
stuff. The South produces the *Long Red Cayenne,* which is
easily dried and the *Tabasco,* a small yellow variety that
gives the hot sauces produced in Louisiana their heat.

Seasons   Both Bell and chili peppers are on the market year
'round. The peak season is August and September. The supply comes from Mexico from early December through April,
and around this time they are usually higher in price.

Marketing Practices   Peppers are very sensitive to climate.
Too much heat, cold or rain will affect the crop and the
prices you pay. So when you hear a weather report of late
frost or exceptionally wet weather in Florida, Louisiana,
Texas or California, expect to pay higher prices.
        Peppers are usually sold loose by the pound.

How to Buy   When you're buying green Bells, keep in mind
what you're buying them for and you'll get your money's
worth. For stuffing, buy the large well-shaped "Fancy"
grade. For other cooking and salads buy the much cheaper
U.S. No. 2, also known as "Choice." You'll just cut them up
anyway, so as long as they're firm and fresh, they'll serve just
as well and cost much less.
        Look for firm dark green peppers. It's usually easy to
spot immature peppers by their sickly look—pale, soft and
thin-skinned. Overmature ones will have a dull appearance.
In addition, avoid green Bell peppers that are starting to
turn red or look shriveled, wilted and generally tired out. Be
sure to check out the stem end, too, that's where decay
usually starts. And, during winter months especially, watch
for black spots caused by rain.
        Be on the lookout for the arrival of big, sweet, fully-ripe
red Bells late in the season. They have many uses in cooking,
but here's an additional tip. If the price of tomatoes is high,

buy these sweet red peppers instead. They'll add color, flavor and nutrition to any salad.

Nutrition   Obviously, a few strips of pepper aren't going to make much difference in your diet, but in larger amounts, they're loaded with nutrients. One-half raw pepper will fill your daily quota of Vitamin C. They are also high in vitamin A. Red peppers are higher in vitamin A and vitamin C than the green ones.) Peppers also contain small amounts of calcium, phosphorus, iron, sodium and magnesium, as well as thiamin; riboflavin and niacin. Are you sold on peppers? Here's another plus: they're very low in calories.

Uses as Food   Peppers are versatile. A Bell, of course, can be cut into one or two cups and stuffed with a variety of rice and meat mixtures to make attractive main courses for dinner. They lend flavor to stews, especially veal, because the meat is so bland in taste. Both the green and mature red make good and nutritious additions to salads or snack trays.

Hot chili peppers are essential to a wide variety of Mexican and Latin-influenced dishes, including Creole cookery. Besides their use for flavoring in sauces, these peppers lend their names to such favorites as Chili con Carne, Chili con Juevos and Chiles Rellenos.

One word of caution to remember when you're handling the fiery little chiles. The natural chemical called Capsicum that gives peppers their bite is present in the form of a volatile oil. It can cause severe irritation if rubbed into your eyes. So prepare the hot ones, especially the yellow wax variety, under running water and wash your hands throughly in soapy water after handling them.

If you've never tasted roasted red bell peppers take my word for it, they're out of this world. Here's the recipe: Bake the peppers in a slow oven for 1½ hours. Remove from the oven and cover with a cloth until cool. Then remove the skin and seeds, slice and add a little olive oil or vinegar and salt and pepper to taste. Use the same day or place in a closed bottle with enough oil to cover and store in the refrigerator. The slices make a great side dish with meat, fish or fowl and can also be used in salads and sandwiches.

POTATOES

PARDON THE PUN, but here's a potato's-eye view of history: If the potato crop hadn't failed in County Wexford, Ireland, in 1848, then Patrick Kennedy, great-grandfather of Robert and John Fitzgerald Kennedy, might never have left to seek his fortune far from the Auld Sod. And think of how the history of our times would have changed.

A Dutch chemist once called the potato an "ill-starred root," and its history does seem to be connected with wars and famines. On the other hand, potatoes come close to being a complete though low-protein food, so they do have their redeeming social significance. Many people consider the potato to be the most important single vegetable in the world today. Certainly, pound for pound, potatoes are the most economical and nutritious buy you'll find.

Potatoes were probably domesticated first in Chile. Europeans discovered them when the Spanish explorer Pizarro went on a treasure hunt in Peru that destroyed the Inca Empire. He never would have believed that the potatoes he found were more valuable than the gold he was seeking. The Incas, by the way, anticipated modern food-processing methods by many centuries. They exposed their potatoes to freezing temperatures, then dried them in the sun. These dehydrated potatoes were kept from harvest to harvest, to be pounded into flour or cooked whole.

The first European country to adopt the potato was—you guessed it—Ireland. Cultivation started in about 1565 and has continued ever since. So few staples were grown in addition to potatoes that when a potato crop failed it meant starvation for thousands. The famous Great Famine of 1845 and following years was caused by late blight attacking the potato crop. It started waves of emigration to England, Scotland, Australia, Canada and the United States.

People in other countries resisted the potato, although

their leaders strongly urged their cultivation. In Scotland, devoutly religious Presbyterians objected because potatoes weren't mentioned in the Bible. In Prussia, King Frederick William I threatened to cut off the noses and ears of all peasants who refused to plant them. Bribery seemed to work better. Frederick the Great distributed seed potatoes free, along with instructions on how to plant and cultivate them. But the thing that firmly established potatoes on the continent of Europe was the famine that accompanied the Seven Year's War (1756–1763). A Frenchman, Antoine Auguste Parmentier, who was fed potatoes as a prisoner in Germany during that war, set up soup kitchens for his starving countrymen when he returned to France. Louis XVI told him, "France will thank you some day for having found bread for the poor." The thanks came in the form of naming a potato soup after him. You can find recipes for Potage Parmentier in cookbooks today.

Many supposedly educated people still weren't convinced. In Holland, a chemist named Mulder wrote that "potatoes cannot become a staple diet without the eaters not only dwindling in physical condition but growing more dull and torpid in intellectual, also ... potatoes have produced a growing lumpishness and so-to-speak potato-mindedness in the people." If you've ever seen Van Gogh's paintings of the Brabant peasants, called "The Potato Eaters," you might be inclined to agree.

Potatoes finally returned to the Western Hemisphere when Irish immigrants brought them to Londonderry, New Hampshire, in 1719. Since they are a cool-weather crop, most potatoes are grown today in Aroostook County, Maine, in Idaho, in the ocean-cooled areas of Long Island, New York and New Jersey, and in the high elevations of Colorado and the foothills of California's Sierra Nevada.

Varieties   There are many different ways to talk about kinds of spuds, which is what we always call potatoes in the produce trade. I could divide them up by shape, by color, by growing area, or by use. The best way, I think, is by combining shape and color. Of the 15 or so varieties grown in quantity commercially, chances are the ones you find in your store will be:

ROUND WHITE: Maine produces the Kathadin and Kennebec, the Midwest grows the Cobbler. These potatoes are good for boiling, baking and French fries. Other varieties in this grouping are the Chippewa and Sebago.

ROUND RED: The main varieties are the Red Pontiac, Red LaSoda, Red McClure and Triumph. They are mainly used for boiling.

LONG WHITE: The main variety is the White Rose, produced in 12 states, mostly in the West. It is best for boiling, good for baking and frying, too.

LONG RUSSET: Idaho, Washington and Oregon produce the Russet Burbank, which is ideal for baking, but good for every other purpose, too.

Seasons   There is no peak season for potatoes. They are on the market in almost equal amounts every month of the year. There are several reasons for this. Any one variety can be planted over a long period of time, which extends the harvest. Also, potatoes from different areas mature at different times. Finally, mature potatoes store well so they can be released into the market over a period of several months.

Marketing Practices   Federal inspectors grade the potatoes you buy. Much of this grading is based on American buying and eating habits. We expect our baking potatoes, for example, to be large, light and pure white. In parts of Europe a yellowish color is preferred but any potatoes with this characteristic would be graded low here.

For best quality buy the U.S. No. 1 grade, which should assure uniformity of size and freedom from blemishes, inside and out. Mature baking potatoes of this grade will weigh six ounces or more.

Potatoes are sold loose in the bin and priced by the pound, or packed by two's or three's in cellophane, or by the sack. The small family with limited storage facilities is better off buying potatoes loose. Large families can save money by buying the largest sack they can afford or carry.

The best buy is probably the 10-pound bag, usually referred to as the multi-purpose bag. The size of the potatoes in one will range from small to large, providing the right potato for every use and every member of the family.

Often a retail merchant will advertise one brand of 10-pound bag of potatoes at a ridiculously low price. Right next to them will be another brand selling for up to almost twice as much. The two brands may be the same quality—the only difference is the bag, and that's not what you should be paying for.

Sometimes you'll see a 20-pound bag of potatoes priced very low. I've found that most of the potatoes in a "bargain" sack will be second-rate, often misshapen and with splits and cracks. Unless you intend to use a large number in a very short time—potato salad and potatoes for the annual Sunday School Picnic and Potato Race—I'd avoid them. The number you'll throw out due to decay will make this a very expensive bargain.

How to Buy   Potatoes are marketed as new, meaning immature, or old, meaning mature. Choosing between these two types, depending on how you want to use them, should be your first decision.

New potatoes are used for steaming, boiling and potato salads. They have a high moisture and sugar content and are low in starch. They tend to have a slightly waxy texture. Look for well-shaped firm potatoes of fairly uniform size. A little skinning, which makes the surface look like it's peeling from a bad case of sunburn, is normal in new potatoes and doesn't affect the quality.

Mature potatoes are used for baking, mashing or French fries. Look for dry, well-shaped potatoes, without skinning or sprouts.

Green areas or a greenish cast indicates that a potato has been exposed to light too long. This can happen in the field when the potato isn't completely covered by soil and sunlight hits it. It's more likely, however, that greening has occurred from the potato being stored or displayed under artificial light for a long period of time. Avoid these potatoes, they will have a bitter taste.

To keep your potatoes from greening or sprouting once you get them home, store them in a cool, dry, dark place. Never put them in your refrigerator, the temperature is just a little too cool. At room temperature, potatoes should keep for two to three weeks.

Nutrition Most people think potatoes are fattening. They're not. It's the butter, sour cream or gravy served with them that adds the calories.

For instance, a medium-sized boiled potato contains only 76 calories, about the same as one boiled egg. A larger baked potato contains 139.

Potatoes are high in carbohydrates, lack fat, and are a fair to good source of vitamins B_1, C and niacin. They have a good amount of iron and potassium and also contain calcium and phosphorus.

You probably wouldn't want to try this diet, but in one experiment volunteers ate nothing but potatoes with a small amount of fat for five months. At the end of that time they were all in good physical health. Also pretty bored, I'd imagine.

I should mention one special nutritional use for potatoes. Converted into flour for bread and rolls, they are literally a life-saver for children and adults on gluten-free diets.

One more thing. Processed potatoes—frozen, powdered or flaked—may seem more convenient. But you'll be paying a premium price for potatoes that have lost over 50% of their valuable vitamin C in the form of acsorbic acid.

Uses as Food   There are almost as many ways to serve potatoes as there are ways to cook. Roasted, baked, steamed, boiled, mashed, fried, creamed, browned, French fried, hash-browned, whipped, diced, riced, scalloped. Have I left any out? In potato salads, both cold and hot German-style. In hot soups, such as M. Parmentier's, and cold ones, such as Vichysoisse.

Here are some tips on preparing potatoes.

When you bake potatoes be sure to puncture the skin.

Otherwise you may set off an artillery barrage in your oven. An aluminum or stainless steel kitchen nail, or skewer, or even a metal knitting needle poked through the potato you're baking will help it cook more quickly and evenly. If you intend to eat the skin, and everyone should, a little butter or oil rubbed in the skin before baking will make it even more delicious.

For best nutrition and the least amount of waste, potatoes should be boiled in their jackets. The skin will be easy to peel after cooking if you score a circle around the potato with a paring knife, or remove a narrow belt of skin from the middle, before dropping it into the pot.

Finally, here's a trick that can avert a cooking disaster. If somehow your soup gets over-salted, cut a potato in slices and boil them in the soup until the saltiness disappears. This way, you'll discard a potato instead of a whole kettle of soup.

PUMPKINS

HENRY DAVID THOREAU, who was the original believer in "doing your own thing," said, "I would rather sit on a pumpkin and have the seat all to myself than be crowded on a velvet cushion." I hope once he got up from his pumpkin-seat he took it home to Walden Pond to make ˜pie—the reason I prefer pumpkins to velvet.

Pumpkins have been growing in the Americas for thousands of years. They were a staple Indian food and were widely used by the early New England colonists as well. We serve pumpkin pie at Thanksgiving to remember the Pilgrim's first harvest feast, which probably did include pumpkin because an old verse went:

"For pottage and puddings, and custards, and pies,
Our pumpkins and parsnips are common supplies.
We have pumpkins at morning and pumpkins at noon;
If it were not for pumpkins, we should be undoon."

Somehow I get the feeling the poet was getting a little tired of all that pumpkin, don't you?

Varieties Pumpkin is really just another type of hard squash, indistinguishable from the others botanically. It has the same nutritional content and uses—aside from being the raw material for Jack o'Lantern sculpture. In fact, canners often use or add other hard squashes, such as Hubbard or Banana, to their prepared pie-filling mix.

A variety called Connecticut Field is the traditional Halloween pumpkin.

Seasons About 80% of fresh pumpkin sales are made in October. Only 3% of the annual crop is marketed in November. Perhaps the mysterious Great Pumpkin who disappoints the kids in "Peanuts" every year is working some special witchcraft to prevent us from enjoying our traditional Thanksgiving pie.

Marketing Practices Many pumpkin growers offer "bargains" to passing motorists just before Halloween. Professional buyers have usually bought up the good-quality fields by that time, so ingenious farmers use this gimmick to sell off the few fields that have been passed over. Few customers can judge the market value of a pumpkin in the field, so once the car has stopped and Junior has chosen his favorite pumpkin—and had his picture snapped with it—the deal is closed. It's probably worth the price just to give city children a chance to see produce growing in a field.

I'm willing to bet that 99.99% of these pumpkins wind up as Jack o'Lanterns anyway, so the eating quality isn't really important. If this is what you buy a pumpkin for, at least dry (or roast) and salt the seeds. They're delicious.

Uses as Food   Let's face it, fresh pumpkin is not a convenience food. It's quite a job to prepare a homemade fresh pumpkin pie. You have to cut it up, clean out the seeds, bake it, scrape the pulp from the shell, put it through a ricer or strainer, and then season carefully with a number of spices. Few people go to all this trouble when they can grab a can of pumpkin from the supermarket shelf. This is especially true during the Thanksgiving season, which is a hectic one for any cook.

But pie isn't the only way to cook pumpkins. Look in any traditional American cookbook and you'll find recipes for cream of pumpkin soup, pumpkin bread and many others. I was surprised to find pumpkin recipes even in one of the Haut-est of Haute Cuisine French recipe books, including one called "Le Potiron Tout Rond," or pumpkin served inside the pumpkin shell.

RADISHES

SOME PEOPLE LOVE radishes. They've been cultivated and eaten, mainly pickled, in the Orient for thousands of years. The great Italian composer Rossini esteemed them so highly they're one of the subjects of a composition called "Four Hors d'Oeuvres." (The other three are butter, anchovies and pickled gherkins.)

Others have mistrusted them. A "Plague Pamphlet," published in London in 1665 said the dread disease had been caused by, "Eating radishes, a cat catter wouling, . . . immoderate eating of caviare and anchoves, tame pigeons that flew up and down an alley, drinking strong heady beer."

Varieties Radishes can be round (ranging from cherry to basketball size), oval or oblong. They can be white, red and white, solid red or black. Whatever the size, shape or color, the flavor is practically the same.

The small round ones are the most common in the United States. Cherry Belle and Comet are two popular red ones. The White Icicle is an attractive white radish, which is narrow and grows up to 5 inches long.

The spectaculars of the radish family are the Orientals. The Japanese Daikon is a big white variety, which can grow to several feet in length.

Seasons The growing time for small varieties is less than a month. Planting, growing and harvesting continues throughout the year, peaking between April and mid-July.

Marketing Practices When you pick up a plastic bag of radishes from the supermarket bin, your hands are almost the first to touch them. Large producers have the process entirely mechanized. A large harvesting machine can lift and top six rows of radish plants at a time. The machine, operated by one man, is said to replace 300 manual laborers. I hate to speculate about what happens to the 299 other manual laborers, but I do know what happens to the radishes. They are mechanically sorted, washed, cooled in ice-cold chlorinated water, popped into a bag, automatically weighed and sealed, and sent on their way in refrigerated trucks.

If your retailer puts bunches of radishes on special, double-check his price for bunched green onions. People buy these items together, so sometimes retailers will offer low-priced radishes and make up the difference by marking up the green onions accordingly. It's the old practice of robbing Peter to pay Paul, with you being Patsy, who does the paying.

Radishes are marketed in bunches or in plastic bags weighing six to eight ounces. They are priced by the bunch or bag.

How to Buy   Unlike most other root vegetables, the condition of the tops does not affect the eating quality. However, the leaves will certainly tell you whether the radishes are fresh or old. When buying radishes with tops, look for fresh green crisp leaves and radish roots that are smooth, bright-looking, firm and well-formed.

If you want to experiment with the giant Daikon, you'll have to settle for a large sample. In San Francisco, anyway, they come in bunches of two or three. Considering their size, that's a lot of radish for the average family.

Remove the tops of small radishes before refrigerating them. They should be used within a few days at most. The Daikon is not as perishable and can be stored for a longer time.

Nutrition   The Italian word is *niente;* and that goes for calories. But they are a good source of vitamin C.

Uses as Food   Radishes can be eaten whole with green onions, or sliced into salads. They also make an attractive garnish on a platter. It's easy to make radish roses, just make thin cuts in the red skin from the top almost to the base. When you drop them into iced water, the petals will turn back.

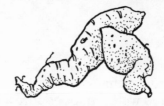

SWEET POTATOES AND YAMS

A SWEET POTATO by any other name would taste as sweet because it's not a potato at all. That is if you think of potatoes as the white, "Irish" type. And a yam, in the United States at least, is a variety of sweet potato, not the true yam that grows in the tropics.

Our sweet potatoes and yams are members of the morning-glory family. You'd recognize that if you ever saw a sweet potato flower. They hardly ever blossom in the United States, however, so you'd have to travel to Mexico or Central America to prove it.

The Incas of South America and the Mayas of Central America called the plant cassiri. They grew many varieties, including one that artists used as a coloring material.

When Columbus and his shipmates ate their first boiled sweet potatoes they compared the taste to chestnuts. The Spaniards took the sweet potato to the Philippines and the East Indies, the Portuguese to India, China and Malaya. Attempts to introduce it to Europe were unsuccessful because of the climate. It's still almost unknown there. But in the Orient sweet potatoes are so commonplace they're often called Japanese potatoes.

Sweet potatoes were quickly adopted by the early settlers in America. They served as a staple for livestock as well as humans. It's said sweet potatoes helped the South survive during the Civil War and Reconstruction days.

Between 1836 and 1936, Georgia remained the leading state in production of sweet potatoes. Then cultivation of new varieties in other states, especially Louisiana, started cutting down on the lead. During the past decade, for instance, Louisiana, North Carolina and Virginia have outproduced Georgia every year.

Varieties Most of the types now popular supposedly stemmed from plants of the Mameya variety brought to

Louisiana from Puerto Rico by an unknown migrant worker. They were probably brought in surreptitiously, and if you've ever tried to get so much as one bonsai tree or one box of chocolate-covered cherries through U.S. Customs you'll know why. (This isn't to say that strict laws on importation aren't necessary to prevent plant diseases from spreading.)

That name Mameya means "yellow yam" in Puerto Rican dialect. They've increasingly taken over from the drier, more mealy sweet potatoes in popularity.

Next time you're shopping notice what your market is selling as "sweet potatoes." If the bin if filled with light yellowish-tan tubers, they're true sweet potatoes. If the skin is coppery or brownish they're what we call yams. The eating part, or flesh, varies, too. Sweet potatoes are light yellow or pale orange inside; yams a deep orange.

Seasons   One variety or another is available year 'round. Sweet potato supplies are lowest from the first of June through early August. Yams are in best supply from November, in time for Thanksgiving, right through the Easter season.

Marketing Practices   Sweet potatoes and yams that are shipped to produce markets fresh are washed, graded and packed right after harvesting. Those going into storage, unlike most other produce, are cured at high temperature and humidity. Taken from storage, as much as three months later, they are washed and graded just before being packed for shipment.

U.S. grades for sweet potatoes aren't of much interest or use to the consumer. If you're buying them loose, you can do your own grading for size or quality at the time of purchase. Sometimes you'll also find a few of uniform size in plastic-wrapped trays. Pricing is by the pound loose, and by the unit packaged.

How to Buy   Small- or medium-sized sweet potatoes that taper at both ends are usually the best quality. Look for firm, well-shaped ones with smooth skin. Avoid any with growth cracks or damp areas, as well as discolored or shriveled ones.

Sweet potatoes and yams will store well at home in a dark, fairly humid place for at least two weeks.

Nutrition Sweet potatoes and yams are very valuable nutritionally, but the exact amounts of calories, vitamins and minerals can vary widely, and not only according to different locations or varieties. From season to season, the same variety grown in the same field will test out differently. So this information should be taken generally, not specifically:

One large baked sweet potato will provide almost three times the vitamin A an adult needs daily and two-thirds the vitamin C.

Uses as Food A baked yam is about the best convenience food you can imagine. It looks good, tastes good, is good for you, and requires no preparation except a good washing. The sweet potato serves the same purpose, but most people nowadays seem to prefer the sweeter-moister-tasting yams.

Instead, sweet potatoes are usually used for more complicated dishes. Candied, or as a sort of pudding with marshmellow topping, they're almost a must for Thanksgiving and other festive fall occasions.

In San Francisco we have the opportunity to sample a wide variety of ethnic specialties. I recommend Japanese tempura-style cooking for sweet potatoes. It's not greasy deep-fat frying, although the cooking is done in hot oil. What actually happens is that the vegetable quickly steam-cooks inside a thin coating of almost transparent batter. In any larger city you can find tempura batter mix at supermarkets or Oriental grocery stores. It combines rice and wheat flour with other ingredients. Follow the directions on the package, then dip slices or cubes of raw peeled sweet potato into the batter and drop into hot oil. Remove as soon as they're lightly browned and tender. Drain on paper towels and serve with side dishes of soy sauce or hot mustard, or both mixed. This unique and delicious cooking method can be used with many other vegetables, too, including broccoli, stringbeans, zucchini—take your pick.

SHALLOTS

THIS ELEGANT COUSIN of onions and garlic is the darling of the French gourmet. Any haute cuisine recipe for sauce or soup that's worth its salt will probably call for a half-dozen or so of these delicately-flavored members of the lily family.

In looks the shallot, sometimes called by its French name, eschalot, is half-onion and half-garlic. The bulb has the reddish-brown skin of an onion but is divided into cloves like a garlic bulb. The flavor is also somewhere between the two—but much more subtle.

Some say shallots originated and took their name from the Palestinian city of Ascalon. During the Crusades they were brought back to Europe as a "new" food and were immediately adopted and cultivated by the French. It was Frenchmen, followers of the explorer DeSoto, who introduced them to the United States in 1543.

Varieties There are several varieties of shallots grown commercially, but the average consumer would have a hard time telling one from another.

Seasons English gardeners have a proverb for shallots: "Plant on the shortest day, lift on the longest day." Commercial growing more or less follows this calendar, too. Shallots are at their best (and lowest in price) from late July to the end of October. Later in the year they are still available, but come from storage.

Marketing Practices Until about 20 years ago, Louisiana produced as many as 15 million pounds of fresh shallots per year. Today you'll see few or none on the market. Apparently increased production of less expensive green onions put the fresh shallot industry out of business in the U.S.

Long Island and New Jersey still produce some mature shallot bulbs for the metropolitan New York market, and a few are grown in California, Indiana and Illinois. But most of our shallots are now imported from France, Belgium or the Netherlands. French shallots are generally the largest and best in quality, but each season is different. The commercial importer has to have gambling blood: he usually contracts for a harvest in advance, before the season starts.

Occasionally you may see shallots sold loose by the pound, but you're more likely to find them in small tubs covered with clear plastic. Just because some unscrupulous customers used to slip loose shallots into the bottom of a brown paper bag and camouflage them with cheaper onions on top, everyone now pays more for the packaging.

How to Buy   In the wholesale market shallot buyers test each shipment for freshness by slicing a few bulbs in half to see if they're fresh and firm. I'm sure your grocer wouldn't appreciate it if you tried the same technique. You'll just have to go by exterior appearance.

Look for large firm shallots with bulbs about ¾-inch in diameter. The outer skin should be smooth and dry without any of the shriveling that shows dehydration or age. Of course, those that are sprouting should be avoided, too.

Shallots should be kept cool and dry. Store them in your refrigerator in a tightly-closed bag or a capped jar.

Nutrition   Shallots are consumed in such small amounts that it's ridiculous to talk about their nutritive value. I'd rather you consider them the catalyst that leads to the consumption of other more nutritive foods.

Uses as Food   Just consult your favorite collection of French or Continental recipes and you'll find a mouth-watering array of soups, stews and sauces flavored with minced shallots.

If the shallot is new to you, here's a simple way to taste-test its subtle flavor. Peel several medium-sized shallots and blanch in boiling water until they're tender. Then use a mortar and pestle to combine them with an equal amount of softened butter. (If the mortar and pestle reside in your druggist's window and not in your kitchen, you can use a blender, I guess.) Spread the shallot-butter on melba toast or crackers and, as a famous French chef says, bon appetit!

SPINACH

WHETHER YOU'RE OF the Saturday movie matinee or the TV cartoon generation, I'm sure you think of Popeye as soon as I say spinach. I don't know what method mothers used to get kids to eat spinach before that feisty little sailor with the bulging muscles became the world's most effective spinach salesman. I've heard that in Texas, our major spinach-growing state, one town even put up a statue in his honor.

As vegetables go, spinach is a newcomer to most of the world. It originated in Persia, or what's now called Iran, and was unknown in Europe until the Moorish invasion of Spain. In fact, as late as the sixteenth century, Englishmen were still calling spinach "the Spanish vegetable."

Varieties There are two main types of spinach—smooth-leaf, used mostly by food processors, and crumpled-leaf, which is sold fresh. The varieties planted commercially are predominantly Bloomsdale Dark Green and American. Both have dark green leaves that are large and crinkled.

New Zealand spinach is also marketed. It's not from New Zealand and it's not spinach. But it is a close relative, with small, very thick leaves that can be used just like spinach.

Seasons Spinach doesn't grow well during long hot summer days or in wet weather. So, it's harvested in regions with mild winters—Texas and California—during the winter months and then progresses northward into the Northeastern and Midwestern states in spring and fall. That means one region or another is growing spinach and shipping it into the produce market all through the year. The supply is at its peak from March through June.

Marketing Practices Retail customers used to complain that when they bought a pound of spinach they actually brought home a half-pound of greens and a half-pound of sand.

Now most producers provide clean bunches that need only a good rinsing in cool water. You may find these bunches loose, and priced by the pound, or in cellopack bags weighing about 10 ounces.

There are government grades for fresh spinach. Your food store is most likely to sell U.S. No. 1 grade, which should be fairly clean and well-trimmed—and free from foreign material, disease, insects and other unpleasant surprises for the cook.

How to Buy   Select fresh, crisp-looking bunches with large dark leaves. Reject any with wilted or bruised leaves, yellowish ones, and bunches which appear untrimmed and full of grit.

It's best to buy spinach as you need it because, even in the refrigerator, three to five days is the outside limit for storage. If you buy in bulk and the spinach seems gritty, then trim off the roots and wash the leaves in a sinkful of warm water. The leaves will float to the top and the sand will sink. Then rinse well in cold running water, drain and store in the refrigerator in a plastic bag or covered container. Prewashed spinach needs only a final rinse just before cooking.

Nutrition   Spinach is a good example of how nutritional information can be misinterpreted by the public. When it was found that spinach was a good source of iron, tons of it (quite a bit of which was overcooked, watery and gritty, I bet) was forced down children to "make them strong." Later it was found that spinach contained oxalic acid, which made the calcium unable to be absorbed by the body. Overreaction again—now spinach was a villain. Actually, the truth is somewhere in-between. As long as calcium is obtained from other sources, such as milk, there's no cause for concern. And spinach does have an abundance of other valuable nutrients.

A half-cup of cooked spinach provides about twice the vitamin A, half the vitamin C and up to one-fifth the iron an adult requires daily. In addition, spinach ranks with that health-food standby, brewer's yeast, as a source of folic acid, one of the essential B vitamins. The food-energy content of this amount of spinach is just 28 calories.

Uses as Food   Spinach is delicious when steamed in a covered pan for five to ten minutes, using only the water that clings to the leaves after a final rinsing. Or, it can be cooked in a small amount of water uncovered for about ten minutes. I even like it pan-cooked in a little olive oil with garlic.

Cooked spinach can be served with butter and lemon juice; some people prefer it with vinegar. Or it can be chopped or puréed and creamed.

Every year tourists discover how good raw spinach is when they visit many San Francisco restaurants where the "house salad" is raw spinach with crumbled bacon.

You may think of spinach as a prosaic sort of vegetable, but it's the base for a variety of Italian gourmet recipes. Whenever you see a dish listed on a menu as "alla fiorentina" (a la Florentine in French) you can be sure it's made with steamed or puréed spinach.

Here's my recipe for *Sole alla Fiorentina,* a delicious and economical dish. That's an unbeatable combination. This amount serves four: Put two cups of water and 1 teaspoon salt in a skillet and bring to a boil. Simmer 1 pound filet of sole in the salted water for ten minutes. Remove the fish to a plate while you steam, drain and chop 1 pound fresh spinach. Put the spinach in a baking dish and lay the filets on top. Now make a cream sauce by melting 3 tablespoons butter in a saucepan and blending in 3 tablespoons flour. Season with ½ teaspoon salt and a dash of pepper. Gradually add 1¼ cups milk. Cook, stirring constantly, until the mixture is smooth and thick. Fold in ¼ cup heavy cream, whipped. Pour this sauce into the baking dish and sprinkle ¼ cup grated Parmesan cheese on top. Place under the broiler until the top is browned.

SQUASH

An AZTEC OR Inca of Columbus' time or even earlier might have trouble recognizing the tomatoes we grow today, their looks have changed so much. But not squash. Many of our present-day varieties have been growing in the Americas for close to 5000 years.

These relatives of gourds and pumpkins had spread throughout North America by the time the Pilgrims arrived in New England. They shortened the Indian word *askootasquash,* which meant "eaten raw," to squash, and immediately started boiling and baking them.

Europeans quickly adopted squash, especially the Italians, who named two of today's popular varieties, zucchini and cocozelle.

Varieties If I went along with the common distinctions of "summer" and "winter" you'd know immediately what kinds of squash I meant. The only trouble is that these days, anyway, both phrases are incorrect. A better way of considering squash is as one of these three groups: soft-shelled, small and immature; hard-shelled, small and mature; and hard-shelled, large and mature. There are countless varieties within each group, so I'll just cover the most widely-marketed and used.

SOFT-SHELLED, SMALL, IMMATURE increasingly dominate the market. They are harvested when about half-grown, before their seeds have become hard. There's Zucchini, or Italian, squash, which is cylindrical in shape, with fairly square ends. The skin color is actually yellow but a network of green, more concentrated in some areas than others, gives it an appearance of light and dark green stripes. The size can vary from small to jumbo, as much as a foot long. *Cocozelle,* or Italian marrow, is very similar in looks to zucchini, straight with alternating stripes of dark almost greenish-black and pale greenish yellow. It's at its best when 6 to

8 inches in length. *Yellow Crookneck* was once called crane-neck and it does look like a plump yellow bird with a long curved neck. This light yellow squash is usually 6 to 8 inches long. Its close relative is *Yellow Straightneck.* Just imagine that the "bird" has stretched out its neck and you'll have no trouble identifying it. *Scallop,* popularly known as summer squash, also known as Patty Pan or Cymling, is a pale green bowl-shaped squash. Prominent ribbing gives the edge its scalloped appearance. They are usually small, about 3 or 4 inches in diameter.

HARD-SHELLED, MATURE, SMALL   three varieties are grown in quantity commercially. *Acorn,* also called Table Queen, Danish or Des Moines, is a deep dull blackish-green when picked but turns orange in storage. You may find either color or a combination of the two. Distinctive wide furrows or ribs run the length of its hard thin skin. Inside is tender pale orange flesh surrounding a fairly large seed cavity. The *Butternut* is fairly large, from 9 to 12 inches in length. It's smooth and buff-colored and shaped like a giant peanut. The flesh is yellow or orange. *Buttercup* is easy to spot by its light-colored turban capping the blossom-end of a drum-shaped body with ivy-green and gray-green stripes. It may weigh up to 4 or 5 pounds. The orange flesh is dry and sweet.

HARD-SHELLED, MATURE, LARGE   these are the so-called "winter" squash. There are many varieties but these two are commonly seen in the supermarket, often pre-cut because they can grow to enormous size: *Banana* is several feet long and cylindrical in shape. The smooth skin changes from pale olive-gray to creamy pink in storage. The eating-part is orange-buff in color. *Hubbard* is a real old-timer, recognized by its green warty skin. Twelve to 15 pounds is average. The flesh is yellow and sweet.

Seasons   With new growing areas, refrigeration and better transportation "summer" and "winter" have mostly changed to "all-year."

The soft-shelled ones are always available, although the supply is at its peak from June through August. From mid-December through March we depend on the Mexican crop.

Acorn and Butternut squash are marketed all year, Butter-cup from late summer through winter. The Banana is available year 'round and in peak supply in October and November. During April and May they come from Mexico. The Hubbard is seen most commonly in December, but the season runs from October through March.

Marketing Practices A picture of a giant "winter" squash (and the farmer or, even better, the farmer's beautiful daughter) is a newspaper standby on a "slow news day." They can grow as tall as a fence and weigh hundreds of pounds. The ones that get to your market aren't that large, but they're big enough to be too big for the average family. So retailers often saw them into pieces weighing just a few pounds, remove the seeds and overwrap the pieces with film. These pieces are priced by the pound.

Even so, the sale of these traditional big hard types has fallen off while the demand for the young tender varieties continues to increase. These soft-shelled squash are sold loose by the pound or in cellopack bags.

How to Buy The soft-shelled varieties are best when small to medium in size. The rind should be so tender that a fingernail will puncture it easily. If you try this, for heaven's sake buy the ones you test out or you'll be a very, very unpopular customer and I don't want to be held responsible! Avoid any that show soft or watery areas.

When selecting pre-cut Banana or Hubbard squash look for crisp, clean flesh and reject any that appear bruised and discolored or show other signs of age.

Zucchini and other soft-shelled varieties are quite perishable. In fact, your retailer should display them in a refrigerated rack and sprinkle them occasionally to prevent dehydration. At home use them at once or refrigerate them in a plastic bag for a day or two at the most.

Nutrition All varieties of squash are quite low in calories. A half-cup of cooked soft-shelled squash contains about 14 calories. The same amount of hard-shelled squash, boiled and mashed, contains 38.

In general the soft-shelled varieties are good sources of

vitamin C, the hard-shelled ones excellent for the vitamin A they contain. Both are very low in sodium.

Uses as Food   The small immature varieties are usually cut in slices and steamed or sautéed. Very small ones need only be cut in half lengthwise before cooking. They may be called squash, but they should never be cooked to the point where they're squashy or mushy. Al dente or firm is the way these young tender varieties taste best. As a matter of fact, zucchini is becoming increasingly popular as a raw ingredient in salad or as an appetizer, cut in sticks and served with dips.

The small hard-shelled varieties are usually baked. Often brown sugar and butter are added. When the seeds are removed the cavity forms a natural cup for stuffing. This can be anything from sausage meat to onions to fruit.

The hard-shelled varieties are usually boiled or baked and then mashed. Since they are close relatives of the pumpkin, they can be used in any recipe calling for pumpkin. I'll bet that many of the "pumpkin pies" you've eaten have really been Banana or Hubbard squash pies.

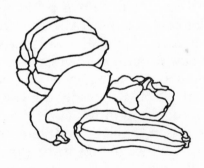

TOMATOES

IT TOOK TWO Italians, traveling in opposite directions, to provide the makings for spaghetti with tomato sauce. The Venetian, Marco Polo, to bring back the pasta from China, and the Genoese, Christopher Columbus, to discover the land of the tomato.

Early explorers in Mexico found the Indians growing a strange plant they called the *tomatl.* Its fruit was probably yellow, not red, because when tomatoes were brought to Europe the Italians called them *pomo d'oro,* meaning "apples of gold." The romantic French misheard the name as *pomo d'amore* or "love apple" and that was the first name they were known by in English, too.

It's never become as well-known as the story about his cloak, but Sir Walter Raleigh is supposed to have given the first Queen Elizabeth a tomato as a token of his affections. It seems rather bold of him because the name "love apple" had given the tomato a reputation as a powerful aphrodisiac.

I don't know if Puritan America objected to tomatoes on moral grounds or because they belong to the Nightshade family, some of which are deadly. Maybe it was just that early tomatoes could only grow in a very temperate climate. Whatever the reason, in the United States tomatoes weren't considered food—although they were grown as ornamental plants—until the middle of the nineteenth century. They finally became a commercial crop in the 1880's.

Now tomatoes are among the top three vegetables in dollar sales, just about matched by the lettuce they're usually served with, and outclassed only by the lowly spud. I've seen the quality and quantity improve every year I've been in the produce business. More efficient transportation and agricultural development are among the main reasons.

In the old days all tomatoes that were shipped any distance were picked in immature, hard, green condition and individually wrapped in paper. Wholesalers put these green tomatoes in basement ripening rooms. Like the old banana ripening rooms, these were just warm boarded-up areas with a can of water to provide humidity. Sometimes the paper wrappings on the tomatoes would be wetted down, too, for more humidity. As the tomatoes began to color-up, the produce men would strip the paper and sort the tomatoes by color, placing the green, pink and ripe ones in different boxes. The ripe and pink ones were then re-packed into baskets and moved upstairs for sale to the retailers. These tomatoes usually didn't color-up well and the flavor wasn't good.

Florida, Mexico and California still ship some green tomatoes, but more and more people today demand the better-tasting, mature, vine-ripened tomato.

That term "vine-ripened" needs some explanation. It covers different stages of maturity. For shipping long distances, the tomatoes are picked when the fruit is mature but the skin is still green. During shipment they begin showing some red on the blossom end. In this stage they're known as starbreakers. Others are harvested when the tomato is light pink. This is the preferred stage for picking them in the West. The tomatoes then get red but stay quite firm. They should be sold within two or three days. The last stage is red-ripe. These are the delicious local ones you get when tomatoes mature in your immediate area.

Sprawling suburbs have overrun the tomato fields that used to be on the edges of San Francisco and other large cities. But on weekend drives you can sometimes spot roadside stands featuring local tomatoes. When you do, pull off the road and stop. In season you can make some wonderful buys of real vine-ripened, fresh-picked tomatoes. It's the next best thing to standing in the field yourself and pulling a tomato off the vine to eat. (Just remembering the unforgettable smell of tomatoes with the sun shining on them makes my mouth water.)

The greatest contrast to this is the flavor of a greenhouse or hydroponically-grown tomato. You've probably tasted some. You probably also remember that they looked great and were expensive.

Varieties   Every year new varieties of commercially-grown tomatoes come on the market. They are developed specifically for the growing area, for disease resistance, or for better eating qualities. The varietal names are less important than how they were grown and when they were picked.

During the summer you'll sometimes see Beefsteak tomatoes advertised. There is a variety by this name that produces large, flat, rather irregularly-shaped tomatoes with a delicious flavor. In the market, though, the term is often used for any variety of large red tomato picked in firm condition.

Cherry tomatoes are easy to identify. They are round and bite-sized usually about an inch to 1½ inches in diameter. They can be grown just about anywhere in the United States but, from the commercial point of view, California and Mexico are the major producers.

Seasons   Good quality tomatoes are now available year 'round in most parts of the country. May through August is the peak season and prices usually come down during these months.

Marketing Practices   Standards for tomatoes are set by the Department of Agriculture and apply nationwide. As far as size goes, when I first started in the business, tomatoes were packed in what were called Los Angeles lugs. These were standard-sized containers made to hold three layers of tomatoes, sorted according to size. Very large tomatoes might pack into 4x4 rows; some were as small as 7x8 to the layer. The flats we use now are packed just two layers deep.

Tomatoes are sold by the pound loose, or pre-packed three or four to a tray or tub and priced at so much per pack. Cherry tomatoes are shipped and displayed in strawberry cartons and priced by the individual basket.

Often you'll notice tomatoes selling for two or even three prices in the same store. The most expensive will probably be greenhouse-grown or hydroponic ones, grown in mineral solutions instead of soil. Many stores sell vine-ripened tomatoes in several sizes. The larger ones may cost 10 cents or 20 cents a pound more. Unless you're planning to stuff or slice them, smaller tomatoes are your best buy, especially if you're going to cut them into salad or use them in stews or sauces.

How to Buy   Look for red, ripe, firm tomatoes. Their interesting combination of sweet and sour taste, actually sugar and acid, is dependent on proper ripeness. If a tomato's too green, the flavor is flat and sour; too ripe, and the taste becomes bland and sweet.

Tomatoes should be clean, unblemished and well-shaped. Avoid any that are split or spongy. Soft ones, which markets often throw out because they're not suitable for salads, are fine for cooking. I hate to see produce wasted and I wish more stores would mark these soft tomatoes down instead, providing their customers with a good, nutritious bargain.

Ripe tomatoes should be eaten or refrigerated at once. If you're buying for later use, get pale pink tomatoes and ripen them at home.

Nutrition   Tomatoes are low in carbohydrates and rich in vitamins and minerals, which makes them popular with dieters. A medium-size tomato contains only 30 to 35 calories and provides 57% of the vitamin C an adult needs daily. A raw tomato, that is. Cooking reduces the vitamin C content.

Uses as Food   I'm willing to bet most tomatoes are eaten raw in salads. I like them as-is with a relish made by mixing finely-chopped garlic, parsley, salt and pepper with olive oil. Sometimes I lay salted anchovies on top of sliced tomatoes, then add this relish.

But there are loads of other uses, too. You can stew, broil or bake them to serve as a hot vegetable. Or, you can put them in a blender, along with other fresh vegetables, and make your own vegetable juice cocktail.

For centuries tomatoes have been the basic of Italian cooking. Here's my recipe for making *Neapolitan Sauce:* Blend 12 fresh tomatoes in an electric blender until juice forms, then pour into a saucepan and bring to a boil. Reduce to a slow simmer while you heat 3 tablespoons of olive oil in a skillet. Slice 4 cloves of garlic into the oil and saute slowly until golden brown. Pour the hot tomato juice into this garlic mixture, add one sliced onion, a bay leaf and salt and pepper to taste. Simmer slowly for one hour if you're using it as spaghetti sauce. For vegetable dishes, simmer about 15 minutes, then add your favorite vegetable—zucchini, carrots, peas, beans, eggplant, even hearts of artichokes—and continue cooking until tender. I use this sauce so often that I make larger quantities and store some in the refrigerator or freezer until I need it.

TURNIPS & RUTABAGAS

SINCE TURNIPS AND rutabagas are such close relatives, are used the same way and usually are found side by side in a produce bin, I'll discuss them together.

Let's get one thing out of the way first. Some people don't like them. I'm sure they're the people one writer was thinking of when he said that the ingredient lacking in the middle-class American diet was hunger. The proof of this is that turnips, and to a lesser extent rutabagas, have been highly regarded as a staple winter food for centuries where no other produce was available.

Turnips have been cultivated since ancient times. They're supposed to be native to Russia and Scandinavia but the Romans knew many kinds—including round, long and flat varieties—before the start of the Christian Era and used them for food as well as feed for stock. They were one of the few vegetables known and available in Northern Europe up to fairly modern times.

They were introduced to North America by the earliest explorers and colonists. Jacques Cartier brought them to Canada in 1541. They were planted in Virginia in 1609 and in Massachusetts in the 1620's.

Rutabagas, on the other hand, are fairly modern. They seem to be the result of a meeting of a swinging Swedish turnip and an equally willing cabbage. They were introduced to England, where they're known as Swedes or Swedish turnips, at the end of the eighteenth century. Most of the U.S. supply for the East Coast comes from Canada, which accounts for their often being called Canadian turnips in this country. On the West Coast, most of the supply originates in Washington and Oregon.

Varieties Turnips look like old-fashioned spinning tops—half white, half purple. Rutabagas aren't as colorful, they're mostly plain yellowish-tan. In general, commercially-grown turnips have white flesh, while that of rutabagas is yellow. The leaves are different, too. Rutabagas have smooth leaves, turnips have somewhat rough ones with a few stiff "hairs" on them.

Many different varieties of turnips are grown commercially. Their shape and skin color may vary but they all taste about the same. The Purple-Top White Globe and the Purple-Top Milan are popular varieties grown for their roots. The Shogoin, an Oriental turnip, is one of the varieties grown for its tender greens. Pulled with tiny roots attached they are sold by the name rapini.

Two of the most widely-known rutabaga varieties are the Laurentian and the Purple-Top Yellow.

Seasons Both turnips and rutabagas store well for use as a winter root vegetable. They are available all year and especially plentiful during the fall and winter months.

Marketing Practices Turnips may be marketed with the greens attached or topped. With tops they are sold by the bunch. Topless, they may be purchased in plastic bags or by the pound, loose.

Rutabagas are almost always topped because the greens show deterioration long before the root does. They are usually sold by the pound.

How to Buy Look for roots that are firm and heavy for their size. Avoid any with cuts or punctures from mechanical harvesting, as well as very large ones, which may be woody or pithy.

Bunched turnips should have fresh, crisp-looking greens. Yellow wilted ones are a sign of age.

Turnips and rutabagas store well in a cool humid place. Turnip greens, however, are perishable and should be refrigerated and used as soon as possible.

Nutrition Turnips are a fair source of vitamin C. A ⅔-cup serving of cooked turnips provides about ⅓ the ascorbic acid an adult should get daily. The food-energy count for a serving this size is 23 calories. Turnip greens are rich in vitamin A.

Rutabagas are more nutritious. Half a cup cooked will provide almost ½ the vitamin C recommended, as well as more vitamin A and much less sodium than turnips. This amount contains 35 calories.

Uses as Food   I'm afraid most people associate turnips with Mammy Yokum serving up L'il Abner a mess of pork chops and turnip greens in the comics. But Julia Child, the popular "French Chef," calls the turnip ". . . a wonderful vegetable when given the treatment required to bring out its delicious qualities," and goes on to describe turnips braised in butter, parslied turnips, turnip and potato pureé, glazed turnips and turnip casserole. I'd add that it goes for rutabagas, too, because they can be cooked the same ways.

But if you don't like turnips cooked, try them raw and you may be pleasantly surprised. They are mild and sweet when cut into sticks to dunk in your favorite dip or shredded into salads.

Turnip greens can be prepared like spinach or other greens. In the southern states, they are usually cooked with salt pork to add flavor.

WATERCRESS

SOMEWHERE ALONG THE line this pungent herb of the mustard family got the reputation of being terribly, terribly refined and suitable only for dainty finger sandwiches at English garden parties. But Xenophon, the Ancient Greek general, and the Persian King Xerxes ordered their soldiers to eat it to keep them healthy. One thing's sure, they found watercress in good supply—it's a native of Asia Minor and the Mediterranean area.

Watercress will grow wild wherever there's shallow slow-moving water. In England it's been cultivated for sale in the markets of London since about 1800. And it was probably gathered wild a long time before that.

Early settlers brought watercress to this country and it can now be found from Washington in the Northwest to Florida in the Southeast, and all other points of the compass, as well. Not too long ago you could gather it from the edges of small streams on hikes or camping trips. Now widespread water pollution makes it safer to stick to commercially-produced 'cress.

Varieties Watercress has a lot of landlocked close relatives: peppergrass (also called curly cress), upland cress, lamb's cress, cuckoo flower, lady's smock, mayflower, pennycress, and even nasturtiums. Some of these must have grown near Stratford-on-Avon, for Shakespeare immortalized them in *Love's Labour's Lost* by saying:

"When daisies pied and violets blue,
And lady-smocks all silver-white,
And cuckoo-buds of yellow hue
Do paint the meadows with delight."

But there's only one variety of watercress. Its scientific name is *Radicula nasturtium-aquaticum.* It has long stems and small thick leaves.

Seasons Watercress is on the market all year but the supply peaks from May through July, just about coinciding with salad season. It is grown locally in many areas with supplementary supplies to the market from Virginia, Pennsylvania, Maryland and about eight other states.

Marketing Practises Since watercress is an aquatic plant, the way it's harvested is unique. Men in hipboots wade through the beds, cutting the stems with sharp slender knives. When a full handful is gathered it's bound with cord and tossed into a tub floating nearby. The full tubs are brought to a packing shed where the watercress is precooled until it's chilled. Then the bunches are packed in paper-lined containers with lots of crushed ice, called "snow." The containers are packed loosely, otherwise the leaves will yellow in as little as six hours.

There are no standard grades for watercress. But growing areas are checked by Food and Drug Administration inspectors, assuring that the watercress you buy has been raised in unpolluted water.

Watercress is marketed and priced by the bunch.

How to Buy Cress is perishable and retail stores that value their produce display it with the stem ends in cool water. Select bunches that look fresh, bright and clean. Avoid any with yellowed or wilted leaves.

As soon as you get it home, untie the bunch and sort out any bad sprigs. Rinse the rest gently in cool water, drain on paper towels and store in a plastic bag in the crisper bin of your refrigerator. It may keep a week this way, but I hope you'll use it within a day or two.

Nutrition A sprig or two won't do much of anything but in quantity watercress is valuable for its vitamins A and C, as well as calcium and iron.

Uses as Food I'm sure you already know that watercress is a tangy addition to salads and an attractive garnish for any platter. Combined with cream cheese it makes great canapes. But I recommend this recipe for watercress soup, which the French call Potage Cressonniére: Melt 2 tablespoons butter in a large saucepan, add thin slices of 4 new potatoes and 2 medium-sized onions. Add 2 cups water, salt and pepper, and cook slowly until mushy. Then add the leaves and stems of a large bunch of watercress, broken into small pieces. Cover and cook another minute or two. Now the classic recipe recommends rubbing through a sieve— but I liquefy the mixture in the electric blender. Return the mixture to a pot, add a cup of milk and ¾ cup of light cream (what's often sold as "Half & Half") and reheat, making sure it doesn't boil. Serve hot. I usually double this recipe, which serves four, so there will be enough left over for a cold treat later, because it's equally good that way.

Fruit

APPLES

JOHN CHAPMAN, BETTER known as "Johnny Appleseed," gets all the credit for planting apple trees across the country, but more should go to a Quaker pioneer named Henderson Lewelling. Without him, for instance, the State of Washington might never have become our largest apple-producing state. In October 1847 he arrived in Oregon's Willamette Valley from Iowa with a covered wagon loaded with 700 grafted fruit trees, all less than 4-feet high: pears, quince, plums and cherries as well as apples. It's said he had tended those trees more carefully than his children on the journey! The trees got their water first every day, the rest of the family got what was left. When his first apples ripened, just in time for the Gold Rush, Lewelling took off for San Francisco with the entire crop—100 apples—which he sold for $5 each to prospectors hungry for fresh fruit. He put the money back into his orchards and very soon his part of the Pacific Northwest was noted for its "woolen socks, big red apples and pretty girls." The orchardists who followed him made fortunes but Henderson Lewelling's pioneering spirit was his undoing. He sold his property and went off to found a colony in Honduras. He went broke there and returned to the States where he died, almost penniless, in a suburb of San Jose, California.

Unless you've studied horticulture you probably missed the important part of Henderson Lewelling's story. He worked with *grafted* trees, not seed. From Roman times on it's been known that grafting or budding is the only way to insure that a variety of apple will run true: a hundred seeds from the same tree will produce a hundred trees all differing from each other and the parent tree. But it is the chance seedlings that produce improved varieties occasionally and they are treasured. There are even monuments to some. In Wilmington, Massachusetts, you can see a pillar topped with a huge stone apple commemorating the place where the first Baldwin apple was found, and in the province of Ontario in Canada a statue marks the spot where John McIntosh discovered the apple tree that bears his name still.

The first apples were probably small and sour, like our crabapples. Pomologists, or apple experts, think they originated somewhere between the Caspian and Black Seas, in Southwest Asia. It's hard to pin down the time and place accurately because by Stone Age times apples had spread over much of Europe. Roman texts on agriculture mention 22 varieties, there were undoubtedly more, as well as giving instructions on grafting that could be used today. In the seventeenth century 56 different kinds of apples were part of the menu for a banquet given by the Grand Duke Cosmo III of Tuscany.

Apples were also among the earliest English fruit trees. The climate was ideal for them since a winter dormant period is necessary for good fruit.

European colonists all brought native varieties of apples to America with them; the English to Virginia and New England, the Dutch to New York, the French to Canada. The first commercial nursery was established on Long Island, New York, in about 1730. By 1823 its catalog included four varieties that are still popular—Winesap, Yellow Newtown, Rhode Island Greening and Baldwin.

Varieties   Today the U.S. Department of Agriculture lists 7000 varieties of apples. Of these 20 are considered valuable and only eight account for three-quarters of all commercial production. They are Delicious, McIntosh, Golden Delicious, Rome Beauty, Jonathan, Winesap, York and Stayman.

The apple you're partial to is almost certainly the one you ate as a child. An apple expert could practically predict what part of the country you came from on that basis. If your favorite isn't on the list it probably means you were eating apples produced quite near home. When oldtimers ask me why they can't find certain varieties anymore I have to tell them the apple they remember as being so good really wasn't and has been replaced by other varieties that are more disease-resistant, have better flavor and looks, produce more prolifically, and will ship and store well.

Here's a rundown on the "Big Eight":

RED DELICIOUS   by far the number-one eating apple in the United States, accounting for more than 25% of the total crop each year. It's one apple you won't have trouble identifying in the market: just look for the five characteristic bumps on the bottom, or blossom end. It has a rich red color with some areas that range from lighter red to yellowish. It's a crisp, midly tart apple that's great for eating but it's definitely not a cooking apple. The State of Washington is the big producer and growers there think the best fruit in the world comes from their irrigated valleys east of the Cascade Mountains. Michigan, New York and California also produce good quality fruit of this variety. They are on the market fresh in September and October but can be held in storage into May or June.

McINTOSH   a multipurpose apple especially popular in the Northeast. Its color can vary from yellow-green to red with light stripes of pale red to deep purplish-red . It has a firm skin but when you bite into this apple it just seems to burst with juice. It's best for eating out of hand but can be used for sauce, pies and baking if you remember it takes less cooking time than "pie" or "baking" apples. The McIntosh is grown primarily in New York, New England and Michigan. The influx of Easterners to the West Coast following World War II created a demand for this variety, filled by shipments from Oregon and British Columbia as well as from the East Coast. The time to look for fresh McIntoshes is from early September to early October, although they are sold from storage into June.

GOLDEN DELICIOUS   as the name implies a gold or bright yellow version of the Red Delicious. It's a very versatile apple, juicy and sweet, that can be used for every purpose. It's highly recommended for fruit salads since the flesh doesn't turn brown as quickly as other varieties. Washington, Illinois, Virginia and many other states harvest this variety from late August to November. Marketing from storage continues into June.

ROME BEAUTY   a bright red apple, with a yellowish undercast. It varies in size from medium to extra-large which makes it ideal for baking. The season is from September to early November but they can be held until the end of June.

JONATHAN   a small to medium-sized bright apple which may show light red stripes over yellow or be deeply-colored red darkening to purple in some areas. This all-purpose apple is grown mainly in Michigan, Washington and Illinois and harvested in September and October. From storage it can be marketed into May.

WINESAP   the name describes the juicy tart taste of this firm, crisp, good-eating apple. It's also good for sauce and pies. The skin is bright deep red with areas that look almost purple. Grown mainly in Washington and Virginia and harvested between mid-September and mid-November, this all-purpose apple is released from storage as late as the end of June.

YORK (or York Imperial)   characteristically lopsided with light red or pinkish skin dotted with yellow. Since the flavor is often rather flat, this variety is used mainly for cooking, pies and baking. Virginia, Pennsylvania and West Virginia are the main growing states, harvesting most fruit during October. They are available into March.

STAYMAN   a juicy and slightly tart apple with skin that's either dull mixed red or has a striped effect. They are grown mainly in the Southeast and harvested in October and November. From storage they are available through April.

These are the national favorites. The list leaves out two of my favorites, admittedly local prejudice again. First of all, the *Gravenstein.* 95% of these exceptionally good eating apples are grown in Sonoma County, just across the Golden Gate Bridge from San Francisco. Early in the season these medium to large apples are in green condition and excellent for sauce or pies. Later you'll see yellowish amber-green ones, with red stripes. This is the time to eat them out of hand. July is the main month for Gravensteins, although you can find them through mid-September. Like other summer varieties they don't store well, so buy and eat them while you can. My other favorite is the *Newtown Pippin,* also known as the Albemarle or Yellow Newtown. This apple is grown mostly in California and Oregon. Three-quarters of the California acreage is practically next-door to San Fancisco—the Watsonville area in Santa Cruz County and the Sebastopol area of Sonoma County. When the color is yellowish-green these apples are at their best for pies. That's not just my opinion, they're the favorite of companies that produce pies commercially. When it turns yellow the Newtown is at its best for eating out of hand. Unlike some other yellow varieties, this one doesn't get mealy but stays firm and crisp even when completely mature. Newtowns are usually on the market, starting in late September and can be held in storage up until June.

You'll find many other good but less common varieties on the market. They may even be best-sellers where you live. Among these are the *Astrachan,* a summer apple formerly very popular, especially for sauce and pies; the *Baldwin,* an Eastern all-purpose variety; the *Northern Spy,* another multi-purpose apple grown in Michigan and New England; the *Rhode Island Greening,* tart and used mainly for pies; and the *Grimes Golden,* a juicy sweet apple good for fruit salads and eating out of hand.

Seasons   Until about 50 years ago, apples were about the only fruit available all winter long. Now they have a lot of competition from other fruits.

The Bible says, "To everything its season . . . " That goes for every variety of apple, too. The summer season, late June or late July, is the time for Gravensteins, Astrachans, and other early varieties that are used mainly for cooking but can be eaten out of hand when mature. The fall season begins September first and includes varieties such as the Jonathan, Grimes Golden and Wealthy. Overlapping them come the winter varieties such as Delicious and McIntosh. From November on, until the next round of the apple seasons begins, all apples are brought onto the market are from storage.

Marketing Practices   When most of America was rural, and before anyone thought of child labor laws, apple picking was the chore for children that marked the end of summer vacation. The first American *Farmer's Manual* said: "Let your children gather your apples. Children are the farmer's richest blessing, and when trained to habits of industry, they become the best members of society ... Let them eat apples, too, for nothing will strengthen and preserve young teeth more."

Now farming is half Applied Science and half Big Business and the whole process is highly mechanized from seedling to store.

Nostalgia buffs may lament the "good old days," but when you're talking about apples, one positive result of the change is that good-tasting apples are now available year 'round. That's because of the development of controlled atmosphere storage. (In the produce trade we call it C.A. storage.) This means that each variety of apple is now carefully refrigerated at a particular temperature and humidity, with carbon dioxide added to the atmosphere to retard the natural oxidation process. At room temperature an apple takes on oxygen, gives off carbon dioxide, and deteriorates rapidly. All the C.A. treatment does is stabilize the apple's natural chemistry, for months even, and allow us to market fresh crisp apples throughout the year.

The other big change is packaging. They used to come in boxes, now every year an increasingly large amount come into the market in plastic bags. This is true mainly of smaller apples. Before, when small apples were displayed in bulk, they suffered in contrast to the bigger ones, and were practically unsalable. Packed in bags these small apples have more appeal. The advantage isn't just to the sellers, customers are getting good apples that are kid-size or snack-size and usually a very good buy.

Grading of apples is based on many factors, but the Fancy and Extra Fancy grades are based mainly on surface color and appearance. That doesn't affect the quality of the fruit inside. So, unless you're setting up your own "Still Life with Apples," ones with less color will taste just as good and be a better buy.

Apples are displayed in bulk and mostly priced by the pound, or in overwrapped trays or poly bags, which are priced by the unit.

How to Buy   In the old days, before the time of the electric can opener and the modern array of highly processed foods, people bought apples with a clear idea of how they would use them. They specifically shopped for apples to eat, apples for pie, or even crabapples to convert into spiced apples or homemade jelly.

Now people seem to buy on impulse and unfortunately most markets display apples with no indication of their best use. Almost all apples are good eaters but, since there's a communication gap between the shopper and the invisible supermarket produce man, it's a good idea to learn which apples to buy for any other purpose. For pies and sauce: tart varieties like Gravenstein, Greening or Newtown Pippin. For baking: large firm-fleshed varieties with thick skins. Rome Beauty if available. If not, then Jonathan, Golden Delicious or Newtown Pippin.

Look for apples that are firm and well-colored. Avoid any that feel soft or have bruised areas. Large apples, like large potatoes, command a premium price on the market. If smaller ones meet your need they'll usually be a better buy.

Refrigerate apples until you use them. Depending on variety, they'll last two weeks or more.

Nutrition   A medium-sized apple, about 2½-inches in diameter, will contain between 66 and 87 calories, depending on how tart or sweet the variety is. A 3-inch apple, baked with two tablespoons of sugar, goes up to 188 calories.

Now, I'll surprise you, I think. As a fruit apples aren't particularly high in vitamin content, although they do contain some A and C, as well as small amounts of various minerals. I'm also sorry to say that storage causes apples to lose their vitamin C fairly rapidly. That doesn't mean apples aren't good for you. Like other fruits they're low in fat and sodium and can be used in diets calling for low intake of these substances. They are rich in cellulose which contributes bulk to the diet and aids digestion. In cooked form they are bland and one of the first fruits given to infants. Apple juice, with vitamin C added, is almost a must for infants who can't take orange juice.

I've read that a British scientist claimed apples were more effective than a toothbrush. Actually apples are great substitutes for candy and other snacks that are high in refined carbohydrates, and they do provide good exercise for the jaws and gums, BUT don't let your kids throw away their toothbrushes, apples or not.

Uses as Food Let's start out with a drink. There's apple juice and apple cider, hard and soft. In Colonial days cider was served where we'd offer water. Even more potent is applejack or apple brandy. Normandy, the great apple-growing province of France is famous for Calvados, an apple brandy that rivals any made from grapes. It seems hard to believe now, but during Prohibition days in the United States more than one apple orchard was cut down by ax-swinging temperance workers when a farmer was suspected of producing applejack as a sideline.

Now to food. It's hard to beat a chilled apple eaten out of hand. That reminds me, any cultured Italian will tell you that Americans eat apples like children. Here's the way they do it. Impale the apple on a fork, peel the skin away in one continuous peel, then cut sections off and convey them to your mouth on the blade of the knife. If you can do this gracefully, without breaking the peel or cutting your tongue, and carry on a polite conversation all the while, you're better than I am.

Other uses for apples seem endless. They're a great addition to fruit salads. (To keep apple slices from darkening, place them in cool water to which you've added a little salt, or sprinkle on a little lemon juice.) Homemade applesauce is great as a sidedish with pork, as well as for dessert. Baked apples, especially ones stuffed with nuts and raisins, make an attractive dessert. The list could go on and on with pies, tarts, fritters, pancakes, dumplings. Just look in any cookbook.

Here's my recipe for applesauce: Peel and slice apples and put them in a pot with a small amount of water. Cover and cook over low heat until the apples soften enough to mash easily. Add a little sugar to taste. Cook a *very* little time longer, then mash and cool. Does this sound dull? Then serve it as the Danes do. Make 2 cups of fine bread crumbs out of dried white or French bread. Mix with about 2 tablespoons sugar. Brown the mixture in ½-cup melted butter. When cool, put a layer of crumbs into a serving dish or individual sherbet glasses. Add a layer of applesauce. Continue alternating the two until the dish or individual serving pieces are full, ending with a layer of crumbs. Chill. Just before serving top with whipped cream.

APRICOTS

HAVE YOU EVER heard of the Hunza people? They live in the Himalayas in a remote kingdom that sounds like a low-budget Shangri-La. They're amazingly healthy and live to be incredibly old. Books written about the Hunzas give a lot of the credit to their diet—which consists chiefly of apricots.

This beautiful fruit undoubtedly does a lot to keep the Hunzas happy and healthy, but I'm sure that freedom from air, water and noise pollution, as well as traffic jams, time clocks and other annoyances of Western life, have just as much to do with it.

Apricots seem to inspire poetry and legend wherever they're grown. A Persian poet described the fruit as the "golden seed of the sun." And the Chinese, who were probably the first to cultivate apricot trees more than 4000 years ago, thought they had special powers. Confucius is said to have worked out his philosophy sitting under an apricot tree.

From China apricots traveled westward to Europe. Before the days of Alexander the Great they were being grown in the warmer Mediterranean regions. Some of the first settlers brought apricots to North America, but the East Coast was no place for apricots. California was destined to be the apricot capital of the world. You can thank the Spanish padres, who planted them in the gardens of the Missions they founded during the late 1700's, for the delicious California apricots you enjoy today.

In 1971 California produced 90% of the total U.S. production and just about 40% of those grown worldwide. The explanation is the Golden State's areas with just the right climate for apricots. They're early bloomers that need a fairly warm spring, allowing the fruit to mature before the summer heat comes on. The trees will not produce good fruit where there are early frosts or too warm a climate. Ten California counties seem made to order for apricots. The states of Idaho, Washington, Colorado and Utah also produce some apricots commercially.

Varieties Four of the varieties produced in California are so similar they're all marketed under one name. They're the Royal, Derby, Steward and Blenheim, all distributed as "Royals." The true Royal variety was imported from France in 1850 and planted in the Winters area of Northern California just a year later. This district has been producing and shipping apricots ever since. The Royal and the Blenheim, which originated in England, account for 80% of California's total apricot production.

In the 1920's another large apricot-producing area developed near Brentwood—not the fashionable Los Angeles suburb, but a town in Contra Costa county northeast of San Francisco. The main variety grown there is the Tilton, which accounts for another 18% of the California crop.

Other popular varieties are the Perfection and the Moorpark.

Seasons The apricot season starts in mid-May and runs through the month of August. About 55% of the crop is picked during June and July.

In larger cities you may find imports from South America during December and January.

Marketing Practices Apricots have to come off the trees fast, so picking usually takes place within 15 to 20 days. Harvesting for the fresh market comes first, then for canning, last for drying.

There's a pleasant practice among our local apricot growers. On weekends certain orchards are opened to the public so families can pick their own fresh fruit. It makes a nice outing—a real treat for kids—and the price is usually attractive, too, for delicious tree-ripened fruit.

Commercially, most California apricots are shipped in boxes called Brentwood lugs that hold 25 pounds net weight of fruit. Some are packed loose, others are face-packed with one or two neatly-arranged rows on what becomes the top of the box when it reaches the retailer. (See the chapter on cherries for a full description of face-packing.)

Apricots are graded as to size: jumbo, extra large, large or small. They are almost always sold loose by the pound. At roadside stands, and possibly in some independently-owned supermarkets, you may be able to buy them by the box.

How to Buy As far as I'm concerned apricots are one of the finest-flavored fruits grown. And they have beauty to go along with the flavor.

Ideally, apricots should be golden-yellow with a red blush and a soft velvety feel. In my opinion the riper the better, even to the point of being soft and mushy.

If you live in the East or Midwest, you'll have more trouble finding some in this condition, because for long-distance shipping apricots have to be picked hard, with just a little yellow color showing. The fruit will ripen and color up after picking but, let's face it, the taste and flavor won't be quite as good.

But if you live near an apricot-producing area you have it made. You can buy beautiful golden-colored tree-ripened apricots, with wonderful aroma and delicious flavor.

The apricots you buy should look plump and juicy, with the beautiful color I've described. Avoid any that are shriveled, dull-looking or firm and pale yellow or greenish-yellow in color.

Firm apricots will ripen in a few days at room temperature. Ripe ones are quite perishable and should be used immediately. At the most, store them a day or two in a plastic bag under refrigeration.

Nutrition Do you remember the Apollo 13 moonflight? Apricots were a required part of the astronauts' diet, in such quantity that the crew got tired of eating them. The reason space doctors chose apricots was their high potassium content, vital to keep heart muscles healthy, especially during long periods of weightlessness.

Getting back down to earth, apricots are a valuable addition to anyone's diet. They are high in natural sugars but fairly low in calories.

Two or three medium-size apricots will contain about 51 calories and provide more than half the vitamin A an adult should get daily. They're also a fair source of vitamin C and contain some iron.

Uses as Food   My recommendation is: eat them fresh, out-of-hand. Oh, I know they can be used in sherbets, pies and delicious preserves. Apricots are great stewed, too. Just use a little water and sugar and cook for a few minutes—it's that simple.

BANANAS

WOULD YOU BELIEVE me if I told you bananas are berries? And what they grow on isn't a tree at all, but just a huge tropical plant? Both are true. Also a fact, and more believable, pound for pound the banana is the most widely sold fruit in the United States.

In the tropics bananas have been a food staple as far back as history can be traced. They were cultivated in Southeast Asia long before most other fruits were domesticated. The banana's botanical name, *Musa sapientum,* meaning "fruit of the Wise Men," comes from the legend that Indian gurus sat in the shade of its large leaves while they meditated. It brings a strange picture to my mind of a yogi sitting cross-legged and peeling a banana, about as incongruous as watching a Supreme Court Justice lick a popicle.

Food discoveries seem to go along with great events in history. It's said that Europeans first saw bananas when Alexander the Great and his Greek troops invaded India. But it took the Arabs to introduce the fruit to the Near East and the Mediterranean. In the early 1400's the Portuguese took banana plants to the Canary Islands. Just a few years after Columbus' voyages, bananas traveled to the Caribbean Islands and Mexico. They spread so rapidly that later visitors thought bananas were native to the Americas.

As early as 1850, Yankee clipper ships were bringing bananas to East Coast ports and regular shipments to the United States started right after the Civil War. They remained a rare tropical luxury—which you can be sure means expensive—until the early 1900's. When steamships began transporting cargoes of bananas from large plantations located throughout Central America and southern Mexico, they became the readily available, inexpensive fruit they are today.

During my time in the business the packaging and shipping of bananas has changed as much, if not more, than any other produce. I remember when all the bananas arrived by boat on stalks, which were unloaded one by one and brought to the produce market by truck or wagon. There they were passed down into basement ripening rooms, which were no more than boarded-off areas with a gas jet for heat and a can of water for humidity. Sometimes a huge hairy tarantula or other unpleasant tropical insect came along for the ride. You can bet that the men checked pretty carefully before putting stalks on their shoulders to carry down to the ripening rooms. But every once in a while they'd come up with one and then there would be plenty of excitement!

Retailers bought their ripened bananas by the stalk to hang on display prominently, often where they could be seen through the store window and hopefully lure in customers. Each stalk contained clumps of bananas which the oldtimers called hands. (Today produce men, retailers and customers alike just say bunches.) When customers chose the hand, or bunch, they wanted from the hanging display, the retailer would cut it from the stalk. Later, as stores increased in size, wholesalers started cutting the bananas in bunches and marketing them in wooden tubs. This meant about 20 handling operations and disposing of the stalks in quantity became quite a dumping problem.

Today there's no waste and very little handling. Since the early '60s, all the bunches coming into the market are cut, cleaned and packed into cartons right at the plantation. There are advantages to this. Convenience, of course. And the fruit is better protected from damage in shipment.

There's one disadvantage, though. I think it's a shame that children today don't get a chance to see those pretty displays of whole stalks of bananas hanging in the stores.

Varieties Practically speaking, a banana is a banana. Chances are the banana you buy will be a Cavendish, also known by its trademark name Valery. A secondary variety is the Gros Michel. The only way to distinguish one from the other is by the shape of the tip. The Cavendish (or Valery) has a blunt end, the Gros Michel comes to a more tapered point.

Often retail stores promote their bananas by the brand names of major importers. United Fruit Company has made "Chiquita" a radio and TV personality, while Standard Fruit and Steamship Company markets their bananas under the name Dole, which you probably still identify more with pineapples.

If you live in an area with a large Latin population, you may find plantains on the market. They are larger than our largest bananas. Plantains are a staple food in the tropics, appearing in one form or another in almost every meal. When green they are starchy and take the place of our potatoes. In fact, plantain chips are as common a snack in Latin America as our potato chips. As the plantain ripens it gets sweeter and softer. In our markets, plantains are sold by the each and priced by the pound.

Seasons   Bananas are consistently available and consistently good throughout the entire year. About the only things that affect the supply are revolutions and strikes.

Grading and Pricing   There are no official grades for bananas, although the major importers have their own standards of size, form and quality.

Bananas are almost always (I'm tempted to say always) sold by the pound. Because they are such a staple item, many stores (especially larger chains) feature them at low markup, making bananas a good economical buy week in and week out.

How to Buy   First of all, it's a myth that tree-ripened bananas taste better than artificially ripened ones. Bananas are one of the few fruits that don't improve in flavor by ripening on the tree. If bananas were allowed to ripen before harvesting and shipping, you'd probably have a choice of starchy and mealy or burst and rotten fruit, in either case inedible. That's why all bananas arrive on the market dead green.

Today's ripening rooms—air-tight with scientifically controlled heat and humidity—assure uniformly ripened fruit, with almost all of the starch converted into sugar for good taste.

The riper bananas get the more susceptible they are to damage from handling, so retailers like to buy bananas in what is called green-tip condition. That means the body of the banana is yellow but the tip is still green. That's the best way for you to buy them, too. A green-tipped banana will ripen at home in two or three days. After a banana is ripe, never before, it can be put in the refrigerator where it will keep in good eating condition for several days. Don't worry if the skin darkens after refrigeration; the fruit inside will still be good.

A banana is in prime eating condition when its solid yellow color is flecked with brown specks. These are called sugar flecks and indicate the fruit inside will be flavorful and sweet-tasting.

One good tip when buying bananas is to check whether the retail produce man has taken precautions to protect the fruit. There should be a mat or other soft surface under the fruit. Bunches should not be piled on top of each other. Overripe ones and single bananas, which unthinking customers have stripped from bunches, should be sorted out and priced for quick sale.

Look for plump, well-filled fruit when you buy. The peel should be a bright yellow color. Avoid spindly or misshapen fruit—it was probably not mature when picked. Another danger sign is a discolored area on an otherwise bright banana. It indicates a bruise that undoubtedly goes through to the inside. When the entire skin is discolored, the fruit inside will be soft and mushy. In fact some people prefer their bananas this way, but it doesn't appeal to my taste.

Chilling is harder to recognize. If the banana has a dull-yellow color and cloudy or smoky appearance, it has probably suffered cold damage. And once the regular ripening process has been interrupted by cold, normal ripening won't occur even when the temperature is raised. Avoid these bananas—chances are the flavor won't be too good.

Nutrition Often the first fruit an infant gets is mashed bananas. They remain one of the most easily digested and nutritious natural foods throughout life, right up to advanced old age. Like other fruits, they're recommended for low-fat and low-sodium diets but, in addition, they're the only raw fruit that's ideal for most special ones, especially bland, low residue, soft diets.

Bananas contain about 22% carbohydrate, practically all of which the body utilizes. They are an excellent source of potassium and contain some vitamins A and C.

A medium-size banana has about 125 or 130 calories. Compare this to the 162 "empty calories" (meaning with little or no nutritive value) in a one-ounce bag of potato chips or the 160 in a pint bottle of a carbonated cola drink. No wonder bananas are a recommended between-meal snack, especially for children.

Uses as Food   Most bananas are eaten out of hand, and that's the way I prefer them. They're a lunchbox standby, since they come already wrapped. Also, they are easier for children to eat than harder fruit, such as apples. Other good uses for raw bananas, sliced, are on breakfast cereals and in fruit salads and gelatin desserts.

We have a favorite banana snack around my house. Put a cup of milk and a whole peeled banana in the blender. You can add a raw egg for extra nutrition and a little nutmeg for taste. My children grew up on these banana shakes; now *their* children are enjoying them.

There are also many delicious ways to cook bananas. You can find recipes for baked bananas and banana fritters, as well as banana pies, cakes and breads.

To sum it all up: for convenience, nutrition and economy, in addition to just plain good taste, bananas are one of the best food buys you'll ever find.

BERRIES

BLUEBERRIES

IF YOU EVER want to get a good fight going try to convince someone from New England or the Pacific Northwest that cultivated blueberries are better than the wild ones. They'll agree that they're bigger, but stick by their native wild ones for flavor. I really can't argue the point with them because up to 25 years ago or so, we hardly saw any blueberries on the San Francisco market—it took mass-cultivation to make this delicious berry available here and in many other areas.

Blueberries are the most widely distributed fruit in the world. They grow wild in Scandinavia, the British Isles, Russia and North and South America. They grow in the Arctic regions and are an important part of the Eskimo diet. This widespread distribution led to the berries being called by many different names: blueberries, hurtleberries, huckleberries, bilberries, whortleberries. This abundance of wild blueberries was also the reason that cultivation started so recently. The big plump cultivated blueberries you buy in your supermarket today are only 60 years away from the wild state.

A New Jersey woman named Elizabeth White deserves most of the credit for "taming" the blueberry. Every year she used to offer prizes for the largest wild blueberries. A Department of Agriculture botanist got interested and started cross-breeding the winners in 1909. The result was the superior berries we have today.

Varieties There are three types of blueberries: low bush, rabbit-eye and high bush. Low bush blueberries grow in the Northern U.S. and Canada. They produce most of the wild blueberries that are picked for local markets, from Maine to Minnesota, and for canning.

The rabbit-eye is a Southeastern type that grows up to 30 feet high. Ladders are used to pick the berries, most of which are processed. They're not considered important commercially.

That leaves the high bush type, which represents most of the commerical plantings in the United States. Most of the blueberries harvested belong to the "Big Seven," all developed since 1949. They are Earliblue, Collins, Blueray, Bluecrop, Berkeley, Herbert and Coville. They are all large, light blue in color and fairly firm.

Seasons   Blueberries are on the market from May through September. July and August are the heaviest months of production. The principal producing areas are New Jersey, Michigan, Maine, North Carolina, Washington and Oregon. Some are imported from Canada in August and September, and from Poland in October.

Marketing Practices   Blueberries are now the second-largest seller among berries, topped only by strawberries. Production has increased more than 500 percent in the past 10 years or so. As a matter of fact, increased acreage is being put in on only two kinds of berries: raspberries and blueberries.

Blueberries are a perishable fruit and there's usually less than a week between picking and retail sales. They are marketed in ½-pint or pint containers, called "cups." These wooden or plastic baskets are almost always covered with cellophane or plastic film, held in place with rubber bands; usually the grower's name and sometimes the varietal name are printed on the covering. The baskets are priced by the each.

How to Buy   Look for plump blueberries with a fresh appearance. Avoid any baskets that are stained with juice. It's usually an indication that the berries are soft, watery and overripe. If the berries have started to shrivel, it means they've been held too long since harvesting.

Store blueberries in the container they came in in your refrigerator. They'll keep a couple of days, but I'd recommend using them quickly—the same day you buy them if possible. When ready to use, rinse them in cool water and pick out any stray stems or leaves that may have gotten into the basket. (Also, you can freeze them in bags or containers just as they come out of the cups—no washing or preparation necessary.)

Nutrition   Blueberries supply the Eskimos with vitamin C. We have better sources available, but still, a cup of fresh blueberries will provide one-third of your daily requirement. They also contain natural sugars and some minerals as well. A cup adds up to about 87 calories.

Uses as Food   Blueberries are beautiful in color and taste. Eat them uncooked by themselves with cream and sugar, or on cereal, or in fruit cups, fruit salads, or with ice cream.

They are excellent stewed, or cooked in pies and tarts. (Children love to eat blueberry pie and then compare tongues to see whose has turned bluest.) They also make great additions to muffins and pancakes.

For a really special dessert, place blueberries in meringue shells and top with whipped cream.

BLACKBERRIES & RASPBERRIES

ANY GARDENER WILL tell you what a nuisance black-berries are. They grow like crazy, even under a fence from your next-door neighbor's yard, and seem determined to scratch the eyes out of anyone who tries to control them. That's because blackberries (and raspberries, too) are mem-bers of the rose family and have the thorns and brambles to prove it. Each berry is actually a collection of small fruits called drupelets.

Blackberries and raspberries are native to Asia, Europe and North America. Like blueberries, blackberries and raspberries grew wild so abundantly that cultivation is a fairly new development. Farmers were much more likely to plow them under than to cultivate them.

Varieties It's easy to get confused with all the different names blackberries and blackberry hybrids are known by. First of all: blackberry plants can be erect or trailing, and the trailing types sometimes go by the name dewberries.

Among the erect blackberry varieties are the Eldorado, which is also called the Stuart, Lowden or Texas. It origi-nated in Ohio and is one of the best varieties grown in the Eastern U.S., producing berries that are large, firm and sweet. Another is the Lawton, also known as the New Ro-chelle, which produces large sweet berries. Although it originated in New York State, it is now grown in Texas, Oklahoma and California.

The earliest dewberry variety was the Lucretia, some-times called the bingleberry, grown first in West Virginia right after the Civil War. It's considered very hardy and is grown even in northern States.

The Youngberry was produced first in Louisiana and named after its breeder, B. M. Young. The berries are large, wine-colored and sweet, but the quantity and quality of fruit aren't too dependable, so they've been pretty much re-placed by boysenberries, which grow in the same localities.

Experts disagree about the Loganberry. Some say it's just another blackberry hybrid, others that it's a cross be-tween a blackberry and raspberry. The fruit originated in the garden of Judge J. H. Logan at Santa Cruz, California. Loganberries are the oldest dewberry (or trailing black-berry) variety on the Pacific Coast. The berries are large and long, and dark-red in color. The taste is rather acid. Maybe that's why they've been declining in importance recently.

The Olallie is a cross between a youngberry and a black loganberry. Grown extensively in California, it's bright black and medium in size.

The Boysenberry was developed by Rudolph Boysen in 1920. California plant breeders had said it was genetically impossible to cross black, logan and raspberry varieties. But he did it. That could have been the end of the story right there because Boysen never cashed in on his discovery. In 1933 these plants were rediscovered and a Southern Califor-nia grower named Walter Knott started planting them ex-tensively. They became the keystone of his family's fortune at Knott's Berry Farm in Anaheim, California. Boysenber-ries are large and long, dark reddish-black when fully ripe. They're so prolific that five tons per acre yield is common. They're still grown mainly in California, although Oregon and Texas produce some, too.

Somewhere between the erect blackberry and the trailing dewberries is the semi-erect type, introduced from Europe early in the nineteenth century. Of this group, I remember the Himalaya blackberry, which was quite com-mon in San Francisco in the 1930's. And we still have the thornless Evergreen blackberry, produced in Oregon and Washington. It has large and exceptionally sweet berries.

Raspberries aren't as complicated. There are two com-mercial types: red and black. The most popular varieties of red raspberries are the Latham and June on the East Coast; the Ranere, grown in New Jersey and California; the Sunrise in the South and Midwest; and the Surprise in Southern California.

As far as black raspberries are concerned: the Black Pearl is the Midwestern favorite; New York is partial to the Bristol and Shuttleworth; the Logan is grown throughout the East; and the Plum Farmer in the Central States and the Pacific Northwest.

Seasons   Blackberries are in season from May through August and in heaviest supply during June and August.

Raspberry season also starts in May, but June and July are the two heaviest months. The July harvest represents 58 percent of the total crop.

Marketing Practices   Blackberries and raspberries are both sold by the basket. Half-pints and pints are the most common sizes, but blackberries sometimes come by the quart, or even the crate, in some parts of the country. That's the way to buy them if you're putting up preserves.

How to Buy   There's one notable difference between blackberries and raspberries. When raspberries are ripe they drop their cores, leaving little hollow cups. Blackberries don't lose their cores and unlike raspberries, when they're red they're "green." However, both kinds of berries do lose their caps when ripe.

Look for fully-colored plump berries. They should be fresh-looking and well-shaped. Reject any stained baskets, that's a sign that at least some of the berries are overripe and have started to soften and decay.

Berries will keep a couple of days in the refrigerator, but it's best to use them as soon as possible. Sort out any bad ones before storing, but don't wash the berries until you're ready to use them (water causes mold to form).

Nutrition   Blackberries   and   raspberries   contain   fair amounts of vitamin C. Like most other fruits, they're fairly low in calories, less than 60 to a 3½-ounce serving.

Uses as Food   Berries are delicious raw with cream. They are also a good addition to cold cereal for summer breakfasts.

Raspberries make tempting shortcakes, while blackberries are often used in pies and tarts.

Both are favorites for home made jams and jellies.

CRANBERRIES

ANYONE INTERESTED IN organic farming that produces good quality produce should study the cranberry industry. The luscious cranberries we enjoy with our Thanksgiving and Christmas turkeys are grown by cooperating with rather than interferring with nature. Pesticides are kept to a minimum. Instead, flocks of geese are set loose to weed the bogs, and birdhouses are built to attract the swallows that eat insects that would harm the vines. Some cranberry growers even rent beehives and place them on the edges of the bogs to aid pollination and insure continuing good crops. And still growers produce over 100 million pounds of cranberries a year with about the highest standards of quality in the produce trade.

The cranberries we eat aren't much different from the ones the Pequot and Narragansett Indians were gathering from the bogs and swamps of Massachusetts, before the Pilgrims landed at Plymouth, quite near Cape Cod, where more than half of our cranberries are grown today. The Indians either cooked them with honey or maple sugar, much as we make cranberry sauce today with sugar, or used them in pemmican, a mixture of cranberries and dried deer meat pounded into a pulp, then shaped into cakes and dried in the sun. Cranberries had other uses, too. They provided a beautiful red dye and were used as a poultice to prevent blood poisoning from arrow wounds.

Varieties The varieties grown today actually are the result of selecting the best wild cranberries, rather than scientific cross-breeding. The Early Black variety represents more acres than any other variety. These medium-sized roundish cranberries are dark red in color. They are grown mainly in Massachusetts and are the first variety to ripen each year. Three other varieties are also grown in quantity: the Howe, another Massachusetts variety, is the most attractive cranberry marketed—shiny, bright red and oval in shape; the Searles Jumbo, a large bright-red berry, grown in Wisconsin; and the McFarlin, a large well-colored variety, developed by a Cape Codder who wandered off to start his cranberry bog in the State of Washington.

Seasons   Almost 200 years ago there were laws against picking cranberries before September. I don't know if those laws are still being enforced, but the fact remains that the cranberry season runs from September through December. November, of course, is the heaviest month.

Marketing Practices   Cranberries have been called "bouncing berries" because that's what the good ones do. In olden days they were rolled down a short flight of stairs: good ones bounced like little rubber balls, soft ones stayed on the steps. Today grading machines are used but they work on the same principle. Each berry is given seven chances to bounce over 4-inch high barriers as it passes along a conveyor belt. If it doesn't pass the high-jump test it's discarded. Obviously, cranberries are hardy, no other fruit could go through this sort of treatment without being bruised and unfit to eat.

Cranberries are marketed in cello-bags or 1-pound boxes with cellophane windows that are priced by the each.

How to Buy   Cranberries are one of your most foolproof produce buys since inferior berries are sorted out during the packing process. Check through the bag or window to make sure that the cranberries aren't soft, crushed or shriveled. They should look bright and plump. Don't go too much by color, it varies depending on variety.

Cranberries will keep between four and eight weeks in the refrigerator. I'd leave them in the container you bought them in until ready to use. Never wash them before using, moisture is the one thing that will make them spoil. And, if you want to extend cranberry season, you can freeze them in their original wrapping without any preparation at all.

Nutrition   In large quantity, cranberries provide vitamin C. They were carried on early whaling ships as a scurvy preventitive, since they kept better and were more available than citrus fruits. But the amount you eat as relish isn't going to provide much of anything but calories—178 to a ½ cup to be exact—because of the sugar that's added in preparation.

Uses as Food   I'll start out with a use that's decorative, not edible. Cranberries make beautiful garlands for an old-fashioned "organic" Chirstmas tree. Children love to string them in long chains, alone or alternated with popcorn.

The cranberries you have left can be used in delicious cranberry nut bread, cranberry and orange relish, or that traditional favorite, cranberry sauce. The recipe is pretty basic: 2 cups of cranberries to each cup of water and sugar. Rinse the berries and cook them in the water until they're soft and the skin breaks. Then stir in the sugar and refrigerate. If your taste is more refined you can strain the berries through a sieve and remove the skins before adding the sugar. I don't, but you can.

STRAWBERRIES

THE ENGLISH HAVE been eating strawberries and cream for centuries and I'm sure that it was this dish—one of my favorites, too—that inspired an Englishman to say, "Doubtless the Almighty could make a better berry—but He never did."

Wild strawberries grow on many continents and in many climates. There are records of the Alpine strawberries the French call *fraises des bois,* or "strawberries of the woods," being cultivated as far back as the 15th century. The flavor was great (and still is) but the fruit remained small and sparse.

So early colonists in North America were amazed to see strawberries growing in abundance. In Maryland one wrote: "Wee cannot sett down a foote but tred on strawberries." And Roger Williams, the Nonconformist minister who founded Rhode Island, said that "this strawberry was the wonder of all fruits growing naturally in these parts ... where the Indians have planted, I have many times seen as many as would fill a good ship ..."

These strawberries, which the Indians crushed and mixed with meal to make bread, were given the scientific name *Fragaria virginiana* and were carried back to Europe where they were accepted enthusiastically.

Then, in 1712, a Captain Frezier found a variety "large as walnuts" in Chile and brought them to Europe, too. By cross-breeding the ancestor of our cultivated strawberries was produced. It returned to the Western Hemisphere in the nineteenth century.

Varieties When an American horticulturist managed to cross-breed several varieties of strawberries successfully in 1838 it was the first fruit variety of any kind that originated in the U.S. by breeding. It was named the Hovey after its "inventor" and became popular in all sections of the country immediately. About 30 years later a newer variety, the Wilson, gained popularity.

But strawberries stayed a locally-produced, limited-season crop until after World War II. The big change came with the introduction of the University variety, developed by the University of California Agriculture Station in 1945.

Experimentation continues constantly to come up with hardier, more prolific strawberries that produce for a longer season and can be shipped long distances. One new variety that's widely accepted is a Tioga hybrid known very unromantically as "63.120-11." It really takes a California strawberry grower to love a plant with a name like that.

For jam and other preserves, a popular variety is the Marshall, which grows best in Washington and Oregon.

Seasons   Strawberries always used to be the first fruit of spring in temperate lands. Strawberry time was something to enjoy for one, two, or at the most three months and remember, or look forward to for the rest of the year. Some people say we Americans lost our feeling of being part of the earth and nature when the seasons stopped having meaning and crops like strawberries became commonplace by being available all year long. Does familiarity breed, if not contempt at least indifference? All you strawberry fanciers will have to answer for yourselves.

The fact is the strawberry season is still a short one in most states. But in California, strawberries may be harvested from February through November—and sometimes into December.

May is still Strawberry Month, though, because that's when production is heaviest all over the country, including California.

Marketing Practices   Many things helped change strawberries from a local crop to a national, or even international, commodity. The new varieties, of course. And processing, which actually started in the Pacific Northwest in 1909 when the first strawberries were frozen. Then there are better transportation (including airfreight) and improved growing and harvesting techniques.

It's interesting to watch trends develop and big changes happen in the produce business. For as long as I could remember, right up to a year ago or so, most strawberries were being frozen. But then frozen strawberries started coming in from Mexico at a price U.S. and Canadian growers found it difficult to compete with. In Toronto, Canada, growers threaten to plow up their strawberries and Michigan is practically out of business.

But not California. The acreage planted in strawberries is less than half what it was 15 years ago, but the yield per acre has almost tripled—so more strawberries are being harvested today than ever before. And more than ever are coming onto the market fresh. Fifteen years ago only 36 percent of the crop was marketed fresh, while 75 percent of all the delicious California strawberries harvested went to the fresh market in 1970.

When I said "international commodity" before, I meant it. California doesn't just ship all over the U.S. Air-flights to Europe are big business. One exporter alone flies up to 200,000 crates of strawberries into European markets between March and May. Most of these berries wind up in bakeries, restaurants and hotels—those that do reach the public sell for as much as $3 a basket.

Your retailer receives his strawberries in a flat packed with 12 baskets. The weight of a flat runs between 11 and 12 pounds. So by simple arithmetic each basket should weigh 14 ounces at the very least and 16 ounces, or one pound, maximum. They key word there is *should.* Some markets sell baskets with a minimum weight of 12 ounces, gaining 2½ extra baskets out of every flat. This practise is called "dinking." I should think with the high cost of labor these days it would hardly pay, considering the time involved, but retailers continue to "dink." So, if you're buying in quantity, to make jam or jelly for instance, buy by the flat and make sure you're getting your money's worth. In that quantity, it means an extra 2 pounds of berries.

How to Buy   The strawberry is the only member of the

berry family privileged to wear a cap as a sign of maturity. The ones you buy should have them.

Look for bright, plump, well-shaped strawberries that are solid in color.

They will keep about 3 days in the refrigerator. And don't wash or hull strawberries until you're ready to use them.

Nutrition Ten large strawberries contain just 37 calories but supply a whole day's quota of vitamin C. Fresh ones, that is. Since vitamin C is water-soluble, up to 50 percent may be lost in frozen strawberries over the time they're stored. Strawberries are also a source of iron in small amounts, as well as other minerals.

Uses as Food It seems silly to suggest ways to eat strawberries because I don't know of a fruit that more people eat more of or like better.

Strawberries and cream are No. 1 on my list, even though I must admit that the ones grown now don't seem to give off as much juice as strawberries used to.

Strawberries with lemon, or wine, are a flavorful treat. Some people like them with sour cream or Yoghurt. And, of course, there's strawberry short-cake and strawberry ice cream.

Here's a recipe for Italian strawberry ice that's delicious and simple to make: Wash and hull 2 quarts strawberries and purée in an electric blender. Boil 1 cup sugar and 1 cup water together for 5 minutes. After this syrup cools, add the berry purée and the juice of a small lemon. Pour the mixture into a refrigerator tray and freeze until mushy, stirring occasionally.

CHERRIES

I ONCE RECEIVED a beautifully and no-doubt expensively printed card saying, "This is to inform you that we're not sending out Christmas cards this year." In the same vein I inform you that I'm not going to start out this chapter with the story of George Washington and the cherry tree.

Cherries have been eaten and enjoyed since pre-historic times. Not just by people, either. Originally sweet cherries were called "bird cherries" because birds were so fond of the fruit. Actually they were responsible for spreading cherry trees throughout a wide area of the world by a very effective although unglamorous natural process.

Cherry trees were probably cultivated first in Asia Minor near the town of Cerasus, which loaned its name to the cherry or cerise. But people were enjoying the wild fruit long before that. Cherry pits have been found in Stone Age caves in Europe and prehistoric cliff dwellings in America.

Today cherries are grown from the Arctic Circle to the Tropic of Cancer in a belt that circles the world's temperate zone.

Varieties There are native American cherries, called sand cherries and chokecherries, that still grow more or less wild in the Plains and Rocky Mountain states. All of the commercially-grown varieties, however, originated in Europe or are sub-varieties of European cherries.

Cherries can be divided into sweet and sour types. The sour varieties—Montmorency, Early Richmond and English Morello—are found mostly in cans for use in pies and tarts. These days you'll hardly ever see them in the fresh produce market. Michigan, New York and Wisconsin are the main producers.

The most popular sweet cherry is the Bing. It developed as a chance seedling from an older variety called the Republican, carried to Oregon in a covered wagon by a family of horticulturists named Lewelling. They named the Bing after a Chinese workman in their orchards. It is an extra-large, heart-shaped fruit. The smooth glossy skin ranges from maroon to almost black when ripe. The flesh is firm, meaty and has a luscious flavor. This variety is in the greatest demand because it ships and keeps so well.

The Royal Ann, sometimes called the Napoleon, is easy to spot. It's the only light-colored cherry that's marketed commercially in any quantity. Look for large, heart-shaped yellowish fruit with a reddish blush. It's a good eater but it does bruise easily, so many wind up in cans or are bottled as maraschino cherries.

Other popular varieties are the Chapman or Early Chapman, a very large round cherry that's purplish-black in color; the Tartarian, a large almost black variety that originated in Russia; and the Burlat, which is large, round and dark red. The bulk of the sweet cherry crop comes from the seven western states, primarily from California, Idaho, Oregon and Washington.

Seasons Sour cherries are harvested from mid-June to mid-August. The sweet varieties are on the market from late April through August. Chapman, Tartarian and Burlat cherries are early varieties, the Bings and Royal Anns are marketed later in the season. Latest of all are the Lamberts and Republicans. June is the peak of the season when supplies should be greatest and prices lowest.

Marketing Practises Most consumers never even think about the work required to prepare produce for shipment to the retail market. Cherries are a good example. Experienced teams of pickers gather the cherries from the trees (a good tree can produce up to a ton of cherries each year) and pile filled boxes in the shade. Trucks carry the boxes to a packing shed and empty them onto a conveyor belt. Bad fruit, leaves and foreign material are removed; the remaining cherries are graded for size, washed and dried, and then boxed. The boxing takes skill. If you've ever made a pineapple upside-down cake you'll understand the process, which is called face-packing. Nimble-fingered women line up rows of cherries, stems up, covering the closed end of the box. Loose cherries are then piled in to fill the box and the cover is nailed down. This cover is actually the bottom of the box. The boxes are then moved quickly to refrigerated trucks or boxcars and shipped on their way.

Until quite recently when a crate of cherries arrived in a retail store the produce man removed the covering of the face-packed end so that the carefully arranged rows of beautiful cherries formed their own display right in the shipping container. Waste often ran as high as 20 percent when shoppers made a shambles out of the delicate fruit while making their selections.

You'll still find some cherries displayed loose for sale by the pound but more and more stores are selling them in overwrapped trays that hold ½ or 1 pound of cherries.

Only the best-grade cherries—judged by size, maturity, color, condition and shape—get to travel. This often gives local residents a real price advantage. For instance, doubles or twins (they really should be called Siamese twins since they're attached in midsection and share one stem) and those with spurs are culled out and sold locally. There's absolutely no difference in the taste but there sure is in the price, which can be half the going rate or even lower.

How to Buy   Dark-colored stems are a sure sign that cherries have been around too long. Avoid them. Look for plump, shiny, well-colored fruit with green stems. Personally, I've found that light red or pink Bing cherries just don't have the flavor of the darker ones.

As I said before, there's nothing wrong with doubles or spurs, and they're often for sale at reduced prices, so don't hesitate to buy them. The same goes for the more expensive, higher-grade, well-formed cherries in overwrapped trays.

Your retailer should refrigerate his cherries and so should you. Rinse them in cool water just before using. Cherries are highly perishable and will soften and rot in a short time if not used. But they're so delicious and tempting I doubt they'll hang around your home that long.

Nutrition   Ten large sweet cherries contain about 42 calories. They have good amounts of vitamins A and C and some minerals, too.

Uses as Food   You can keep your cherry pies, cherry tarts and even Cherries Jubilee. Ever since I was a young child I've loved eating them out of hand. I used to hunt for the ones with two or three cherries joined at the stem ends and hang them over my ears like earrings.

I've found that children today enjoy them just as much as I did. They make great lunchbox surprises and afternoon snacks. But don't let the kids get all of them—save some for yourself! Take them along on a picnic, or serve them for a simple dessert that's simply out of this world.

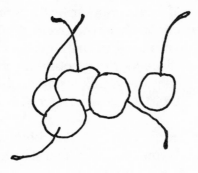

COCONUTS

IN THIS BOOK I've avoided referring to any item as an oddity because what's unusual to you may be a staple to others. The coconut is a good example of this. In tropical regions the coconut palm has been cultivated for many uses for so long that its origin isn't even recorded in written history.

Here's what a coconut palm produces: Copra, the dried oily white meat of the nut, is a money product which is sold to manufacturers of soaps, margarines and other products; the fibers of the coconut's husk are made into mats, ropes or brooms; the leaves are used to thatch roofs; the sugary sap of the tree can be distilled into a potent alcoholic beverage known as arrack; the watery milk inside the nut is a refreshing liquid, especially in areas where fresh water is difficult to find.

There are a number of varieties, both wild and cultivated, but don't ask your produce man which one he has in stock. It's practically guaranteed he won't know. And it won't affect the taste of the coconut meat anyway.

Coconuts are available year 'round in large diversified produce departments, and most abundant during our fall and winter months. They are imported from Honduras, the Dominican Republic, Puerto Rico and other tropical areas. They are sold by the each.

The only way I know to pick a good fresh one is to shake a couple and choose the one that seems to contain the most liquid. Without liquid they aren't for you. Once you have one home, refrigerate it until ready for use.

The major problem is getting the watery milk out and separating the meat from the hard shell. The stem end or base has three spots which form a monkey-like face. In fact the word coco means "grinning face" in Portugese. Puncture one or two of these spots with an ice pick, awl or small screwdriver and drain the liquid into a container. You can drink this "milk" if you wish.

Methods vary on how to separate the meat from the shell. One way is to attack the nut from all sides with a hammer until it cracks open. A second way is to heat the coconut for about 30 minutes in a 350-degree oven. This technique separates the flesh from the shell, which usually splits or cracks easily. An alternative is to place the nut in your freezer for an hour or two and then break open the brittle frozen shell with a hammer.

Fresh coconut can be broken into small chunks and eaten out of hand. It is also delicious toasted, just place in a 350-degree oven for about 15 minutes, until it's light brown. It can also be grated in a blender and used as a condiment with curry, or baked in cakes and cookies.

DATES

DATES HAVE BEEN called "candy that grows on trees." They probably were the world's first sweet-tooth gratifier; the trees were cultivated in Mesopotamia and the Nile Valley as early as 3500 B.C. The date palm grows best in warm dry areas and, like its relative the coconut palm, each part of the tree serves some use to its owner. But while the coconut may grow on a tiny island surrounded by the sea, the date palm is often seen growing in a small oasis, a dot of green surrounded by a sea of lifeless and forbiding sand. In these arid lands the fruit, which we call dates, can be stored for a long time if they are dried and pressed into cakes. Date honey is made from the juice of the fresh fruit. Flour is made from the soft central parts of the tree, oil is extracted from the seeds, an alcoholic beverage is made from the sap. The leaves are put to many uses and fiber from the tree is used to make rope. There was good reason for the ancient people of the Middle East to have deep respect for the life-sustaining qualities of this palm in a harsh and rugged environment, and even today palm leaves play a religious role in Palm Sunday ceremonies and the Jewish Feast of the Tabernacles.

Early Spanish missionaries introduced the date palm to the coastal areas of Mexico and California but they didn't thrive in the damp climate. But in the early 1900's Dr. W. T. Swingle of the U.S. Department of Agriculture brought the Deglet Noor variety from Algeria to California's dry interior valleys where it flourished. Other pioneer growers introduced more varieties from Algeria and Iraq.

Now the city of Indio in the Coachella Valley in Southern California has date gardens that qualify it as the date capital of the Western Hemisphere. The valley looks like a giant oasis and you might even expect to see Rudolph Valentino as "The Sheik," riding in from the nearby Colorado

Desert in his flowing white robes seeking a beautiful tourist to carry away as his prize.

Varieties Date varieties are classed from soft to dry, and also by the type of sugar they contain. Some, like the Deglet Noor, contain sugar in the form of sucrose. Others, like the Halawy, have invert or fruit sugars, called dextrose and glucose. There are over 100 varieties grown in the Coachella Valley alone, but the principal variety is the Deglet Noor, accounting for about 85 percent of all the dates produced.

Deglet Noor means "date of the light." It is a semi-dry variety, medium to large in size. When fresh and ripe the color is amber, after curing it becomes a deeper brown.

Invert or fruit sugar varieties are the Halawy, Khadrawy and Zahidi. The Halawy (meaning sweet) is an early date which is light amber and has good flavor. The Khadrawy (meaning green or greenland) is one of the earliest dates. It is dark in color and is popular in health food stores. The Zahidi is an amber-colored date that is small to medium in size.

Seasons Dates store well under controlled refrigeration and are available year 'round. The fresh crop extends from September through May, with most available in November. Dry varieties store very well, but the softer, moist dates are perishable and must be dried or refrigerated. Imports from the mid-East supplement our domestic production.

Marketing Practices Dates are most commonly sold in flat cardboard boxes with open plastic-covered tops, but you'll sometimes find them in plastic bags, too. They are usually pre-packed in pound or ½-pound weights. Some now have the seeds removed and this is a practical convenience for the buyer. Most dates you see will be fresh. Processing is minimal: they are cleaned, pasturized, and certification of quality is mandatory.

How to Buy Fresh dates should be plump and golden brown, with smooth skin that has a glossy appearance. Quality is generally good but avoid any that look dull or shriveled. They will generally have been on the shelf too long.

Refrigerate your fresh dates in sealed containers to keep them from absorbing odors from other strongly flavored foods.

Nutrition   Dates are about 75 percent sugar. In addition, they have small amounts of essential minerals and are a good source of calcium and a fair source of B complex.

All sugars come from natural sources. And while some dates contain sucrose and others levulose and dextrose there's no difference in human metabolism because sucrose is quickly broken down to levulose and dextrose: In other words, sugar is carbohydrate, regardless of its origin. Calorie-counters and mothers concerned with the number of cavities their children accumulate should view dates as a fruit candy to be eaten in moderate amounts with meals and avoided as between-meal snacks. One date has about the same number of calories as an ounce of raisins.

Uses as Food   Fresh dates can be used to enrich the flavor of breads, cookies and other foods. They can be stuffed with nuts or cream cheese as a rich confection. They are probably at their best nutritionally with cooked cereals or in fruit salads. Small amounts of carbohydrate are essential to a balanced diet, and if dates are used as a natural and flavorful mealtime source of sugar in its most natural form, they serve their purpose well.

FIGS

DURING SOME PERIODS of history the leaf of the fig tree seems to have been more important than the fruit. After all, when Adam ate that apple and discovered his nakedness it took a handy fig leaf to restore his dignity. And during the Dark Ages artistic censors were kept busy protecting the public by strategic placement of fig leaves on the scandalous naked gods and goddesses of pagan times.

But the Greeks and Romans appreciated the fruit itself, which is one of man's most ancient fruits and originated in western Asia and the Mediterranean region. The Greeks valued them so highly that Solon, the ruler of Attica, decreed against exporting them. An ancient Greek botanist named Theophrastus even described the process known as caprification that's still used today to "set" the fruit so it matures on the tree. The Romans considered figs a gift of the god Bacchus, especially to the poor people who could eat them fresh in summer and dried in winter.

The Spaniards introduced figs to America where they flourished in warmer climates. But when commercial cultivation of the calimyrna variety started in California in about 1885, growers were almost ruined by fruit dropping off the tree before it matured. I'm sure they had never heard of Theophratus but they followed his advice and planted one wild or capri fig tree with resident Blastophaga wasps to every hundred cultivated trees. At the proper time the caprifigs were gathered with the wasps in them and hung in small bags on the fruit-bearing trees. When the wasps crawled out, covering themselves with pollen in the process and crawled onto the cultivated trees they pollinated the flowers. The fruit that developed would stay on the tree to maturity. Today's growers are still using this ancient process.

Varieties There are hundreds of varieties of figs; some

round, some oblong and varying in color from almost white to purple-black. I'll mention just six, the ones you're most likely to find fresh.

The Mission, which you probably know in its dried form, is even better-tasting fresh. It's dark purple, almost black and has small seeds.

Another variety that's often processed is the Kadota. It's small, has few seeds and a thick yellow skin.

The Calimyrna gets its name from a combination of *Cali*fornia and *Smyrna,* the place in Turkey where it originated. It's large and squat with smooth thick yellowish-green skin.

The Adriatic, an Italian-type, has light green skin and dark pink pulp.

The Southeast produces the Brown Turkey and the Brunswick, as well as other less common varieties.

Seasons You may see fresh figs in the market from June through October.

Marketing Practices Fresh figs for the Eastern market are packed as carefully as eggs, with cardboard separators between each fig to prevent bruising. Air freight has become important in the shipment of this perishable fruit.

If you live closer to the source of supply, of course, the figs you get won't need or get quite the same de luxe treatment and the price will be lower as a result.

Figs are usually priced by the pound, but you may find a few in small plastic-wrapped tubs that are sold by the each.

How to Buy In order to be good and sweet, figs must be really ripe. As a matter of fact, some of the better-eating figs that come to local markets are extra-ripe ones classified as No. 2 grade because they're too ripe to ship—give that fig to an Italian every time.

Size isn't any indication of ripeness or maturity. Also, a ripe fig that's been partially dried or is shriveled and wrinkled from the sun's heat shouldn't be rejected, far from it. Excessively overripe ones will have a sour odor caused by the juice inside fermenting. Avoid bruised fruit, too, it will deteriorate rapidly.

A Mission fig must be almost black to be really ripe. In other varieties, such as the Adriatic, Calimyrna and Kadota, look for fruit that's fairly soft and has a rich color.

Fresh figs are highly perishable and the sooner you eat them the better. I'd say the same day you buy them if possible, if not I'd set 4 or 5 days in the refrigerator as the outside limit.

Nutrition   Two large figs will contain about 80 calories. They're rather low in vitamins A and C for a fruit, but do have some minerals. Because of the bulk they supply they are often recommended as a natural laxative. When eaten dried they provide fair amounts of iron.

Uses as Food   If you're more familiar with figs in their dried form or canned in syrup than in their natural state you've been missing a delicious treat. Try them out of hand or sliced with a little cream as a breakfast fruit.

One of the delights of old-time Italians is figs with proscuitto, the delicious Italian ham that's often served with other fruit, too, such as melon and pineapple.

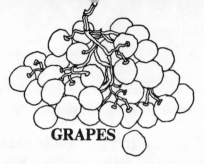

174

GRAPES

"And Noah began to be a husbandman
and he planted a vineyard." (Genesis 9:20)

THERE'S THE MOST condensed history of agriculture you'll ever find. Grapes were probably one of the first fruits cultivated; since such ancient times, in fact, that the experts aren't even sure where they originated. Their educated guess is Asia Minor, between the Caspian and Black Seas, where so many other kinds of fruit got their start.

You can find grapes on Egyptian mosaics, Greek friezes, Roman murals. You can read lyric descriptions in ancient Greek, Hebrew and Latin. But while the early artists and poets were immortalizing the grape, practical farmers and ancient produce buyers were developing an agricultural economy based to a large extent on "the fruit of the vine." One of the earliest Roman books on agriculture discusses the same things that interest growers today: the yield per acre (or Roman equivalent), the man-hours of labor needed to bring in a crop, how to raise money on grape "futures." When you're talking about grapes, at any rate, there's nothing new under the sun.

Grapes weren't just limited to Europe and Asia Minor, either. When the Norsemen visited the Northeast coast of North America, centuries before Columbus, they found grapes growing wild in such profusion they called the land Vinland.

These native American grapes, such as the Northern Fox and Muscadine, were the forerunners of today's commercially grown American grapes, such as the Catawba, Niagara, Delaware and Concord.

But most of the grapes we eat today are Old World grapes of the species *Vitis vinifera*. They are very sensitive to climate and just didn't do well when they were introduced into the Eastern part of the United States. They flourished in California, however, and about 90 percent of the table grapes produced each year come from this state. As a matter of fact, they're sometimes called "California" grapes.

Not all grapes are grown to be eaten fresh, out-of-hand. Many are processed into wine, grape juice, raisins, fruit cocktail and jelly. Some—like the Concord and Thompson Seedless—are sold as table grapes and processed as well.

Varieties & Seasons   Even limiting myself to table grapes, the list is long.

First, the native American grapes, produced mainly in New York State and available fresh for a very limited time in the fall of the year. They're apt to have a wild, winey flavor and are known as slip-skin varieties because the pulp separates easily from the skin as you eat them. The best-known varieties are the large round Concord, almost black-ish purple and covered with a silvery bloom; the large purplish-red Catawba; and the small pink Delaware.

Any description of California table grapes has to start with the one that accounts for 50 percent of the total acre-age planted: the Thompson Seedless. Of course, you recog-nize it. Even if you've traveled in British-influenced countries you've encountered it as the "sultana." It's a medi-um-sized oval grape that's yellowish green, or straw color with a touch of amber, when really ripe and at its sweetest. The season is from early June into November. (Incidentally, most of the raisins you eat are a dried form of this variety, but that's another story.)

Another seedless variety that's often confused with the Thompson Seedless is the Perlette. The main difference is the shape, rounder than the Thompson. The Perlette has a waxy, white appearance. It's the first seedless grape on the market each year, but the supply seems to come and go through July, as different growing areas come into season.

There are several varieties of red seeded grapes to choose from. The first to appear, in June, is the Cardinal, a large grape usually more than one-inch in diameter. This variety is actually a cross between the Flame Tokay and the Ribier.

Red Malagas are on the market from late July through September. This grape varies in size from medium to large and in color from pink to reddish-purple. Red Malagas are crisp and hard, with a sweet flavor. They ship so well, even cross-country, that we don't see too many locally in the San Francisco market.

The Tokay (or Flame Tokay) is a large, very pretty red grape that's marketed from September through November. It gets the name "Flame" from its brilliant color. Practically all the Tokays marketed are grown in a very small area around the town of Lodi, California. Wholesalers and retailers look forward to Tokays coming on the market because they're considered the best of the red varieties and customers are sure to be pleased when they buy these beautiful grapes.

In the past few years, however, another large red variety, the Queen grape, is cutting into the Tokay's territory. It's a hardier variety, more loosely bunched, which helps them keep better. It also colors up better.

The last red grape to appear on the market is the Emperor. The flavor of these large, elongated, light-red grapes isn't equal to other varities, but they have other things going for them. They store and ship remarkably well. Emperors mature in September and can be sold from storage right through winter into late April when the fresh grape cycle begins again.

Until recently you wouldn't have had any trouble identifying the Ribier. This large grape has a rich purple-black color and sweet flavor. It's on the market from July into February. But during the past few years a variety named the Exotic has been introduced. It's also large, black and sweet and, personally, I think it's the better of the two.

Some table grapes that come onto the market in smaller quantity deserve mention. Some are rather thin-skinned and tender, which makes them perishable, but you may find them in some of the fancier stores.

The Lady Finger is a big elongated grape that is delicious and tender. There are several members of the family, including the Khardahar, Rishbaba and Olivette; the Calmeria, which stores well and is on the market from October to April; the Almeria, another late white grape with seeds that aren't too big; and the Black Rose, with the oval elongated shape that characterizes this group of grapes.

Old-timers often ask me what happened to the older varieties of Muscat grapes, such as the Alexandria Muscat and the White Malaga. They were good-flavored, and are still grown as wine grapes, but they've been phased out as table grapes. Their replacement is the hardier Italia Muscat. This large round yellowish grape has sweet flavor and is on the market from August to November.

In general, grapes are on the market year around. Late May and April is the slack season and during this time some Ribier, seedless and Emperor grapes are imported clear from Chile and Africa.

Marketing Practices   Bulk display of grapes allows retail customers to examine and pick the bunches they want. This is great for customers but not so good for the grapes and the retailers who sell them. The more bunches of ripe grapes are handled the more "droppers" fall off. These represent a total loss to the retailer and lessen the chances of the bunch they came from being sold, as well.

This happens most often with seedless varieties in September and October. That's when they're amber-colored, sweet as sugar and fully ripe. Actually at their best. But some retailers won't accept grapes in this state because of the shedding problem. This is unfortunate for the customer but understandable from the retailers' standpoint, I guess.

One solution, being used more and more, is pre-wrapping grapes in plastic bags or overwrapped trays. It cuts down on damage from handling so it benefits retailers and consumers both. This is just good business practise and in your interest, so don't avoid these packs.

Loose or packaged, grapes are sold by the bunch by weight.

How to Buy   These rules apply to grapes regardless of variety. First and foremost: use your eyes. Grapes, like other produce, should look fresh and bright. Choose a nice medium-sized bunch with good laterals, or side bunches. The bunch should be fairly loose so sections can be separated easily for eating and so air can circulate, preventing moisture accumulating and causing mildew.

The individual grapes should be plump and well-developed. Avoid bunches with "shot" berries. These are small green berries that just didn't develop and ripen properly. They'll be sour.

Another important indication of good grapes is "bloom." This is the velvety powdery look you see on the skin of nice, fresh grapes. If the bloom is gone and the grapes look shiny, they've probably been handled too much. Don't always blame the retailer for this, some customers just aren't as careful and considerate of this delicate fruit as they should be.

Okay, the bunch looks good, the grapes on it are inviting, does it go in your shopping cart? Not until you check one more thing—the stem end. When grapes are in season look for a green, firm, healthy stem. If the stem looks dry and has turned brown or black in color, the grapes will have started to age and lose flavor, too. Supposedly, every rule has its exception—and grapes are no exception to that rule. The stems of Emperor grapes sold from storage in the winter and spring months *should* have woody stems. In this case a woody-looking stem just indicates that the bunch has been properly cured for storage.

On the vine, grapes thrive in hot temperatures, up to 100 degrees Fahrenheit, but once cut they must be cooled quickly to prevent dehydration. Most grape harvesting is done during the cool morning hours and grapes are moved as quickly as possible to warehouses kept at about 45 degrees Fahrenheit. The shipper, wholesaler and retailer do their best to deliver chilled grapes to you in prime condition.

So when you bring your grapes home get them into the refrigerator as fast as possible. First, pick off any bad grapes, then put them in a plastic bag for storage. They should keep for up to two weeks in the refrigerator.

When you're ready to serve them, rinse and use at

once. I know grapes look pretty in a fruit bowl, but after any length of time they won't look or taste too good.

Nutrition Grapes provide natural sugars and small amounts of various vitamins and minerals, mainly vitamin C and potassium. Twenty-four fresh grapes contain about 68 calories.

Uses as Food For my money it's difficult to improve on the flavor of fresh grapes eaten out-of-hand. But this is a versatile fruit and combines well in fruit cups, fruit salads and fruit compotes, too. Grapes are good in combination with avocado, grapefruit sections, melon balls or strawberries.

Memories of my grandmother's homemade grape jelly still makes my mouth water. It's almost worth the long, tedious process of jelly-making just to smell the aroma of grapes being cooked down before being strained and bottled.

Beyond this, I advise consulting your favorite cookbook.

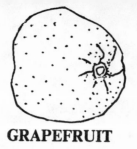

GRAPEFRUIT

IT'S HARD TO imagine a time when a grapefruit on display with other fruit would stop customers in their tracks or when a hostess could get a reputation for imagination by serving grapefruit to her guests. That was the case up to the start of this century when grapefruit was practically unknown anywhere in the world outside of Florida.

Grapefruit evolved from a citrus called pummelo, pomelo or shaddock that's native to the Malay Archipelago. A Captain Shaddock brought some pummelo seeds to the West Indies in 1693. By 1824 a naturalist described "a fruit not larger than a good orange which is borne in bunches like grapes and is designated by the English as Forbidden Fruit or smaller shaddock."

Undoubtedly this was grapefruit but botanists can't decide whether it was a mutation of the pummelo or a cross between it and an orange.

About the same time the fruit was first recorded in the West Indies, a former surgeon in Napoleon's army, Odet Philippe, planted some in Florida. Not only was this the start of Florida's commercial grapefruit industry—the state still produces 70% of all the world's grapefruit—but these trees were the parent trees for all the grapefruit varieties grown today everywhere.

Varieties Your store probably "shelf-talks," or posts signs, that identify grapefruit as seedless or pink. Actually there aren't that many varieties of grapefruit. There's Duncan, a direct descendant of M. Philippe's trees. It has a medium-thick yellow rind that's sometimes tinged with green or russeted. The fruit usually runs 3½ inches to 5 inches in diameter, and can be oblate (flattened at the poles) or round. You'll probably find 30 to 50 seeds inside.

So, when a tree producing nearly seedless fruit was found in about 1890, it was a real breakthrough for the grapefruit industry. It's called the Marsh, very similar to the Duncan in appearance except the rind is usually lighter in color. But inside: only 3 to 8 seeds. This variety is now grown in Texas, California and Arizona, as well as in Florida, and can even be found growing in Israel and Australia.

Pink grapefruit was developed mainly in the Rio Grande Valley of Texas. The main varieties are Pink Marsh, also called Thompson, and Ruby, which has the distinction of being the first citrus fruit ever to be patented.

Seasons You'll find grapefruit on the market every month of the year, but supplies are small from June through September.

Florida produces grapefruit from September 1 to July 31; California from October 1 throughout the year; Texas from October 1 to June 30; and Arizona from October 1 to July 31.

Marketing Practices All grapefruit comes into the market tree-ripe. As a matter of fact, it can be stored on the tree for months, becoming sweeter all the while. One of the grading tests is for maturity and fruit ready for marketing has to have little or no starch left for conversion to sugar.

Once picked the fruit is washed, scrubbed, coated with wax and polished. Then it's sized and packed in cartons weighing 36 to 40 pounds. The 18 size is large, weighing in at about 2 pounds each. It sounds like an oldtime math exercise: How much do 40 size grapefruit weigh? The answer is about one pound each and they're the best sellers.

Grapefruit are sold by the each, the pound, or in cello bags. Because customers prefer them, for no other reason I know, seedless and pink varieties are usually priced a bit higher than other grapefruit.

How to Buy When grapefruit are in season it's hard to pick a bad one. Fruit with lots of juice should be thin-skinned and feel heavy for their weight. The smoothness or roughness of the skin is a direct indication of how thick it is. To determine weight or heft, bounce the grapefruit in your hand. It's easier when you juggle one in each hand. Don't worry about minor skin defects, russeting or scars. They won't affect the quality of the fruit inside. But do avoid any grapefruit that's soft and puffy or has a pointed end.

Once you get it home, grapefruit will keep at room temperature for 5 or 6 days, and in the refrigerator for several weeks.

Nutrition Recently a grapefruit diet became quite fashionable. Fad diets can be dangerous and unless your doctor recommends large amounts of any one food I wouldn't experiment. But grapefruit is low in calories, only 40 to a half, and makes a good dessert or snack for anyone trying to lose weight by cutting down on their calorie intake.

Like almost all fruit, grapefruit is low in sodium and fat and high in vitamin C. About half the ascorbic acid you should get each day is contained in one grapefruit half. Pink varieties provide good amounts of vitamin A, and all grapefruit contains small amounts of various minerals.

Uses as Food Breakfast, lunch, dinner and any time in-between is a good time for a half grapefruit. Some people sprinkle salt or sugar on the fruit. I don't see why.

Sections can be used in fruit salads and in combinations such as avocado and grapefruit. The juice is refreshing by itself or with other fruit juices.

Grapefruit becomes a more elegant dessert when honey or brown sugar, butter, and perhaps some sherry or rum, are added on top of each half and they're placed under the broiler until browned.

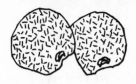

KIWIS

HOW DO YOU go about marketing a completely new fruit to the American public? Especially one that's a real ugly duckling as far as looks go? That was the problem New Zealand businessmen faced with the fruit they called the Chinese gooseberry.

They decided a new and provocative name might do the trick and they settled on Kiwi, after the New Zealand national bird. I don't know how smart this was because it always makes me think of a brand of shoe polish. But that's the name they're sold by in the United States, although the fruit has also been called monkey peach, sheep peach, yang tao, and Ichang gooseberry. None of these names do this delicious and exotic fruit justice to my mind.

The reaction to seeing a Kiwi for the first time is usually, "What on earth is that?" The fruit won't win any beauty contests for sure. It looks like a small new potato with three-day's growth of beard. But once you cut this brown, furry, egg-shaped fruit in half the picture changes. It has a creamy pale center with lines radiating out like rays of sunshine into beautiful green flesh the color of lime ice. Tiny black seeds surrounding the center provide more color and texture. (Like strawberry seeds, they're completely edible.) The flavor is wonderful: an almost perfumed combination of sweet and tart tastes that's been described as watermelon with a dash of strawberry. I predict that this fruit will become more and more popular as the supply increases. Once all Kiwis arrived by ship from Down Under, now they're being air-freighted in. And, in addition, California has started producing this delicious and unusual fruit. Between 1962 and 1970 the amount of Kiwis coming into the market increased 100 times and I'm sure sales will continue to skyrocket as the public "discovers" them.

Varieties & Seasons   Kiwis imported from New Zealand are primarily of the Hayward variety. They start arriving by air in May and by ship in mid-June. Shipments continue through December.

The Chico variety is the one grown in California. It's harvested in November and December.

Kiwis keep from four to six months in storage, so it's likely that one of these days the fruit will be available all year long.

How to Buy   To select a ripe ready-to-eat Kiwi, place one in the palm of your hand squeeze *very* gently. As you add pressure the fruit should give slightly. If you'd rather buy firmer fruit and ripen it at home, place the Kiwi in a plastic bag (some people say adding an apple will help it ripen) and keep it at room temperature for about 3 days.

Nutrition   The Kiwi is high in vitamin C. An average-sized fruit is said to provide a full day's requirement, along with 30 calories. The Kiwi, like the papaya, seems to contain a natural meat tenderizer. Experiments in the Home Science Department of New Zealand's Otago University concluded that rubbing meat with peeled Kiwi fruit not only tenderized it, but added to its flavor as well.

Uses as Food   If there's anything guaranteed to make a New Zealander feel homesick it's mentioning Pavlova Cake. It consists of a meringue shell filled with sliced Kiwi fruit and whipped cream. But you don't have to be that elaborate. Just peel the skin—there are no pits, seeds or stones to remove —and eat it with a spoon, or slice it into a bowl with yoghurt or ice cream. And, remembering the Kiwi's "magic" with meat—try rubbing a sliced half over steaks before grilling them.

I've devoted all this space to what's still considered a "specialty item" even where it's known in the U.S., because this fruit is something special. Try it, you'll like it.

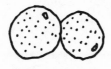

KUMQUATS

ONE OF W.C. Field's best-known lines was, "How about a kumquat, my little chickadee?" It always got laughs, probably because of its strange sound. I bet lots of people who laughed didn't even know what a kumquat was. Actually, it's the smallest orange-like fruit on the market, often used for decoration rather than eating.

The shrubby kumquat tree is native to China and is valued there because it is resistant to cold and grows farther north than other true citrus trees. The name comes from Chinese words meaning "golden orange." They are a very decorative bush and many can be seen growing in gardens in areas near San Francisco, such as Palo Alto, Santa Rosa and Sonoma.

Kumquats are on the market from November into June. Until around Christmas, the crop comes from Florida. After the holidays California starts producing.

The oblong fruit is about 1¼ to 1½ inches long. It is usually sold loose by the pound. Look for fresh bright orange-colored fruit and pick those with leaves attached if you wish to add a decorative item to your fruit bowl. Kumquats may be displayed at room temperature or refrigerated for later use.

But please don't just use kumquats for decoration. They are delicious eaten skin and all, with their combination of sour pulp and sweet rind. First squeeze and massage the kumquat to combine the flavors. When the fruit is soft, pop it into your mouth.

Kumquats make excellent preserves, especially marmalades. They can also be used to make jams, jellies and sugared candies. Whole kumquats can be seen preserved in jars in your supermarket and are quite expensive. Why not be adventurous and make your own? Just consult any comprehensive cookbook.

186

LEMONS

LEMONS MAKE ME think of lemonade—a Norman Rockwell painting of a small freckle-faced kid selling it from a homemade stand at one cent a glass. But in researching this book I've found that the Mongolians started making lemonade about the time of Ghengis Khan. That's an entirely different picture—the Mongol hordes swooping down with fire and sword, sacking villages in their path, and then stopping for a lemonade break.

All our citrus fruits originated in Asia and lemons followed the same path West as the others. To North Africa with Arab traders, to southern Europe with the Crusaders, then across the Atlantic with Columbus.

California and Arizona now grow almost half the world's lemon crop. The California industry got its start during Gold Rush days, when scurvy was more common and dangerous than claim jumpers. Fresh fruit and vegetables were so scarce that lemons sold for up to a dollar each—and the dollar was worth a lot more then.

Lemons are still a profitable crop and not just from what you and I squeeze into our iced tea or salad dressing. They wind up in things you'd never expect: waxes, printing inks, medicines, mirrors and blueprints, for instance.

Varieties There are actually sweet and sour varieties of lemons. In the United States, though, the sweet ones are grown only as an ornamental or novelty plant, not commercially.

The Eureka is the most popular variety we market. It's egg-shaped with a fairly flat nipple at the stem end. The skin is pitted and lemon-yellow in color when ripe. It contains lots of clear, very acid juice and has few seeds.

The other variety you're likely to find is the Lisbon. It's generally smoother skinned and has a longer nipple than the Eureka.

Seasons   If you walked through a lemon grove, you'd see blossoms, buds and mature fruit all on the same tree. This means that lemons can be harvested every month of the year. Not only that, they also store well, allowing wholesalers to market them when the demand is greatest, during the hot summer months.

The Eureka variety is at its peak in summer; the Lisbon produces more fruit during the winter.

Grading and Pricing   I can remember, and it wasn't too long ago, when lemon harvesting and packing were done by hand. Now it's a highly mechanized industry. There are machines that sort the lemons electronically for size and color at the rate of 40 a second. The packing is automated, too.

The packing houses like the change because it's faster and cheaper. I like it because virtually all of the lemons coming into the produce market now are of good quality.

In retail stores lemons are either displayed loose and sold at a unit price ("3 for . . ." or "6 for . . .") or pre-packaged by the half-dozen or dozen and priced by the bag.

How to Buy   The best lemons have a fine-textured skin and are heavy for their size. Rough-looking ones usually have thick skins and less juice. A slight greenish cast to the skin is desirable, since it means the juice will be more acid.

Avoid lemons that are shriveled and hard-skinned or soft and spongy. Look at the stem end; that's where signs of decay or aging will show up first.

At home, store lemons in the fruit drawer of your refrigerator. They should keep up to a month.

Nutrition   Maybe the old saying should be changed to "a lemon a day keeps the doctor away." One will provide between 40 and 80 per cent of the vitamin C you need each day. Lemons have been used for over 200 years to prevent scurvy and have been a popular home remedy for colds for generations.

In addition to vitamin C, lemons contain bio-flavonoids. Some studies have shown the two together help reduce the inflammation that goes along with respiratory infections. So if lemons won't keep you from getting a cold, they may help you get over it. You see, grandma was right!

Lemons are made to order for anyone on a low-fat or sodium-restricted diet. Not only are they low in calories and sodium themselves, but they can be used instead of things that aren't, such as butter and salt (on vegetables) and dressings (on salads).

Uses as Food   Most lemons are used in fruit drinks, but there are many other uses. In salad dressings; on such cooked vegetables as broccoli, asparagus or spinach; with seafoods— lobster or scallops; as a flavoring in cakes and cookies. As a matter of fact, from the wedge served with a tomato juice cocktail to a lemon meringue pie for dessert, lemon can add to every course of a meal.

Here's a favorite lemon recipe of mine: Squeeze 6 lemons. Add ¼ cup olive oil, ¼ teaspoon dried oregano, a small chopped garlic clove and a chopped sprig of parsley. Season with salt and pepper to taste. Stir thoroughly and set aside for an hour before using this tangy sauce as a marinade, salad dressing or barbecue sauce.

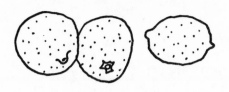

LIMES

HAVE YOU EVER wondered why British sailors are called "limeys"? The nickname is almost 200 years old and comes from the daily ration of citrus fruit issued to British seamen. Sailors from other countries may have laughed at the practice, but it accomplished its purpose. It wiped out scurvy, common on long voyages when the diet consisted of hardtack and bully beef (dry biscuits and pickled beef). Today, of course, we know that vitamin C is responsible.

Limes flourish in a hot, humid climate. That's where the fruit originated, in Burma or southeast India. They were equally at home in Egypt when Arab traders brought them there. The Crusaders were the first Europeans to see limes and carried them to southern Europe. They crossed the Atlantic with Columbus on his second voyage in 1493 and were grown wherever the Spaniards settled. Three of these former Spanish colonies—Florida, California and Mexico—now produce the limes sold in the United States.

Varieties Most limes grown in the United States are of the Tahitian-type, with Persians and Bearss the most popular varieties. Florida, which practically has the lime market cornered, grows the Persian, a large oval fruit with very acid juice and few or no seeds. The few from California are usually Bearss, somewhat smaller and always seedless.

Florida also produces the only Mexican-type limes grown in this country: the Key lime. It is smaller, rounder and more acid than the Persian variety. Many are processed into juice and sold for use in Key Lime Pie.

Seasons It's rare to find a lime tree without fruit on it in some stage of maturity. But each producing area has its peak seasons. When the supply from Florida slackens off in August, the California crop is conveniently at its peak.

Between mid-March and April, when domestic stocks are low, some limes are imported. The West Indies supplies the East Coast; Mexico the West. These limes tend to be small, full of seeds and expensive, so they don't sell too well.

Grading and Pricing   In Florida, the major producing area, much of the crop is processed into juice. So oversized and undersized limes, as well as any with external damage, are diverted to this use.

Limes are hardy enough to be displayed in bulk. They're often sold as what retailers call a "twofer"—for example, 2 for 15 cents, or 3 for 29 cents. Sometimes they're in plastic bags or overwrapped trays, priced by the pack.

How to Buy   Good limes should be green and heavy for their size. Brown spots on the skin are nothing to worry about and won't affect the juice. There are two kinds of limes to avoid. (A good produce man will discard them anyway.) First, yellow-skinned limes—the juice won't have the desired acidity. Second, fruit that's dry, hard and blackened. This is a sign of immaturity dehydration or age and the pulp will be "ricey," a term used when the fruit's juice sacs are grainy and won't yield juice.

Once you get them home, limes should be refrigerated. Sunlight will turn them yellow and they will deteriorate.

Nutrition   As the British Navy found out, citrus fruits such as limes are an excellent source of vitamin C. The calorie count is negligible: 3½ ounces of juice, more than you're apt to consume in a day, contains 26 calories.

Uses as Food   The tangy flavor of lime livens up salads, melons or seafood. If you don't squeeze the juice directly on the food when preparing it, wedges or slices of lime make a decorative addition to a platter or plate. The ascorbic acid limes contain will keep such fruits as peaches or bananas from turning brown when sliced—and add to their flavor.

Bartenders always have a good supply of limes on hand. Daiquiris depend on them and a gin- or vodka-and-tonic isn't complete without a wedge of lime. Lime juice is a flavorful addition to punch, whether you're serving a non-alcoholic fruit punch or the more potent kind.

MANGOES

MANGOES ARE CONSIDERED exotic in the United States, but they're one of the most commonly eaten fruits in the tropical areas of the world. India alone produces about seven and a half million tons of mangoes each year. They probably originated in the Himalayan region of India and Burma, where they've been cultivated for over 4000 years. In the fourteenth century a poet named Amir Khusran wrote, "The mango is the pride of the garden, the choicest fruit of Hindustan. Other fruits we are content to eat when ripe, but the mango is good at all stages of growth."

It doesn't take a poet to be enthusiastic about this delicious fruit. Its delicate flavor is hard to describe: some say it tastes like a mixture of pear and apricot, others a cross between melon and pineapple. What's more, they're attractive to look at. Most of those you see on the market are about the size of a large avocado, with colors that range from green to bright yellow to gold to pink to clear red. Often several colors are blended on the same egg-shaped fruit as it ripens.

Varieties   There are hundreds of varieties of mangoes, ranging from the size of a large plum to seven-pounders or larger. The Hayden from Florida is one of the most widely distributed varieties in the U.S. Other popular varieties are the Malgoba, deep yellow with red on one side that weighs from nine to fourteen ounces, and the Amini, a smaller type usually six to eight ounces in weight. You may also find the Bennett, Sandersha, Paheri, Kent and Manila varieties on the market, depending on the season and where they came from.

Seasons   You're most likely to find mangoes in the average retail store between May and September. June is the peak month, because that's when most Florida mangoes are harvested. The rest of the time the fruit is imported to the East

Coast from the West Indies and Haiti and to the West Coast from Mexico.

Marketing Practices   It seems strange that a fruit so common in what are considered the poorest parts of the world should be so expensive in some parts of the U.S. The main reason, of course, is that mangoes are a tropical fruit and most of our supplies are imported—so by the time it gets to you it is fairly high-priced.

However, as the volume of mangoes increases, as they have been doing in the past few years, particularly imports from Mexico, prices will surely come down as they already have in some parts of the country, notably on the West Coast.

Practically all mangoes sold commercially are a pound or less in weight. They are usually sold by the each.

How to Buy   Look for smooth-skinned mangoes that have started to color up. All-green ones may never ripen properly. At the other extreme is soft, shriveled fruit and those with large black areas on the skin. They are probably over-ripe and should be avoided.

A ready-to-eat mango should be firm but have some "give" to it. Test for this by placing the fruit between the palms of both hands and pressing very gently.

A firm but mature mango will ripen at room temperature in three or four days. When it's springy and ready to eat, either use it at once or refrigerate in a plastic bag for a few days only.

Nutrition   One-half of a medium-sized mango will supply more than half an adult's daily requirement of vitamin C. They are also high in vitamin A. This quantity of mango contains about 66 calories.

Uses as Food   Some people say the only place to eat a mango is in the bathtub. That's because a ripe mango is lusciously juicy and can leave bright yellow stains on tablecloths and clothes. Don't let that stop you—just take precautions.

I've read that in India people eat mangoes from the inside out. The trick is to take a firm ripe mango and keep kneading it *very, very gently* until all the pulp inside is mashed. The description of the mango at this stage is "like a rubber bag full of water." Then *carefully* remove the "scab" where the stem was attached and put the hole to your lips. Suck the juice out, squeezing the "bag" gently until it's empty except for the large stone or pit inside. I'd try this for the first time over a sink until you get the knack of liquefying the pulp without splitting the skin.

· The more usual way to eat mangoes out-of-hand is to score the skin with a knife, going from north to south around the fruit, like the longitude lines of a world globe. Then peel the skin back like a banana, again being careful where the juice goes.

Mangoes can also be served on the half shell like avocado or melon, and sliced into fruit salads. If you're an adventurous and ambitious cook, mangoes make delicious pickles and are practically synonymous with chutney.

For an elegant, yet simple to make, "company" dessert, try this: Slice mangoes, sprinkle with sugar and cover with rum. Chill in the refrigerator for an hour, then serve over vanilla ice cream.

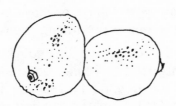

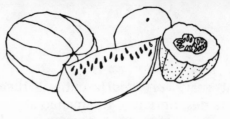

SWEET MELONS

THESE MELONS ARE sometimes called muskmelons to describe their almost perfumed fragrance. The word musk, like the melons themselves, is of Persian origin. From the Near East they spread to Europe. It's said that the Ancient Roman Emperor Tiberius was so fond of melons he had the first greenhouses in the world built so he could enjoy the fruit year 'round. Centuries later an Italian, Genoese not Roman, made sure he'd have melons available, too. His name was Christopher Columbus and he planted them in the New World on March 29, 1494. We know the date because he considered it important enough to note in the record of his expedition.

Melons spread rapidly in the Americas and were popular with home gardeners from the time of the first settlements in North America. Commercial cultivation didn't start until about 100 years ago, though. The first big melon-producing area was Rocky Ford, Colorado. Melon farmers supplied miners in boom towns like Leadville, and shipped melons as far away as Chicago. Now California and the Southwest are the major producing areas.

Varieties To avoid confusion I'm going to vary the usual procedure in this book and talk about each type of melon separately. That means you'll find specific information about seasons and buying tips in this section, and general comments applying to all melons under the usual section headings.

CANTALOUPE is undoubtedly the most popular variety. The fruit is oval in shape, with rough cream-colored raised netting covering the entire surface. The flesh is salmon-orange in color. It has a musky sweet aroma and sweet taste. In the old days we used to call cantaloupes "megs," because they resemble giant nutmegs.

You can buy cantaloupes, from one source or another,

for the major part of the year. Mexico begins shipping its cantaloupes in January. California's Imperial Valley takes over in June. Production then moves northward in California, the largest producing state, through such areas as Bakersfield, Mendota and Los Banos, where production is heavy from July into September.

Beware of advertisements featuring "jumbo" cantaloupes. It refers to the size of the crate the melons were shipped in, not to the size of the individual melons. Cantaloupes are packed in jumbo, standard or pony crates. The number of melons in a jumbo crate ranges from 18 to 72, or from about one to four pounds each. A 1-pound melon is hardly "jumbo" to my mind, and I feel there's a real need to standardize terms.

Cantaloupes should always be *completely* covered with creamy-colored netting. A large "slick," or smooth spot on the surface, is a bad sign—leave those melons on the counter. The melon should have slight "give" when you press it gently, just don't confuse this springiness with softness. Cantaloupes should always be in "full slip" condition. This means a smooth stem end. A cantaloupe picked before fully mature is in "half-slip" condition and will show some rough stem fibers on the stem end.

PERSIAN MELONS look like oversized cantaloupes. When you look closely, however, you'll see it's somewhat rounder and has finer, flatter netting. The meat is a beautiful delicate pink-orange color. Persians have a pleasant aroma and mildly sweet taste.

The Persian is grown almost exclusively in California and is available from July through October, peaking in August and September.

As with cantaloupe, choose a springy melon without any "slicks." Avoid any with dark or greenish-black netting; this is usually a sign of immaturity and indicates a melon that probably won't ripen successfully.

CRENSHAW MELONS are winners in just about every respect. They're a hybrid, or cross between a Persian and a Casaba that started coming into the market in the 1940's.

Crenshaws are large, weighing up to nine pounds, with flattened or rounded blossom ends and rather pointed stem ends. The skin is smooth with slight lengthwise ribbing and no netting. It is a beautiful golden color when ripe. The flesh is a delicate golden-salmon color; pinker than a cantaloupe, more orange than a Persian. It has a rich aroma and juicy, spicy taste.

Crenshaws are available from July through October and are in peak supply during August and September. They are grown in California, Arizona and Texas.

CASABA MELONS resemble Crenshaws somewhat in shape. However, they have definite irregular lengthwise furrows. The skin is a rich golden-yellow color, the flesh creamy-white to creamy-golden and juicy.

Casabas are available from July through November. But they're most plentiful in September and October, and that's when they're best. In fact, when Casabas begin to appear in good supply, it's a sign to produce men that it's getting darn near the end of the year again.

Casabas are one variety you can squeeze. They're thick-skinned and not easily damaged. Choose a golden-yellow one and press gently at the blossom end. Slight springiness is a sign of ripeness.

HONEY DEW MELONS are fairly large, averaging about six pounds, and oval in shape. The skin is usually smooth, although some have patches of slightly raised irregular netting. (Far from being a drawback, this generally indicates exceptional sweetness.) The skin of a ripe Honey Dew is creamy white or yellowish, the flesh a delicate light green color.

Some Honey Dews are available most of the year, particularly on the East Coast, because of imports from Latin America. The biggest months, however, are June through October, when Texas, Arizona and California are producing in large quantity.

Let me sound off briefly about Honey Dews, at least the way they're marketed locally. Vine-ripened Honey Dews used to arrive in the San Francisco produce market packed in lettuce crates. Now they're shipped in standard crates that hold only seven to nine melons, as well as even smaller ⅔-standard cartons that hold four to eight smaller sized melons. This protects the market for the large producers, but the increased handling that's required has raised the retail price to the point where sales have been reduced on one of our best melons.

There's nothing better than a fully ripe Honey Dew but it takes some skill to choose one. First look for color, creamy-white or creamy-yellow. Rind that's dead-white or has a greenish tinge indicates a melon that was picked too soon. Don't you pick it, either. Next, feel the skin for "bloom." A good one will have a soft and velvety feel, slightly sticky or oily. One that feels like a billiard ball—smooth, hard and shiny—was picked too soon. A little give to the rind indicates ripeness.

CHRISTMAS OR SANTA CLAUS MELONS are shaped something like a dirigible or zeppelin. The skin color is green with patches of yellow forming a striped effect. The flesh is similar to the Casaba in color and flavor. They get their name because they're on the market in December. This melon keeps very well, up to a month in storage, but in my experience it's not equal to the other varieties.

Marketing Practices Melons are usually sold by the pound, with the exception of cantaloupes, which may be sold by the each or the pound. Always weigh a melon. What seems like a bargain at 20 cents per pound may not seem like such a good buy when you know it weighs four pounds or more.

How to Buy Just on the basis of the number of people who ask me, "How do you pick out a good melon?" it seems obvious that everyone's been disappointed from time to time.

My answer may sound discouraging at first: the only infallible way is to cut the melon open first, and I'm sure no retailer would stand for customers trying that test. At any rate, thumping, shaking and squeezing aren't the ways to go about choosing melons.

In addition to the specific "rules" for each variety,

there are a few general ones for all melons. First, don't look for soft melons, except to discard them. They will always be overripe. Second, any melon that "sloshes" when shaken will be mushy inside and may have started to sour. Third, reject any melons that are soft and wet at the stem end, they've already started to decay and will deteriorate rapidly.

Melons don't gain in sugar or sweetness after they're picked. But they do become riper and mellower, therefore more flavorful. Holding melons in a warm area out of direct sunlight for three or four days before chilling and serving is a good idea. Many fine restaurants and hotels neglect doing this. They pay premium prices for the best melons, especially the larger varieties such as Persians and Crenshaws, that are impractical for small families, and then some are served before they're ready for eating. When ripe and ready to eat, a melon will keep up to a week in your refrigerator.

Nutrition   Melons are low in calories. Cantaloupes provide vitamin A and C, Honey Dews vitamin C. Generally, the darker orange the meat of a melon the better source of vitamin A it will be.

Uses as Food   Melons are light and refreshing, whether eaten for breakfast or as a dessert. A little lemon or lime brings out the flavor. Melons can be served in wedges, halves or scooped out into balls. They combine well with other fruits, especially berries, for fruit salads and fruit cups.

Italians serve melon with proscuitto as an appetizer. You can usually find this delicious hard-cured Italian ham at better delicatessens. Sliced almost paper-thin and eaten with the melon it makes a delicious combination—the slightly smoky-salty taste of the ham with the sweet-tart flavor of the melon.

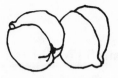

NECTARINES

TIME AND TIME again I've heard people insist that nectarines are either a rather new variety of fuzzless peach or a cross between a peach and a plum. Wrong on both counts. Nectarines are a relative of the peach but are a distinct variety, maybe even older than their other relatives, cherries and apricots. They originated in the Orient before the time of Christ and were known to the ancient Greeks.

The name comes from the Greek *nektar,* which we call nectar. It was the drink of the gods who lived on Mount Olympus and was supposed to grant immortal life to anyone who drank it. To a botanist, however, nectar is the sweet sugar-flavored liquid that attracts insects and leads to cross-pollination. That's the real story of "the birds and the bees."

The great English poet John Keats seemed to agree that nectarines were fit for the gods. In 1819 he wrote a friend, "Talking of Pleasure, this moment I was writing with one hand, and with the other holding to my Mouth, a Nectarine —good God how fine. It went down soft, pulpy, slushy, oozy ..."

Varieties Before World War II most nectarines were white-fleshed. The flavor was excellent. They had everything going for them except shipping quality. The result was this wonderful fruit was rare or even unavailable to people in many parts of the country. But then new varieties, yellow-fleshed instead of white, were developed that are much more hardy. Since the 1950's the industry has really taken off.

Now nine varieties, produced in California's San Joaquin Valley, between Yuba City in the north and Bakersfield in the south, account for 90% of the U.S. crop each year. It takes a real pro to identify the different varieties, which, like peaches, can be Clingstone or Freestone. All are highly colored and have a beautiful bright red blush over a rich amber-yellow skin.

The Red June and the Early Sun Grand are early Freestone varieties. They are followed late in July by the Red Grand and Le Grand, both Clingstones. After these, in August and September, two more Clingstone varieties come onto the market, the Regal Grand and the Gold King.

Seasons The California season runs from late March through September. The heaviest harvest is during July and August. You'll find some nectarines, imported from Chile and Argentina, on the market from January through March.

Marketing Practices Like peaches, nectarines do not gain sugar after harvest and must be picked and shipped at just the right time. Growers, shippers and wholesalers walk a tightrope between marketing immature green fruit and overripe fruit that will spoil before it reaches the consumer. The plentiful supply of nectarines marketed in season now shows they have the technique down pretty pat.

Nectarines are usually sold loose by the pound, although occasionally you'll find them priced by the each.

How to Buy Look for nectarines that are firm, plump and well-formed. Slight softening along the seam indicates ripeness. The skin should show a blush of bright red color over a yellow or yellow-orange background. The background color of Early Sun Grand, Sun Grand, Red Grand and Gold King varieties may have a slight greenish cast or show some green at the stem end and still be ripe.

Avoid hard green or dull-colored fruit. It was picked too soon and will shrivel instead of ripening when you get it home. Soft, spotted or bruised fruit should be avoided, of course.

Mature but firm fruit will ripen at home at room temperature and be ready to eat within a few days. If necessary you can store these nectarines in the refrigerator several days before ripening them.

Nutrition Two medium-size nectarines will provide about one-third the vitamin A and one-fourth the vitamin C recommended for adults daily. This amount contains just 64 calories.

Uses as Food   I can't imagine anything much better than a nectarine eaten raw, skin and all. If you want to try something fancier (and can keep your family from eating them all first) you can slice them into fruit salads or serve with melon. I've seen recipes for nectarine pizzas and nectarine sauces for meat, but I've never been adventurous enough to try them.

But here is an elegant way to serve nectarines, without losing their natural fresh flavor: To serve four, make a compote of fresh nectarine slices (2 cups) and seedless grapes (1 cup). Pour over a marinade of ¼ cup vodka (or fresh lime juice), ¼ cup fresh orange juice, 2 tablespoons sugar, 2 tablespoons grated fresh orange rind and 1 tablespoon finely-chopped candied ginger. Mix gently, then cover and chill about 2 hours, tossing occasionally, before serving.

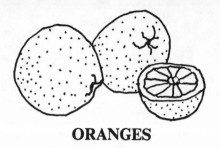

202

ORANGES

IF YOU'D BEEN strolling through London in the early 1600's you might have heard a street peddler hawking his fruit with a song that went:

"Fine Sevil oranges, fine lemmans, fine;
Round, sound, and tender, inside and rine,
One pin's prick their vertue shew:
They've liquor by their weight, you may know."

(I assume that "rine" is the rind.) Today's produce men couldn't advertise oranges much better than that.

Even fairly recently in Northern European countries such as England, oranges were a delicacy because the fruit can't stand frost. In fact, the first greenhouses, called orangeries, were developed to protect trees brought from a more temperate climate.

Oranges are a pretty hardy fruit to market, but there's very little latitude in growing them. Very little north of about 40 degrees latitude, that is. From their native soil in southeast Asia, where they've been cultivated for centuries, they successfully took root in the Near East and North Africa in the ninth century and in southern Spain and Portugal in the twelfth. Thanks to Spanish and Portuguese explorers sailing almost due West in the early sixteenth century, oranges acclimated themselves to the semi-tropics of North and South America. Just by looking at a map you can see why commercial groves in the United States are practically restricted to Florida, southern California, Texas and Arizona.

But where orange trees *do* grow they flourish. So much so that in many places they're a symbol of fertility. In Sardinia the wedding limousine is usually a cart, pulled by oxen with oranges attached to their horns, and in Crete the bride and groom are sprinkled with orange-flower water on their wedding day to make the marriage happy, prosperous and fruitful. Even in this country, brides often carry orange-blossom bouquets or wear wreaths of them in their hair. Of course we call this "a lovely tradition" instead of "a superstitious folk custom."

Varieties   When we say oranges we mean sweet ones, although there are "bitter oranges," which are grown commercially in Spain. They're used for marmalade, candied peel and to flavor the liqueur called Curaçao.

Our sweet oranges are the most popular and long-established citrus fruit in the United States. While many varieties have been developed in the hundred years they've been grown commercially, only six are of major importance.

The Washington Navel accounts for only 10 percent of the total crop, but it's so distinctive I think it deserves first mention. That name, as the spelling indicates, has nothing to do with boats or sailors. It comes from what kids call the "belly-button" on the flower end. You might think that Navel oranges are a modern product but they're not. They were described and pictured as early as 1646. The variety we call the Washington Navel was already being grown in Brazil in 1820. Fifty years later a missionary stationed there sent 12 trees in tubs to the Department of Agriculture greenhouses in Washington, D.C. Two of them were carried to Riverside, California, and alone were the source for extensive plantings in Orange County—now probably better known for conservative politics and Disneyland. For years these Navels went by three different names: Bahia, for the part of Brazil where they originated; Washington, for their first home in the United States; and Riverside, for their commercial origin. The name Washington is most commonly used today. Washington Navels are ideal for eating out of hand because they're so easy to peel and separate into segments. And, they're large, seedless and have a delicious flavor.

Most of the juice oranges you buy will be Valencias. They are produced in Florida, California, Arizona and Texas and make up about half the U.S. crop most years. The Valencia is a round or slightly oval medium-size orange. The rind is thin and smooth. Inside there's lots of juice in which sweet and acid tastes are well-combined for good flavor.

Early in the season you'll often see smaller oranges on display. It's not that they were picked before they grew to full size, they're just different varieties. The Hamlin, grown in Florida and Texas, is considered the best of the early-maturing oranges. Hamlins have a lot of good-tasting juice and few or no seeds. The Parson Brown is another good early orange. It's grown mainly in Florida, although there are groves in Texas, Arizona and Louisiana as well. You probably won't be quite as satisfied with this variety: it has a lot of seeds and sometimes the flavor isn't as well blended as in other varieties.

The Pineapple orange was named for its beautiful aroma. Its size varies from medium to large and its shape from round to oblate (like a grapefruit). It has a glossy deep-orange colored rind. Inside there's lots of everything—seeds as well as delicious juice.

I've left the Temple orange for last, wondering whether to include it with the tangerines and mandarins, where it really belongs. Since it's called an orange, I'll let it stay. Horticulturists consider the Temple a hybrid known as a tangor—a cross between an orange and a tangerine. It's less frost-resistant than a tangerine and more tender to cold than an orange. Florida produces most Temples but California and Arizona are planting more each year. The skin is a deep orange-red color and easily removed. The sections also separate easily, so it's good to eat out of hand. The juice, and there's lots of it, is rich and spicy, with a good blend of acidity and sweetness.

Seasons One or another variety of orange is available every month of the year. The largest quantities are on the market December through April. Supplies are lowest from May through September.

California navels are marketed from mid-November to mid-May. Arizona harvests them from November through February.

Valencias have a late season and are available when

other varieties are off the market. They're harvested in one producing area or another 10 months of the year. The two exceptions are December and January.

Florida harvests its Temple oranges between December and February. The California and Arizona crops then take over through April.

Grading and Pricing   Two grades of oranges are usually sent to market, the Extra Fancy and the Choice. The Extra Fancy grade should be completely free of blemishes and scars. You pay for this. Since the defects on the outer skin of the Choice oranges don't affect the eating quality, they're usually the better buy.

The way oranges are priced varies from store to store and even according to size, variety or packaging in the same store. You can find them by the each, by the dozen, by the pound, or by the pre-packaged bag. It's easier to judge the value you're getting when you make up your own dozen, but it does slow things down at a supermarket counter when checkers have to stop to count them.

The law of supply and demand has a definite effect on the price of the oranges you buy. Weather—mainly frost— is what determines the supply. Frost warnings send growers hurrying for their traditional smudge-pots, or to turn on wind machines to keep air circulating and, hopefully, warmer. Some growers even hire helicopters to hover over their trees and mix the colder and warmer air with their blades. If none of these methods work, your oranges will cost more very soon.

How to Buy   Don't depend on color to determine whether an orange is ripe and ready to eat. In southeast Asia the skin of an orange *never* turns a bright orange color, it stays green even when completely ripe. The same is true of many oranges grown in Florida and Texas. Climate is responsible. Cooler weather, like that found in the less tropical growing areas in California and Arizona, is what makes oranges naturally take on the color named for them. What happens is that lower temperatures destroy the chlorophyll, or green color, leaving the other pigments predominant. Because most people associate a rich orange color with good fruit, Florida and Texas oranges often get a beauty treatment in a harmless dye-bath that affects only the skin. They are always stamped "Color Added." These oranges must pass strict tests for maturity and their quality is not at all inferior.

In California Valencia oranges tend to regreen late in the season and develop a greenish cast, particularly around the stem end.

Instead of judging oranges by their color, look for ones that are firm and heavy for their size. This indicates lots of juice. Most important, choose the smoothest-skinned ones of the variety you're buying, making sure they're also free from soft spots or mold.

Once you get oranges home, store them in a cool place. The refrigerator is okay but not necessary. If mold develops on an orange you're storing, get rid of it before it spreads to the other fruit.

Nutrition   Have you ever noticed how some "orange drink" concentrate is marked "vitamin C added"? That's because some of the natural vitamin C is destroyed by freezing or processing and has to be replaced artificially. I think it's better to get the real thing in a freshly-squeezed glass of orange juice. An eight-ounce glass provides more vitamin C than the charts say you need in a day. Since your body can't store this important nutrient, it's a good idea to make orange juice a daily habit.

Oranges also provide some vitamin A and folic acid, one of the B complex, and are an excellent source of potassium.

Uses as Food   Most people would agree with me that oranges are best out of hand or squeezed for juice. However, they can be used in fruit salads and gelatin desserts, too. If you insist on doing something elaborate with oranges, the juice and grated rind make a delicious sauce for chicken or duck.

PAPAYAS

My FIRST INTRODUCTION to papayas was through a wonderful man named Paxton who devoted his life to growing perfect papayas in his conservatory at Encinitas in San Diego County, California. He used to ship small amounts of fruit—about 4 to 10 papayas in a wooden crate—into the San Francisco and Los Angeles produce markets in the 1930's. We in turn sold them to the real "carriage trade" food stores and the fancy hotels such as the Palace, St. Francis, Fairmont and Mark Hopkins, places that catered to people who could afford high-priced luxury items. This was during the Great Depression, remember, and there were more people selling apples on street corners than there were buyers for such exotic produce as papayas.

Today, in California at any rate, papayas are an everyday item and the price is fairly low. It wasn't until after World War II that sales started to zoom upward. Improved shipping from Hawaii, mainly by air, made the difference.

Even though Hawaii is our main source of supply today (Florida and Puerto Rico produce some for the East Coast, too), papayas aren't native to the Islands. They originated in the Americas, either in Mexico or the West Indies, no one seems sure which, and were brought to Hawaii by the same man who introduced pineapples—a Spanish settler of the late 18th century named Don Francisco de Paula y Marin.

Varieties Many varieties grow in the tropics, ranging from small, wild, bitter fruit about 3 inches long to cultivated varieties that weigh up to 20 pounds. But it's practically certain the papaya in your produce department is a 'Line 10' Solo. This is the main variety Hawaii grows commercially because the plant produces small fruit of uniform size, usually about 6 inches in length.

Seasons May and June are the months when the supply of

papayas is heaviest. But you'll find them on the market all year long at a pretty even rate of distribution.

Marketing Practices   Today papayas arrive in San Francisco from Hawaii by jet airplane faster than you could truck them in from Los Angeles. I've been told that the cost of air freight to the West Coast is within the reach of shippers because cargo planes flying to Korea in the '50's and Vietnam in the '60's and '70s needed freight for the trip back to the Mainland and reasonable rates were set.

Because of the short time in transit we now get freshly-picked papayas—just as ripe as they're eaten in Hawaii. And in my book that's a blessing, because nothing can match the flavor of tree-, plant- or vine-ripened fruit.

Papayas are graded by size and ripeness: ¼-ripe, ½-ripe or ¾-ripe. That ¾-ripe fruit is about as yellow-ripe as you can ship. The fruit comes packed in cartons with a net weight of ten pounds, about eight to 12 papayas to the carton. The fruit is carefully packed to prevent bruising, usually cushioned with shredded paper or similar material. Lately papayas have been coming into the market in individual styrofoam net "sleeves" that my wife says look like little crocheted jackets.

How to Buy   Papayas ripen from the bottom or blossom-end up to the stem-end. If you can find one that's started to color and has speckled yellow over 35% or more of the fruit, it means you have a good papaya that will ripen completely in two to three days at room temperature.

A ripe papaya should have a fruity aroma and yield to slight pressure. Look for a medium-sized one, slightly larger than a large pear. The skin should be smooth, unbruised and unbroken. Avoid any shriveled or overly soft ones. Dark spots on the outer skin are a bad sign. As with avocados or mangoes, these spots will get progressively worse and eventually penetrate through to the flesh and cause bad flavor.

Pay particular attention to the stem-end—that's where decay starts. Sometimes this is hardly noticeable, so press gently to detect softness or signs of wetness.

Treat papayas about the same as avocados. A ripe papaya can be stored in the refrigerator for one or two days.

Nutrition   The papaya plant produces a milky latex or juice that contains an enzyme called papain. It's the ingredient used in meat tenderizers because it breaks down protein fibers. Ripe papaya fruit contains a little papain. Health food stores sometimes bottle papaya juice as a health drink.

Papayas are low in calories. One-third of a medium-sized fruit contains about 39 calories. This amount provides a day's requirement of vitamin C and one-third of the vitamin A recommended for adults.

Uses as Food   Papayas are sometimes called melon-tree fruit. The flesh, orange-colored at maturity, is juicy and fragrantly-sweet with musky overtones.

To prepare papaya, slice the fruit in half lengthwise and scoop out the seeds. That's the way I enjoy them, although you can squeeze on some lemon or lime juice and eat with a spoon. Or put some ice cream in the seed cavity for a dessert treat.

The fruit can also be cut in wedges or slices as a breakfast or dessert fruit. Cut into cubes, it's a wonderful addition to fruit salads or fruit cups.

For more elaborate uses, consult any comprehensive cookbook. You'll find recipes for pies, sherbets and exotic drinks.

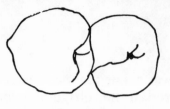

PEACHES

FOR YEARS PEOPLE have been lamenting that vaudeville is dead. This is the joke that probably killed it: "My girl has skin like a peach—yellow and fuzzy."

Peaches are still yellow but now most of them come into the market defuzzed. Isn't science wonderful?

The luscious juicy peaches you find in your store today are far removed from the wild fruit that originated in China thousands of years ago. Then peaches were small and hard with sourish flesh—almost inedible. Confucius referred to the peach in the fifth century B.C.. The tree was considered a symbol of long life and porcelainware with peach blossoms painted on it was often given as a birthday gift, much as we say, "Many happy returns of the day."

From China peaches traveled along age-old caravan routes to the Near East and then to Greece and Rome. Since Persia was about the limit of the world known at that time, the fruit was called the Persian plum or Persian apple. Someone has figured out that in Rome in the first century B.C. you'd have paid the equivalent of $4.50 for one peach.

The fruit remained a luxury for centuries. In the mid-seventeenth century the English poet Andrew Marvell wrote a poem called *"The Garden,"* which includes the lines: "The nectarine and curious peach/Into my hands themselves do reach." There was nothing peculiar about the fruit, it was "curious" because it was still so rare in England.

Peaches were introduced to the Western Hemisphere by the first explorers and settlers. You guessed it, Columbus brought the first ones. The governor of the Massachusetts Bay Colony requested that peaches be included among the first seeds sent to the colony in 1629.

Within a hundred years peaches had spread so rapidly that leading botanists considered them native to North

America. Commercial production started in the early 1800's and has continued ever since.

Peaches are still grown commercially in 35 states, on the Eastern Seaboard from Georgia to Maine, around the Great Lakes, and on the Pacific Coast, especially in California. They're the third most important fruit crop in the United States, outranked only by apples and oranges.

Varieties   The first modern variety developed was the Elberta. Supposedly it happened this way: In 1857 buddings from a China Cling variety were sent to a family named Rumph in Georgia. The trees flourished and the wife of the orchard owner dropped a few pits into her sewing basket, where they lay forgotten for years. Years later, when her grandson was starting his own orchard, she gave him the old, dried-out pits. He planted them and when they blossomed accidental cross-pollination took place, producing a brand-new golden freestone fruit. You'd think he would have named it for Grandma but he didn't. Elberta was his wife. Up to 30 years ago the Elberta represented 75% of the total U.S. production, now it's dropped to less than 50%, including those used by canners.

Another "new" variety from this same source was named the Belle of Georgia. It's still in production, too.

But many of the peaches I knew as a youngster aren't grown commercially anymore. The reasons usually given are that the quality isn't as good as newer ones and that they don't ship as well. I'd guess the second reason is the main one. And, by the same token, I'm willing to bet that many of the present-day varieties will disappear in the future.

One big change in fresh produce is from Clingstone varieties to semi-Cling or Freestone. Many Clingstones are still grown commercially but most go directly to processors for canning.

There are literally thousands of named varieties of peaches. The ones grown commercially vary from area to area. But here are some of the main ones:

The Springtime, as its name suggests, is an early peach. It's small and white-meated. Another very small early variety is the Armgold, a yellow peach. Both are semi-Freestone (or semi-Cling, depending on how you look at it) and make up in flavor what they lack in size.

Some other well-known varieties sound like they belong in a birdcage, not a produce bin. Robin, Cardinal and Redtop, for example. Coronet and Bobcat are popular, too. All of these are excellent in appearance, flavor and texture.

Seasons   Luckily for peach-lovers the season is a long one, extending from early May to mid-September. July and August are the peak months.

The early May crop is mainly semi-Freestone, the Freestones start coming into the market in June.

The last few years the state of Arizona has stolen a march on California for the honor of producing the first peaches of the year. It may not matter to you where peaches come from, but it means less change jingling in the California growers' jeans, and you can bet they care a lot. After all, how often have you bought produce marked "First of the Season"? It may not necessarily be the best and probably will be expensive, but you, and other customers, will probably buy some.

From January through April you may see imports from Chile—the seasons reverse south of the Equator, that's why.

Marketing Practices   Peaches don't gain in sugar after they're picked from the tree and, they're a pretty fragile fruit. So they have to be harvested when they're mature but still firm enough to stand shipping.

After picking, peaches go through cleaning machines that wash and defuzz them. In the East and South they are also hydrocooled in cold-water showers. In the West cooling takes place in refrigerated trucks or railroad cars during shipment.

Grading is on the basis of size, color and appearance. The main distinction between U.S. #1 and U.S. Fancy is usually the amount of surface that shows blushing, the pink or red color on the surface. It makes for a pretty fruit bowl, but your mouth won't know the difference.

Peaches are usually sold by the pound loose or in one-layer containers. Some are sold by the few in cello-packed baskets. Extra-large peaches are often put out in what are known as "selective displays," carefully-arranged rows just one-layer deep. This is to discourage the rummaging and squeezing that produces bruises.

How to Buy   That fancy pink or red color is attractive but not a good indication of ripeness and flavor. Instead look for a yellowish or creamy background color. The fruit should feel fairly firm but have some "give." And follow your nose. Good peaches will have a good peachy fragrance.

Things to avoid: greenish fruit—it won't ripen at home. Soft fruit, unless you intend to use it immediately. Split or bruised fruit with soft indentations or brownish areas—I'm sure you would anyway.

You should store peaches unwashed in the refrigerator. They'll keep up to two weeks.

Nutrition   A medium-size peach, eaten out of hand, contains just about 38 calories. It will have more vitamin A than most other fruit (only apricots, cantaloupe and nectarines are richer sources) and a fair amount of vitamin C.

Uses as Food   I've read that in Queen Victoria's day peaches were served at banquets in little nests of cotton. I think that sort of treatment went out with the pinkie curled away from the teacup.

Just pick up a peach, wash it off, and bite into it. Delicious!

There are many other ways of using peaches, of course, starting with sliced peaches on cold cereal at breakfast. Peaches and cream are almost a cliché but a great tasting combination however you slice them. They can be used in compotes, gelatin molds, ice cream and sherbet, shortcake, cobblers. And don't forget peach jam, peach preserves, gingered peaches and even peach chutney.

A traditional Italian favorite, especially when the firmer Clingstone varieties are available, is sliced peaches in red wine. Here's a more elaborate dessert version, called Peaches Sabayon, the French equivalent of the Italian zabaglione or wine sauce. First make the sauce by beating 4 egg yolks and ½ cup sugar together in the top half of a double boiler. Then add ¾ cup sweet wine (Marsala is best, but you can use port or sherry). Place over hot water and cook, continuing to stir until the sauce is foamy and thick. Then add a tablespoon of brandy, stir, and chill in the refrigerator. About 15 minutes before serving, peel and slice one peach per person. Squeeze on some lemon juice to prevent discoloration and place in the refrigerator. To serve, put the peach slices in a sherbet glass and cover with the Sabayon sauce.

PEARS

THE FIRST OF the twelve lavish gifts the lady in the old Christmas carol got was "a partridge in a pear tree." I think she must have been a princess or pretty close to it, because while the Greeks grew pears and the Romans introduced them into every land they conquered, by the Middle Ages in Europe you could only find pear trees in the gardens of castles and monasteries. Even later, into the seventeenth and eighteenth centuries, growing pears was a popular hobby for wealthy gentlemen. Many of the varieties developed by these amateurs are still grown today.

Pear trees were planted by the earliest colonists in North America. The first tree planted in the Massachusetts Bay Colony in 1630 was still standing in 1875, almost 250 years later, and had grown to a height of 80 feet. Today commercial cultivation is practically limited to California, Oregon and Washington because of destruction of Eastern pear trees by a disease called fire blight.

Varieties Like apples, pears don't come true by seed, so all new cultivation is by budding or grafting. Of the thousands of registered varieties grown in the U.S., not one is known to be native to North America. All of the major commercially-grown varieties are direct descendants of European varieties or hybrids produced by crossing European stock with Chinese varieties, sometimes called sand pears.

You'll notice that the full names of some varieties, mainly those that originated in Belgium, have the word "Beurre" in their name. That means butter in French and describes the soft, melting quality of the flesh. As a matter of fact, pears are sometimes called butter fruit.

THE BARTLETT a summer pear, is by far the most popular one grown. It's medium to large in size and looks like a lopsided bell. The skin is bright yellow, sometimes with a red blush when ripe. This skin is very tender, even fingernail marks show up almost immediately. It's a marvelous pear—juicy, sweet and very smooth—that practically melts in your mouth. In England and France this variety is called the Williams pear. The name-change came about when a Bostonian named Bartlett bought an estate complete with pear orchard in 1817. He didn't know the pears already had a British name and started distributing them under his own. In 1841 the American Pomological Society gave up and accepted the name as Bartlett.

THE ANJOU   or Beurre d'Anjou, is known as a winter pear. It originated in Belgium in the 1820's and was introduced into the U.S. just 20 years later. It's similar in size to the Bartlett but has a shorter neck, making it oval or globular in shape. The skin is yellowish-green, the flesh yellowish-white. The Anjou is sweet in flavor and stores well.

THE BOSC   or Beurre Bosc, is easy to spot because of its goose-necked shape with a long tapering neck. Its color is distinctive, too, a dark yellow to tannish-brown color covered with a lot of cinnamon-colored russeting. I enjoy the yellowish-white flesh of this pear even before it becomes buttery ripe—when it's firm, crisp and chewy. Even when fully ripe the Bosc is not too juicy and not quite as smooth-textured as the Bartlett. But it is sweet. This variety has been a long-time favorite on the East Coast and is just beginning to get the recognition it deserves on the West Coast.

The full name of the *Comice* pear is Doyenne du Comice. I'm told this translates as "best in the show." It must be, because this is the pear shipped all over the country in special gift packs by a group called the Fruit-of-the-Month club. The Comice is very delicate, sweet, smooth and deliciously juicy. It's a fairly large neckless pear, oval in shape, somewhat fuller and stubbier than the Bartlett or Anjou.

Other well-known varieties are the *Winter Nelis,* a small to medium-sized pear with spicy rich flavor that's not as popular as it should be because of the rather unattractive appearance of its dull green skin, which is covered with russet dots; the *Seckel,* a very small brownish-yellow pear, often blushed with red, is a hybrid of a European and Chinese or sand pear, which gives it a characteristically grainy texture; the *Easter Beurre* and the *Beurre Hardy,* both of which have the melting qualities of the other "butter pears."

Seasons The largest number of pears are on the market from August through October. From April through June you may see some imports from Argentina.

Bartletts are available from mid-July through early November; Seckels from late August through December. The Comice is on the market from October through March, with the peak supply in October and very few available after January.

The most popular winter pear, the Anjou, accounts for 75% of sales during its season, which runs from October through May. The Winter Nelis are another variety sold during the same period as the Anjou and extending into June.

Marketing Practices Pears are one of the few fruits that don't ripen successfully on the tree. They have to be picked when mature but still hard. So if you ever see pears advertised as "tree-ripened" remember that it's absolutely no indication of quality.

I'm sorry to say that the amount of pears marketed seems to decline every year. That fire blight disease back East had something to do with it, plus the fact that even in the Northwest pears are difficult to raise and store. Growers would rather bet on a sure thing and concentrate on a hardier crop, such as apples.

The condition of a pear when you buy it is more important than the grade—like Fancy or U.S. No. 1—given it in the packing shed.

Pears are sometimes sold by the each, but usually you'll find them by the pound.

How to Buy If you've ever picked out some nice-looking pears but found them hard and tasteless, blame yourself, not the retailer, because pears must be ripe to be enjoyed. Pears are always picked before they're ripe, but the tests for maturity are pretty foolproof. So, unless the retailer has gone to the trouble of storing his pears until they ripen, you'll have to ripen them at home yourself.

Look for pears that are free from cuts, bruises, dark spots or decay.

The best place to ripen pears is on top of the refrigerator where the temperature is warm and even. If you put them in a plastic bag during the ripening process, be sure to poke some holes in the bag. Ripening will probably take two or three days. You can tell when a pear is "ready" by pressing *gently* against the sides or stem end. When there's a little give, the pear is ready to eat. Ripe pears should be refrigerated.

Nutrition   Half a medium pear has small amounts of various vitamins and minerals, and contains about 61 calories.

Uses for Food   For a dessert or a snack there's nothing better than eating a fresh ripe pear out of hand. And I'd guess that's the way most of them are used. Their sweet flavor and buttery texture really add something to a fruit salad, too.

But if you want a real treat, serve pears the way they do in France or Italy, with a soft cheese, such as Camembert, Brie or Liederkranz.

PERSIMMONS

PERSIMMON TREES ARE beautiful things to see, standing up to 40 feet tall with golden-orange fruit hanging from them like bright shiny Christmas ornaments. The persimmon is a member of the same family as ebony, and its hard wood is highly prized for making the "woods" in sets of golf clubs.

Maybe the growing popularity of golf is one reason the number of acres of persimmon trees in the U.S. has dropped more than 90% in the past 40 years. But the other reason, I'm sure, is that like the old nursery rhyme, "when they're good, they're very very good, but when they're bad they're horrid." Or, as Captain John Smith described the native American persimmon he found in Virginia, ". . . if it is not ripe, it will drive a mans mouth awrie with much torment; but when it is ripe, it is as delicious as an apricock."

There are still some native persimmons growing throughout the U.S., mainly in the South, but they're not important commercially. Without a doubt the ones you see on your supermarket shelf will have an Oriental background. Commodore Perry "discovered" the fruit when he led an American naval expedition to Japan in 1852. Persimmons, which the Japanese call *kaki,* are the national fruit of Japan, almost as popular as citrus fruit. They've been cultivated in Japan for over 1000 years but, like citrus fruit, originated in China. Many of the Oriental varieties brought here from Japan were grafted onto native American rootstock.

Varieties Almost nine out of ten commercially-produced persimmons are of the Hachiya variety. They're about the size of a large peach, sometimes weighing a pound or more. The shape is rather like an acorn, oval and tapering almost to a point. The color is beautiful—a glossy bright orange-red. The Fuyu is another variety marketed in quantity. It's one of the few persimmons that can be eaten and enjoyed while still rather firm.

Seasons You'll find persimmons on the market from late September through mid-December. The supply peaks between mid-October and late November.

Marketing Practices California produces practically all of the persimmons marketed commercially. Half the crop is shipped into the Los Angeles and San Francisco markets, the balance ends up in New York, Philadelphia and Chicago. I'm afraid that if you live outside one of these large metropolitan areas you'll have a hard time finding any, and that's a shame.

Persimmons are very delicate and have to be handled almost as carefully as eggs. As a matter of fact, the newest way of shipping them is in polyvinyl trays similar to egg cartons, with each persimmon nestled into its own protective cradle.

Persimmons are sold by the each.

How to Buy Your retailer should refrigerate his persimmons and display them in a single layer.

If you're tired of having me say "shop with your eyes," you'll be happy to know that appearance is *not* the way to judge a persimmon. Unlike any other fruit, persimmons get their full color before they're ripe. That's unfortunate, because one writer described the experience of eating an unripe persimmon as, "your mouth feels like it's trying to turn itself inside out." And anyone undergoing this the first time they try a persimmon will never be a return cutomer.

To make sure you get a pleasant not puckery taste choose a really soft one, even a little bit shriveled. The fruit should be plump, with smooth glossy skin and the green stem cap attached. Avoid any decayed, bruised or hard ones.

If you buy a persimmon that's still a little too firm for eating, let it ripen at room temperature for a couple of days inside a closed plastic bag. Some people say placing an apple in the same bag will aid the ripening process.

Nutrition A medium-size raw persimmon will supply half

an adult's daily requirement of vitamin A, as well as a fair amount of vitamin C. The caloric content is about 77 calories.

Uses as Food   I'm sure more people would eat this delicious fruit if they knew how to go about it. A fully-ripe persimmon *is* squishy, but don't let this stop you. Either peel it like a banana and eat it out-of-hand, or cut it in half and eat it with a spoon, like a melon.

Some people like their persimmons with cream, or ice cream. They're also excellent for sherbert, puddings and pies.

But I've never found the way I like persimmons best described in a recipe book. Peel back the skin and slice small sections of persimmon into a bowl of salad greens and sliced red onions. Add lemon juice and olive oil and you've got a unique and refreshing combination of tastes.

PINEAPPLES

IF YOU HAVE ANTIQUE English furniture or reproductions in your home you may find pineapples carved on them somewhere as a sign of hospitality. In New England the colonists often carved them over doorways or on gateposts, for the same reason. Some people say the pineapple symbolized hospitality because it was so rare and expensive that offering one to a guest showed you really wanted to roll out the red carpet. Others say it goes back to a West Indian custom where Indians placed pineapples or pineapple tops near their huts to show that strangers were welcome.

These were the Indians who introduced Columbus and his crew to the delicious fruit. They in turn had gotten the fruit from the mainland of South America—the Incas and pre-Incas of Peru were probably the first to cultivate it.

The Spaniards named the fruit piña de Indias, or pine of the Indies, because the fruit resembled a pine cone in shape. Then the English confused things further and called it "pineapple"—although the fruit has absolutely nothing in common with pines or apples. Actually, the best-known relative of the pineapple is Spanish moss, the grey-green stuff than hangs from trees in Louisiana and other southern states.

Pineapples were spread throughout the tropical areas of the world by early explorers and traders. Some were planted intentionally. But more found new homes by chance when pineapple crowns—thrown overboard by seamen who had brought the fruit aboard sailing ships in South America or the Indies—washed ashore and took root. By the end of the sixteenth century they were being cultivated in Africa, Madagascar, India, China, Japan and the Philippines.

In 1790 a Spanish adventurer named Don Francisco de Paula y Marin brought pineapples to Hawaii. They were looked down on as weeds and nuisances until a hundred

years later when Captain John Kidwell, an English horticulturist, introduced scientific growing methods for commercial production.

But fresh pineapple was still unavailable except in the
tropics. The fruit doesn't ripen after it's picked and ripe fruit
spoiled before slow ships reached European or North
American ports. Attempts were made to grow pineapples
under glass. Quite an industry developed in the Azores and
lasted until fairly recently, when development of large pineapple plantations in the tropics and improved shipping facilities made greenhouse cultivation uneconomical.

Varieties There are many varieties of pineapples grown
commercially but, as far as those marketed fresh are concerned, three dominate the market.

Definitely first and foremost is the Smooth Cayenne,
the wonderful pineapple that comes from Hawaii. It's also
grown in Australia, the Philippines and South Africa, but I
doubt you'll ever find any on the market from these areas.
It has the classic pine cone shape and usually weighs in at
between three and one-half and five pounds. This is the most
widely planted variety because it's used for canning as well
as for the fresh market.

Next in popularity is the Red Spanish, grown in Puerto
Rico, Florida and Cuba. It weighs about the same as the
Smooth Cayenne, but it's not as cylindrical. You could describe the shape as squarish. This variety has a tough shell,
which makes it a good shipper, so the majority of the crop
is marketed fresh.

Last is the Sugar Loaf—an extra-large pineapple weighing between five and ten pounds. Mexico is our source of
supply, although they're grown in Cuba, too.

Seasons Pineapples are available year around and in greatest supply from March through June. The price stays fairly
steady all year.

Marketing Practices The pineapple plant can produce fruit
almost indefinitely, but from a commercial standpoint each
plant is allowed to bear fruit for five to ten years only, then
the field is replanted.

You have to know a little botany to understand why the quality of the pineapples on the market varies so greatly. On the pineapple plant a large quantity of starch is stored in the stem, not in the fruit. Just before the ripening process takes place, this starch converts to sugar and is carried up into the fruit. The sugar content of a pineapple can increase as much as 100% in this final stage. If the fruit is picked before this time, the pineapple has no starch reserve to change into sugar. It will not get sweeter after harvesting. But if the pineapple is picked when completely ripe, its chances of getting to the consumer in good eating condition are greatly reduced.

So growers and shippers have to compromise between riper fruit with less market life and greener pineapples that won't taste as good. In the past few years better and faster shipping, including air freight, has led to marketing of riper fruit that shows more yellow to golden color, what's called Hawaiian maturity.

The two biggest shippers—Standard Banana Co. and Del Monte—are shipping this plant-ripened fruit. Standard ships what's known in the trade as X-R (meaning Extra-Ripe) pineapple. It comes into the market in a white carton to distinguish it from the greener fruit that's packed in brown cartons.

Some retail markets now offer pineapples sliced in half and overwrapped with cellophane. This is great for people who live alone or have small families.

Pineapples, whole or sliced, are usually priced by the each.

How to Buy   I wish I had a dime, or even a nickel, for every time I've been asked, "If I pull on a leaf and it comes out easily is the pineapple ripe?" My answer is always, "Maybe."

I've become extremely unpopular with pineapple sellers by insisting that the outside color—yellow to golden orange—is the sign of a good pineapple. I've cut into hundreds of pineapples and better than 90% of the time if the color's right outside, the meat will be a beautiful amber to golden color and taste literally as sweet as sugar.

Now I'll hedge a bit. At certain times of the year, and under ideal weather conditions, a pineapple *may* appear greenish and still have good-tasting meat inside. But it takes an experienced professional to choose a good one in this condition, not the average retail buyer. So for your sake, choose fruit with as much color as possible and you'll come out ahead.

I'd also recommend buying the largest pineapple you can use, because the proportion of edible flesh increases with size, saving you money. After all, there can be only so much rind on a pineapple. For example, half a five-pound pineapple will have more meat than a whole three-pound fruit.

In addition to greenish fruit I'd avoid: pineapples with bruises, discolored areas, soft spots or dried-out brownish leaves, a shriveled appearance or dull color.

I hope I've made the point by now that a pineapple isn't going to get any sweeter or improve with age. So, assuming you've chosen a good ripe one, the sooner you eat it the better. If you must store a pineapple, put it in a plastic bag to keep it from losing moisture and it should keep three to five days in the refrigerator.

Nutrition   One thick slice of raw ripe pineapple (about ¾ inches thick and 3½ inches in diameter) will contain about 44 calories. This amount will provide about one-third of your daily quota of vitamin C. Like most fruit, pineapple is low in sodium.

It's interesting that centuries ago the Indians believed that pineapple stimulated the appetite. Some experiments claim to confirm this. There's no real proof but you might try pineapple if you're planning meals for someone who's trying to gain weight or for a child with eating problems.

Uses as Food   Pineapple can be cooked with pork or ham, or used in sweet-and-sour sauces. It's a good addition to fruit salads and goes well with avocado. It can be used for sherbets and conserves.

All these are great. But I prefer pineapple by itself, cut into slices, spears or wedges. It makes an elegant dessert when sliced in quarters from top to bottom and served as a "boat" with the leaves still attached. Once you have the knack it's easy. After quartering the fruit, separate the meat from the rind by "sawing" with a long sharp knife close to the rind from top to bottom. Then cut the dislodged meat in half and slice in inch-thick sections. (A special pineapple knife, somewhat like a grapefruit knife, is designed to make this job easier.) A little vodka or white wine poured over the fruit will enhance the delicious flavor.

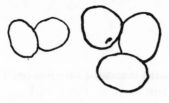

PLUMS & PRUNES

DO YOU KNOW the difference between a plum and a prune? It isn't that one is fresh and the other dried. Today the word plum is used to describe all varieties that are eaten fresh, canned or processed into jams and jellies. In most cases these varieties ferment if dried without removing the stone. Prunes, then, are varieties that can be dried without removing the pit. The term is used even when they're marketed fresh, the way some from the Pacific Northwest are. To avoid confusion and promote fresh sales, the industry is encouraging that they be called purple plums.

Plums are a very ancient fruit, native to most temperate areas. They were gathered and used as food by Stone Age tribes in Europe. Cultivation of the Damson type originated in the Caucasus, and plums of this species spread to the Mediterranean region before the time of Christ. Another species is native to China and has been grown there since ancient times. About 300 years ago they were introduced into Japan. When the famous American horticulturist Luther Burbank brought them to California a century ago, they were called Japanese plums and the name has stuck, even though it's not accurate. There are also native American plums, but none are produced commercially in any quantity. The best known are probably sloes, used to make sloe gin.

Varieties Hundreds of varieties of plums are grown throughout the U.S., ranging from small yellow Japanese plums to almost black European types. In California alone about 40 varieties are grown commercially. Of these, 11 are produced in quantity. The easiest way to talk about them is as early, mid-season and late types.

EARLY VARIETIES: The most important variety by far is the Santa Rosa, conical in shape with purplish-crimson skin and yellow flesh that shades to dark red near the skin. It is very juicy with a rich and pleasing tart flavor. This variety, developed by Luther Burbank in 1907 and named for the Northern California town he lived in, has been called the "Queen of Plums" because it accounts for about 35% of the total crop produced in California. The Red Beaut comes on the market even earlier in the season. The name is accurate—the skin is a beautiful bright red color. It has firm yellow-colored flesh and is noted for its good-eating qualities. The Burmosa is a semi-heartshaped plum with a mild pleasant flavor and fine soft texture. The skin has an attractive red blush and the flesh is light amber in color.

MID-SEASON VARIETIES: The major one is the El Dorado, a heart-shaped plum with black-red skin and light amber flesh that turns pinkish when cooked. Other popular varieties are the Tragedy, a medium-sized oval plum of the European type (it has yellow-green flesh and dark purple skin), and the Simka, even larger, with purple skin and yellow flesh.

LATE-SEASON VARIETIES: There's the Late Santa Rosa, similar to the one already described; the Casselman, an improved Santa Rosa hybrid with lighter red skin and less tendancy to "crack at the seams;" the Nubiana, a recently developed large oval plum that's black-red in color and has firm amber-colored flesh; the Laroda, a large roundish plum with reddish-yellow skin and firm yellow flesh that has a grape-like flavor; and the Queen Ann, a recently-developed richly flavored plum with mahogany-colored skin and amber flesh.

Seasons Plum season extends from mid-May to late August. May is the month for Santa Rosas, Burmosas and Red Beauts. In June the El Dorado and Nubiana come onto the market. The Queen Ann and Late Santa Rosa are harvested in early July. The last heavy producer is the Casselman which appears in late July.

About 90% of the plum crop comes from California. The balance comes from Oregon, Michigan, Washington and Idaho, in that order.

During January, February and March some plums are imported from Chile.

Marketing Practices A good retailer doesn't pile his bulk display of plums too high because he knows the fruit at the bottom will get bruised from weight and from customers digging down to find the best ones. He'll also refrigerate his plums and pick them over frequently to remove any decayed or damaged ones.

Plums are sold in bulk by the pound or by the few in overwrapped trays.

How to Buy First of all, be adventurous. Try different colors and shapes. You'll find each variety has its own unique texture and taste.

Look for good-colored plums ranging from fairly firm to slightly soft. Avoid immature ones that are hard, shriveled or poorly colored and overmature ones that are soft, bruised or split.

If the plums you buy are still firm leave them at room temperature for a day or two until they're slightly soft. Then eat or refrigerate them in a covered container. Most plums are highly perishable when ripe and should be eaten within three to five days at most.

Nutrition Plums vary greatly in caloric and nutritive content. A medium-sized plum can vary between 66 and 75 calories, depending on the variety. They are high in potassium, low in sodium and contain some vitamin A, iron and calcium.

Uses as Food There's nothing better than fresh plums, eaten out of hand, for a refreshing snack or dessert. In season they can be stewed or used in jellies, jams, puddings and cakes.

Just don't try to make an English Plum Pudding with them. This traditional dish is actually made with beef suet, currants, raisins, citron and spices.

Instead, I'd suggest making this plum sauce to serve over vanilla ice cream or pound cake: slice 1 pound fresh ripe plums and purée them in an electric blender. Then strain through a sieve. Stir in ½ cup sugar and lemon juice to taste. You can add ¼ teaspoon almond extract, too, for extra flavor if you wish.

RHUBARB

THESE DAYS YOU'RE apt to hear the word rhubarb more at a baseball game than in the kitchen. It's too bad because as a food, rhubarb is attractive and tastes good, especially mixed with other fruits.

In case you're still wondering how rhubarb and baseball got together, I better explain. Some, including one edition of Webster's, trace the use of rhubarb to mean a disagreement on the baseball diamond this way: the word comes from the Greek *Rha* (Volga River) and the Latin *barbarium* (barbarian) . . . these early rhubarb growers were difficult to get along with . . . so are argumentative ballplayers . . . therefore, etc., etc. That seems pretty farfetched to me. I prefer the explanation that in the early days of radio broadcasting, actors would stand back from the microphone and mumble "rhubarb, rhubarb, rhubarb" to sound like an angry crowd.

In any event those Volga peasants were responsible for the ancestors of our rhubarb. They noticed that a plant growing wild on the river's bank was similar to a medicinal root that camel caravans brought from China. The difference was that the roots (and leaves, as well) of their species contain large quantities of oxalic acid that can be fatal if swallowed in large amounts. It's not recorded how many succumbed before the difference was discovered and only the stalks were eaten.

From Russia, rhubarb spread westward and centuries later arrived in this country from England with the early colonists. By the early 1800's it was being used in New England for tarts and pies. In fact, rhubarb was often called pie-plant.

More recently, in 1947, a court case finally put rhubarb on the record as a fruit, rather than the vegetable it is botanically. With great good sense Judge Genevieve R. Cline—

only woman on the U.S. Customs Court in Buffalo, New York —ruled that, since its principal use in the home was as a fruit, it should be considered one legally. The question wasn't as ridiculous as it sounds—the decision meant a 35% import duty instead of the 50% charged for vegetables.

Varieties There are numerous rhubarb varieties but the only important distinction in edible species is between the field and hothouse types.

Field-grown rhubarb has deep red stalks and green leaves. It has a very distinctive tart flavor. Hothouse varieties range from light pink to light red with yellowish green leaves. It has a milder flavor than its country-cousin and few strings.

Seasons Thanks to hothouse cultivation, rhubarb is now available year 'round. The State of Washington supplies the west, Michigan the eastern states.

I can remember when the arrival of rhubarb on the market meant spring was coming. To a certain extent that's still true. The peak season for rhubarb, when most field crops are harvested, is April and May.

Rhubarb needs to "rest" during a cool winter to thrive. So growing areas are limited to the northern states. Besides Washington and Michigan, the main producing states are California, Oregon and New York.

Marketing Practices Rhubarb is sold by the bunch or by the pound. Every year more and more rhubarb is pre-packed, either at the wholesale or retail level. You may find perforated poly bags weighing about a pound with stalks about 10 inches long. Other one-pound packs contain rhubarb already cut into inch-long pieces. You'll probably be charged a lot more for the cooking-sized pieces, so I'd recommend buying the long stalks.

How to Buy Retailers should always display their rhubarb in a refrigerated rack, because it's very perishable. Avoid any that looks wilted or flabby.

The stalks should be firm, crisp, straight and fairly thick.

Rhubarb meeting these qualifications will be tender and free from strings when cooked.

Plan to use the rhubarb you buy as soon as possible. And be sure to keep it refrigerated until you do cook it.

Nutrition   In the olden days mothers fed their families rhubarb as a spring tonic to "purify the blood." I'm not sure exactly how the rhubarb was supposed to do this. I prefer to say it's good for you because of the vitamins A, B and C it contains.

Don't worry about oxalic acid in the stalks, there's no more than in an equal amount of spinach. But do avoid the leaves. The only use they should be put to is cleaning discolored aluminum pots. Try it. (Boil them in water in the pots.)

By itself, rhubarb is very low in calories. Adding sugar in cooking raises the count, of course. Without sugar an average portion (about ⅜ of a cup) contains 16 calories. Cooked with sugar the same quantity has 141. A good compromise is to combine rhubarb with sweeter fruits and cut down on the amount of sugar needed for good taste.

Uses as Food   Rhubarb can be stewed or baked. It makes an interesting addition to applesauce for both taste and color. Rhubarb and strawberries are another popular combination, either stewed or in pies. You can also strain the juice from stewed rhubarb to add color and flavor to fruit punch.

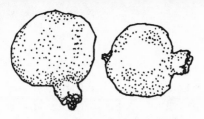

POMEGRANATES

THE ANCIENT GREEKS explained the annual crop cycle with this legend: Pluto, god of the Underworld, kidnapped Persephone, the beautiful young daughter of Demeter, the goddess of agriculture. A bargain was made that the kidnapped girl would be returned if she didn't eat anything during her stay in the Underworld. Persephone couldn't resist a pomegranate and every year she has to spend one month with Pluto for each seed she ate. During that time her mother is so sad that she neglects her duties and the crops don't grow.

Even today pomegranates symbolize fertility in some parts of the world, especially in the Near East where the fruit originated. In Syria and Lebanon, for instance, it's traditional for a new bride to stamp on a pomegranate at the entrance to her new home, scattering the seeds. This is supposed to guarantee fertility, abundance and a happy life.

The name pomegranate comes from two Latin words that translate as "apple with seeds." It's a pretty good description. The fruit is the size of a very large apple and slightly angular in shape. The hard rind—yellow or red depending on the variety—contains a lot of tannin and is used for curing leather and making indelible ink. Inside, the fruit is divided into cells containing lots of seeds, individually wrapped in bright crimson juicy pulp. They look like little jewels and have a delicious flavor, an intriguing mixture of sweet and tart.

Varieties The leading varieties produced in the U.S. are the Wonderful and Red Wonderful. As the names suggest, they have a beautiful red color. The Spanish Ruby is bright red, too, and very large. The Paper-Shell, however, matures with a pale yellow color washed with pink.

Seasons Pomegranates are ideally suited to the warm climates of California and the Gulf States. Commercial production is concentrated in California, however. They are ripe and ready to harvest from September through December. October is the peak month. Maybe that's the reason I always associate pomegranates with Halloween. They make excellent "trick-or-treat" gifts, much better for children than candy.

Marketing Practices   Pomegranates are what's called a "specialty item" in the produce trade. They've never caught on in this country because most people don't know what to do with them. Perhaps if more retailers used signs suggesting uses for pomegranates this interesting fruit would get the attention it deserves.

Most pomegranates are harvested before they ripen fully because the fruit has a tendancy to split in full-ripe condition. It can be stored for a couple of months if refrigerated.

Pomegranates are always sold by the each.

How to Buy   My best advice is, use your eyes. Choose fruit with good color and skin that's free from cracks or splits.

Home storage is no problem. A pomegranate will keep several weeks or more refrigerated in a plastic bag.

Nutrition   The pulp and seeds of a medium-size pomegranate will contain about 90 calories. In small quantity the nutritive content is almost negligible, although they do contain some vitamin C, iron and calcium.

Uses as Food   Children love pomegranates. Maybe it's because opening the fruit and discovering the seeds is like finding the prize in a box of Cracker-Jacks. Neat children (there are some) suck the delicious red pulp from the seeds, most will chew and swallow them whole, with absolutely no ill effects. There's just one thing to remember: pomegranates are also used as dye and without some precautions you're liable to wind up with red polka-dotted clothes, walls or children.

Here's the way I used to enjoy pomegranates when I was a youngster. I'd roll the fruit on a table, or even a window sill, until the juice in the kernels broke down from a solid pulp to juice. When the pomegranate became soft like a sponge ball I'd poke a hole through the skin, usually with a pencil, and then suck out the juice. Occasionally the juice would spurt out through the hole when I removed the pencil and make a real mess—but it was worth the risk.

The more usual way to get at the seeds is by pulling the fruit open and picking the seeds out with your fingers or a nut pick. Fingers work better, I think.

In addition to eating out-of-hand, you can squeeze pomegranates for juice. Grenadine is made from pomegranate juice. Pomegranate seeds also make a beautiful and good-tasting addition to fruit salads or fruit cups.

TANGERINES, TANGELOS
& MANDARIN ORANGES

MANDARINS, TANGERINES AND tangelos are probably best described as loose-skinned oranges. The three names are often used interchangeably by produce men and consumers alike. I'll try to straighten out the confusion, not add to it.

To a botanist, all three are Mandarins. Commercially, we use the name tangerine for all the smallish, deeply-colored mandarins and mandarin hybrids. Since most retailers don't identify mandarins as such, about the only time you'll see the name "mandarin oranges" in a store is on cans. These are actually tangerine sections packed in syrup.

The tangelo is a larger mandarin hybrid. The fruit, as well as its name, is a cross between *tang*erine and pom*elo,* another name for grapefruit.

Like other citrus fruits, the original mandarin oranges were native to Asia. They've been grown and eaten in China and Japan from very early times. At some point in history they traveled to North Africa, where the tangerine took its name from the Moroccan seaport of Tangiers. By the middle of the nineteenth century, people in all the Mediterranean countries were enjoying them. Tangerines arrived in the United States when an Italian diplomat, perhaps homesick for native foliage and fruit, planted some in the consulate garden in New Orleans. The first commercial crops were grown in Florida. Now California and Arizona are major producers, too.

Varieties   The most popular tangerine is called the Dancy, after an early Florida grower. Colonel Dancy nicknamed the fruit a "kid-glove orange" because the rind peeled so easily—you still hear the phrase occasionally. A direct descendant of an Oriental mandarin, the Dancy is small and has a deep, rich, red-orange color. It's decorative as well as good to eat. Unfortunately, it also has lots of seeds.

More and more Kinnow mandarins come on the market each year. They're usually larger and flatter than the Dancy. The rind is yellow-orange and thin, meaning a bit difficult to peel.

The other main varieties are the Clementine and the Satsuma. The Clementine is an Algerian tangerine with a deep orange-red color. The satsuma is a cold-resistant mandarin developed in Japan. It is sweet and almost seedless. Satsumas would probably be more popular but the fruit stays greenish, even when mature. This causes marketing problems, since it's against the law to color tangerines artificially in California and Arizona.

In the spring of 1972 a variety of tangerine-type fruit formerly called the Murcott orange changed its name to the Honey Tangerine. The name-change was more than a promotion or sales gimmick, the fruit *is* sweet as honey. The flesh has a beautiful color—it's too bad the outside color isn't as good. This flat-shaped fruit is very thin-skinned and has quite a few seeds. But it's fairly easy to peel, is heavy and firm for its size, and has good home-keeping qualities. It's definitely a variety I recommend you taste-test. One of these days, if they ever get the color of the skin to match the beautiful color inside, I know sales will jump sky-high.

There are three main varieties of tangelos, all named after regions in Florida where they were developed. The Minneola is considered best. It's good-sized, juicy, peels easily and has few seeds. You can spot a Minneola easily by its nipple-shaped stem end. The Orlando is the size and shape of a tangerine but its color and texture are more like an orange. It's very juicy and has a mildly sweet flavor. Orlandos have two drawbacks: seeds and a thin rind that's hard to peel. The Seminole is similar to the Minneola but has more seeds.

Seasons   The tangerine seems specially designed to fill the toe of a Christmas stocking. Almost half the year's supply comes into the market in December. But you'll probably be able to find some where you shop any time from late fall to early spring.

Tangelos are becoming available later and later in the year. Until recently the season was October to January, now you can find them clear into the spring.

Grading and Pricing Almost all tangerines and tangelos on the market come from states that set standards for citrus fruits. So what the growers ship, wholesalers and retailers market and you buy, will be fairly uniform in size, juice content and color at any given time.

Most tangerines and tangelos are sold by the pound. Sometimes you'll find them in mesh or plastic bags weighing three to five pounds. You may save a little buying them this way, but I think you're better off buying them loose. First of all, most people don't eat them in quantity and you may wind up with more than you can use. Second—and this applies to those packed in plastic film especially—the old saying about one apple spoiling the barrel applies even more to this rather delicate fruit.

How to Buy Look for deep rich color with a bright luster. (Don't worry about small green areas, especially around the stem.) The fruit should feel heavy for its size. A slightly puffy appearance is normal because of the loose skin, but excessive puffiness may indicate overripe fruit. Skin with very soft spots or mold should be avoided.

Tangerines and tangelos are more perishable than sweet oranges and should be handled carefully. Keep them in the fruit bin of your refrigerator until you use them.

Nutrition Both tangerines and tangelos are excellent sources of vitamin C. If you're calorie-conscious, here's good news: one tangelo or two small tangerines will contain just over 40 calories.

Uses as Food Tangerines and tangelos make great snacks and lunchbox desserts because they peel and separate into sections so easily. They're also good additions to a fruit salad.

For a more elaborate dessert, try tangerine sections with sour cream.

WATERMELON

IN NAPLES, WHERE watermelon slices are commonly sold from sidewalk pushcarts, there's a saying that watermelon is "the only way to eat, drink and wash your face at the same time."

Watermelons have been common in Europe, Asia and Africa for so long that botanists weren't quite sure where they'd originated until the middle of the nineteenth century. Then David Livingstone, of "Dr. Livingstone, I presume" fame, settled the question once and for all. He discovered watermelons growing wild in the remotest interior region of Africa. Watermelons were the original canteens in tribal Africa. They were cultivated and stored for a source of water during dry seasons and taken along on long hunting treks when water might not be available.

Watermelons were brought to North America by the earliest European colonists and spread rapidly throughout the continent. They're now grown commercially in 27 states, principally Florida, Texas, Georgia, California and South Carolina.

Varieties The variety you'll find in your store depends on where you live because there are definite regional preferences in watermelons.

In the West, where people seem to prefer solid-green color, the traditional favorite is the Peacock. But the Charleston Gray is a good-seller, too, perhaps because so many people have moved to California from the East Coast and Southwest where they're preferred.

In Canada, smaller sizes of these varieties, weighing eight to 12 pounds are the big favorites during our shipping season. In the trade they're called "Canadians." There are other small melons, often called "icebox varieties," and including the Sugar Baby and the New Hampshire Midget.

Seedless hybrid varieties also are seen on the market occasionally.

Seasons Watermelons are available practically the year around, but they need hot weather for growth and are in greatest demand during the summer months. About 85 percent are consumed during June, July and August. Watermelons and holidays go together: the three big days for watermelon-eating are Memorial Day, which opens the season, the Fourth of July, and Labor Day, which closes the season.

Some watermelons are imported from Mexico from Mid-December to mid-June.

Marketing Practices Most watermelons are packed and shipped by the truckload without refrigeration. In the East and in Canada, many large chains buy and sell these melons by the each. Some shippers sort out melons by weight electronically in different price ranges. In the West they are generally sold by the pound. Sometimes they'll be advertised by the each in some stores and by the pound in others, making it impossible for consumers to judge the best buy without a scale and a slide rule.

Quite often retailers slice watermelons in halves, quarters, or even slices, which they cover with plastic film. I think some overcharge terribly for these few swipes of a knife, but if you live alone or have a small family it's one way you can enjoy watermelon. In addition, there's the advantage of being able to see what's inside, the only real way to judge a good watermelon.

How to Buy I've watched some performances with watermelons that deserve an Academy Award, by customers and retail produce men alike. There are thumpers, slappers and shakers. The watermelon they choose may be a good one but it won't be because of these "tests."

Do You know how the real "pros"—the watermelon shippers—do it? They go into a field that's considered ready for picking and cut a few melons open.

Al Harrison, the "King of the Watermelons," and a major shipper out of western Mexico and Arizona, is so expert he can spot a field that's ripe from a scouting plane. But he still insists that the first 10 watermelons cut from the vine be split open to make sure they are just right.

Still there are a few ways to avoid picking a "lemon" of a watermelon. It should have a somewhat velvety bloom on the rind. Avoid any that look shiny. Then look at the under-side or "belly" where it rested on the ground. The color should be slightly yellowish or amber-colored. Avoid any with a greenish or dead-white "ground spot."

If you're buying a cut watermelon your choice should be easier. Look for firm red flesh and black or dark-brown seeds. Avoid any melons with soft, white, immature seeds, or ones that have broken away from their cavities, or ones with a sugary look around the seeds. There's one more kind that should be rejected: watermelons with a white streak running the length of the melon—it's called "white-heart."

Some stores sell "chilled" melons or display them on a bed of ice. Don't count on these to be properly chilled, because it takes 8 to 12 hours to chill a melon properly, and in season they usually move faster than that.

You can usually hold a watermelon for up to a week in your refrigerator.

Nutrition Watermelon is a good thirst-quencher and fairly low in calories, about 126 to an 1½ inch-thick slice. This amount will provide about 50 percent of a day's require-ment of vitamin A and vitamin C. In addition it contains some iron and calcium. If you thought watermelon just con-tained "sugar water," this should change your mind.

Uses as Food Watermelons and picnics go together. Moth-ers are much more likely to approve of kids literally up to their ears in watermelon when the fruit is being eaten out-doors. When watermelon moves indoors the process still doesn't have to be messy. Either cut slices into smaller wedges for easier handling or make melon balls with a scoop. I've discovered children love to wield a melon scoop as a spoon and do a very neat job of it.

Melon balls also are a great addition to fruit salads and

fruit cups. For a festive buffet dessert, use a scooped-out watermelon half as a boat for mixed fresh fruit.

Watermelons are traditional fare for adult beach parties, too. Sometimes the melon is plugged and vodka or white wine is poured in to "lace" the fruit. I've never done this but friends tell me to start the day before so the liquor permeates the fruit and the melon is thoroughly chilled before you take off. I consider this a real "fruit cocktail."

Some of the best part of the watermelon is usually thrown away. The rind is delicious pickled. Some black people today get very "uptight" about watermelon. They seem to feel it has some connection with Uncle Tom eating watermelon on the old plantation while he sings happy songs to his "Massa." That isn't the picture I get. I think of wonderful black women who managed to create something elegant out of nothing by inventing pickled watermelon rind. Here's how to do it: Remove all the green and pink from watermelon rind until you have four pounds of white rind. Cut it into 1-inch cubes and soak overnight in 2 quarts water with ¼ cup salt added. Drain and cover with fresh cold water and boil until tender. Then, in another pot, mix 2 quarts vinegar and 4 pounds sugar in 1 pint water. Add 2 tablespoons whole cloves, whole allspice and 12-inch pieces of stick cinnamon tied into a cheesecloth bag. Boil the mixture 5 minutes then add the drained watermelon rind and simmer until clear. Put the rind with liquid into hot jars and seal.